ADVANCE PRAISE FOR *LABYRINTH*

"Astute, thought-provoking, and bold. Pawel Motyl has brought important case studies to life brilliantly, revealing deeper lessons for anyone in a decision-making role. This unique book is an essential contribution in truly understanding executive leadership."

MARSHALL GOLDSMITH Thinkers50 #1 in Leadership and World's #1 Executive Coach

"This book is a must-read for any leader wanting to improve how decisions are made. Pawel Motyl demystifies the challenge of decision-making in a dramatically changing world. Using extensive case studies, he points out common decision mistakes and offers specific recommendations. His work is extremely well grounded, researched, and presented."

DAVE ULRICH Rensis Likert professor, Ross School of Business, University of Michigan

"Both enlightening and entertaining, Pawel Motyl has created a dream guide to the art of sound decision-making. Sixteen rules are well articulated and amply illustrated with fascinating examples. They provide the road map for decision-makers to challenge the natural human reliance on precedent in a world where options are increasingly unprecedented, and to wean us from slavish devotion to authority and the status quo so that we can make the innovative, process-driven decisions necessary to be trailblazers rather than bridge-burners."

WHITNEY JOHNSON bestselling author of *Disrupt Yourself* and *Build an A-Team*, and Thinkers50 Leading Management Thinker

"Leadership and life are about making great choices based on sound decision-making. If there's one decision you need to make about must-read books for this year, make this one your first choice!"

MARK THOMPSON *New York Times*–bestselling author and AMA's #1 Growth Leadership Coach

"With a backdrop of history, Pawel shares 'watch outs' and 'ways' to make better decisions that are practical and executable."

GARRY RIDGE president and CEO, WD-40 Company

"Fantastic, gripping read! Brilliantly helping to understand how decisions are made, both one's own and those of others. Highly recommended!"

DOROTA CZARNOTA managing partner, Poland and CEE, Russell Reynolds Associates

"Decision-making is often complex and somewhat overwhelming at inflection points, and thereby in ambiguous times. Pawel Motyl offers refreshing and practical insights on the journey of leadership for decision-making. This is a fascinating read!"

AICHA EVANS chief strategy officer, Intel Corporation

"What an amazing book! Pawel Motyl takes his readers on a fascinating journey through perfectly researched case studies. Each page in the book is both inspirational and practical. This reading is essential."

DAREK LENART senior vice president human resources, North America and strategic growth, Mastercard

"Perfecting the skill of decision-making is essential in a complex, attention-restricted economy. Pawel Motyl gives you the tools you need to move your agenda forward."

BONITA THOMPSON *New York Times*–bestselling author and career strategist

"Some decisions are easy to make. You've already got those covered. But others, leadership decisions, are much trickier. Motyl's substantial book draws on data, storytelling, and leadership principles to share the rules that will help you learn how to make smarter decisions. And smarter decisions mean more successful outcomes."

MICHAEL BUNGAY STANIER author of *The Wall Street Journal* bestseller *The Coaching Habit*

"In an age of unprecedented complexity, uncertainty, and change, the big, important decisions become extremely difficult. Few leaders are equipped with the level of courage and insight that is necessary to make these tough decisions with velocity. Pawel's book provides rules, principles, and vivid examples that actually help leaders make sense of what they are facing so they can make better decisions to drive better outcomes."

DAVID B. PETERSON PhD, director, leadership and coaching, Google, Inc.

"Pawel Motyl took a massive undertaking in analyzing the most complex cases in history where effective decision-making was critical to creating or destroying value for the endeavor at hand. In this groundbreaking book, he offers practical frameworks that will help you prepare for the uncertain future and make better calls at any high-stakes juncture."

SERGEY SIROTENKO executive coach, INSEAD and Ward Howell

"There is real wisdom in this book. You will remember its lessons and its stories long after you are finished reading it. The world would be safer and happier if our leaders made better decisions—and Pawel Motyl shows us how."

ASHEESH ADVANI CEO, Junior Achievement (JA) Worldwide

"In today's uncertain and complex world, we face new assumptions and unprecedented challenges. Through insights backed by numerous case studies, Pawel Motyl presents us with new rules for effective decision-making and launching into leadership success. A thought-provoking read!"

SANYIN SIANG CEO coach and author of *The Launch Book*

"The speed and quality of decision-making is vital in any organization—and Pawel Motyl deeply gets it. In this enlightening book, Pawel has taken real case studies and offered precise and actionable insights to help leaders make more effective decisions. I highly recommend any executive to read and apply the lessons from this powerful book."

PRAKASH RAMAN CEO, Raman Consulting

"If you've ever wondered how catastrophic mistakes, with lives and fortunes lost irretrievably, could have been avoided, you need to read *Labyrinth*. Writing about business and leadership with the pace of a thriller, Pawel Motyl will change your assumptions about decision-making, drawing on lessons learned from high-altitude mountaineering to organized crime syndicates."

AYSE BIRSEL Author of *Design the Life You Love* and one of *Fast Company*'s Most Creative People

LABYRINTH

THE ART OF
DECISION-MAKING

PAGE TWO BOOKS

LA
BY
RIN
TH

Pawel Motyl

Cataloguing in publication information is available from Library and Archives Canada.

ISBN 978-1-98902-531-4 (paperback)

ISBN 978-1-98902-532-1 (ebook)

Page Two Books

www.pagetwobooks.com

Cover design by Taysia Louie

Interior design by Setareh Ashrafolofghalai

Printed and bound in Canada by Friesens

Distributed in Canada by Raincoast Books

Distributed in the US and internationally by Publishers Group West

19 20 21 22 23 5 4 3 2 1

www.pawelmotyl.com

"Life is the sum of all choices."
ALBERT CAMUS

To everyone who taught me to choose better in life.

LABYRINTH

CONTENTS

Introduction 1

1 **Koyaanisqatsi** 15

2 **Turkey Trouble** 27

3 **In This Chapter,
There Is No Good News...** 39

4 **Process** 61

5 **改善** 95

6 **Something in the Air** 139

7 **In Search of Authentic Leaders** 189

8 **My Favorite Enemy** 251

9 **Peering through the Looking Glass** 283

Epilogue 301

Endnotes 325

**Bibliography and
Further Reading** 335

Index 347

About the Author 357

INTRODUCTION

V IJNH BẮC BỘ, better known in English as the Gulf of Tonkin, lies on the coast of northern Vietnam and southern China in the northwestern South China Sea. In the early 1960s, it was the focal point of the US Department of Defense's DESOTO operation, as part of OPLAN 34-Alpha: regular patrols were conducted by US Navy destroyers in order to gather information about the North Vietnamese army's plans and movements. On July 2, 1964, a serious incident occurred. Captain John J. Herrick, commanding the destroyer USS *Maddox*, reported coming under fire from North Vietnamese patrol boats. Two days later, another incident sparked the war in Vietnam: the destroyers USS *Turner Joy* and USS *Maddox* reported coming under torpedo attack. The information about the event was very precise—the commander of the Pacific Fleet, Admiral Ulysses S. Grant Sharp, stated that as many as nine torpedoes were fired, none of which hit any American ships. As a result of this purported attack, President Lyndon B. Johnson forced a bill through Congress—the Gulf of Tonkin Resolution—that resulted in air strikes being launched against North Vietnam, followed by ground troops being sent in. Thus began a nearly decade-long conflict which, according to various estimates, took the lives of between 2 million and 3.5 million people.

THE MID-1980S marked the beginning of the commercialization of Mount Everest. In 1985, a wealthy Texas businessman named Richard Bass spent a small fortune on buying himself a place on the climbing team of the renowned US climber David Breashears. Bass was successful in his mission, conquering the highest peak on Earth, and the event resonated widely; not only among Texan oilmen seeking an adrenaline rush, but also among mountaineers, who smelled a new kind of pay dirt. The following years saw a whole new industry emerge, as a series of commercial expeditions were launched up Everest and the other eight-thousanders. The market leader was Adventure Consultants, founded in 1991 by New Zealander Rob Hall, who could boast of having led thirty-nine amateur climbers to the top of the world. On May 10, 1996, Hall set off with another eight cheerful paying customers. He was supported by two experienced mountaineers—Mike Groom and Andy Harris—and a group of Sherpas led by sirdar Ang Dorje. Several other expeditions were operating on the mountain at the same time: an IMAX television team with David Breashears, a Taiwanese group led by Makalu Gau, a South African team led by Ian Woodall, and a commercial team under the leadership of American Scott Fischer, who had founded a rival company to Adventure Consultants, called Mountain Madness. Despite a few minor problems, the likes of which affect any expedition, there were no portents of the tragedy that would claim the lives of eight people, including Rob Hall and Scott Fischer, and result in numerous others suffering from hypothermia and frostbite. For nineteen years, May 10, 1996, would hold the record as the most lethal day in the mountain's history.[1]

WHEN GABRIEL García Márquez placed the action of his novel *One Hundred Years of Solitude* in the fictional town of Macondo, he could never have imagined that the name would dramatically resurface more than forty years later for reasons entirely unconnected with the world of literature. But that's exactly what happened: at 9:47 pm on April 20, 2010, on the oil platform *Deepwater Horizon*, owned by Transocean and leased by British Petroleum, a catastrophic explosion killed eleven people. But that was only the beginning of the damage. In the weeks that followed, close to 5 million barrels of oil gushed from the damaged well into the waters of the Gulf of Mexico, causing massive ecological carnage and sparking discussions not only about the safety of exploiting mineral deposits in the undersea Mississippi Canyon, but also about the multitude of risk-management mistakes that led to the explosion. The name of the well in Block 252 where the tragedy occurred was Macondo.

AT THE beginning of the 1990s, Porsche was teetering on the brink of bankruptcy. Few believed it could be saved, and opportunistic predators circled the ailing brand, waiting to snap it up. One of the few who believed there was a chance of saving the firm without selling it was a thirty-eight-year-old named Wendelin Wiedeking. He took on what others saw as a mission impossible, and in 1993, he was made President and CEO of the failing automotive legend. Over the following decade or so, he showed that Tom Cruise and

Hollywood directors are not the only ones capable of achieving mission impossible: he rescued Porsche through a series of bold moves, including strategic cost cutting and process optimization—known as the Porsche Improvement Process (PIP)—outsourcing a part of the production process to Valmet Automotive, a Finnish company, and radically revamping the product portfolio by ditching the loss-making 928 and introducing the Boxster and Cayenne models. Wiedeking's moves took the firm back into the black, making him an industry bigwig in the process. His success reached its zenith in the 2007/08 financial year, when Porsche posted record net profits of €6.392 billion. The company was valued at over €13 billion, and it spoke confidently about buying the Volkswagen group. Fast-forward one year: Porsche was back in the red, primarily because of gigantic losses, which exceeded €3.5 billion. As a result of this startling reversal of fortune, Wendelin Wiedeking was obliged to hurriedly clear his desk and leave the building, although the pain of his dismissal was undoubtedly soothed somewhat by a €50 million golden handshake.

WHILE WENDELIN Wiedeking was indisputably among the elite of European management, in terms of economics he was outclassed by Robert C. Merton, winner of the Nobel Memorial Prize in Economic Sciences, which he shared with Myron S. Scholes, in 1997. Merton is famed for his groundbreaking research in finance, including share option pricing (which gave rise to the Black–Scholes–Merton formula), derivatives, and managing investment risk. It would therefore be reasonable to assume that someone who had spent his whole professional life developing ever more effective and precise forecasting instruments would be brilliant at building an investment portfolio. Robert Merton certainly thought so when, in 1993, he co-founded and became a member of the board of directors in a hedge fund management firm called Long-Term Capital Management (LTCM). Hordes of clients shared his belief in his abilities, investing over $1 billion in the fund. After impressive initial successes (annual returns as high as 40 percent!), came a massive meltdown, caused by the Asian financial crisis that ignited in Thailand in 1997 and hit Russia a year later, and in 1997/98 the share price crashed. LTCM's capital fell to under $400 billion, and the total losses suffered by investors was estimated at $4.5 billion. A similar fate befell the Trinsum Group, another company set up in 2007 by the Nobel winner: just a year and a half after its founding (admittedly, in a very difficult period), it had to file for bankruptcy.

WHAT ROBERT Merton was to economics, Harvey Weinstein was to film: co-founder of the legendary Miramax production company, which we have to thank for such films as *Pulp Fiction*, *Shakespeare in Love*, *Kill Bill*, *The English Patient*, *Clerks*, and *The Crying Game*. His influence in the industry, built up over decades, was affirmed by the often-quoted statistic that he got more thank-yous than God from Oscar winners. His remarkable career came to an abrupt halt in October 2017, when the *New York Times* and the *New Yorker* published a series of articles alleging that he had sexually assaulted numerous actresses over many years. His denials of the charges changed little. In the weeks that followed, a typhoon swept through the media, leading Harvey Weinstein to discontinue many of his business activities and resign from The Weinstein Brothers. In addition, he was thrown out of the Academy of Motion Picture Arts and Sciences, and Georgina Chapman, whom he had married in 2007, moved out of the family home.

EARLY IN the morning of January 28, 1986, Dr. James P. Bagian, an astronaut with NASA's space program, took a desperate step: he called on STS-51-L Mission Control to cancel the liftoff planned for that day. He was worried by the unusual weather conditions in Florida, as on the night of January 27, the temperature at Cape Canaveral had fallen to 23°F. The solid rocket boosters used to send the shuttles into orbit had never been used in such low temperatures, and Bagian was concerned that after such a cold night the O-rings separating the rockets from the fuel source might fail. Mission Control ignored his concerns and approved the liftoff of the *Challenger* space shuttle.

SIXTEEN YEARS passed, during which time NASA conducted eighty-nine successful shuttle missions. In 2003, the space shuttle *Columbia* was scheduled to be the first launch of the year. The oldest of NASA's fleet of five shuttle craft, its maiden flight on April 12, 1981, had initiated the entire space shuttle program. Liftoff for the STS-107 mission, led by Rick Husband, was planned for January 16; the aim of the flight was to conduct research in microgravity. The crew of seven consisted of five Americans, one Indian woman, and an Israeli man named Ilan Ramon who was to become the first person from his nation in space. The liftoff was fairly routine. The only anomaly looked at in detail by NASA engineers was a small part of insulating foam that broke off and struck a thermal protection panel on the shuttle's left wing. Although the Debris Assessment Team (DAT) had serious concerns about the condition of the wing, the engineers could not assess the safety risk from the available data. Flight Director Linda Ham decided to continue the mission as planned and to not take any actions in response to the engineers' concerns. Tragically, for over two weeks, NASA managers did not act on the chance to try and save the astronauts onboard *Columbia*. On February 1, 2003, at 8:10 am, the space shuttle initiated its landing procedure. Just before 9:00 am, it burned up on re-entering the Earth's atmosphere.

A SIMILAR double tragedy occurred in Europe. On the evening of January 23, 2008, not far from Mirosławiec Airport in Poland, a military CASA C-295M airplane belonging to the Polish air force crashed. The scale of the catastrophe was shocking. Twenty officers were killed in the disaster, among them almost the entire leadership of the 1st Tactical Air Force Squadron. Some analysts and commentators asked the obvious question: How, at a time when any sensible corporation prohibits all the members of the board from traveling together, could key air force personnel be allowed on board the same plane? Not only was the question never answered but, sadly, no lessons were learned from the catastrophe. On April 10, 2010, one of the most appalling tragedies in the history of aviation unfolded. All ninety-six members of a Polish delegation en route to the village of Katyn, in Russia, onboard a Tupolev TU-154M died when the aircraft crashed on its approach to the Smolensk-North military airbase. Among the victims were MPs, diplomats, and senior military personnel, as well as President Lech Kaczyński and his wife, Maria.

THE FUNERAL ceremonies for Maria and Lech Kaczyński were held a week later, with thousands of Poles turning out to say farewell to the couple. Numerous foreign leaders, though, failed to make it to the funeral for reasons beyond their control: Iceland's Eyjafjallajökull volcano erupted on April 14, spewing enormous volumes of volcanic ash into the skies. Eurocontrol, the intergovernmental agency created in 1960 to manage air traffic in Europe, made an instantaneous and sensible decision: as there had never been a comparable eruption, it was impossible to assess the scale of the problem or level of risk, and so it ordered that flights across the continent be suspended as of April 15. Travel to and from Europe halted immediately. In the days that followed, a total of 104,000 flights, which would have carried some 10 million passengers, were canceled due to the flight disruptions. Of the passengers affected, hundreds of thousands were stranded at airports with no idea how long the crisis would last. Some tried to look for alternative means of transport, borrowing cars or fighting for train tickets; others camped out in the airport terminals in the hope of flights suddenly recommencing. Eurocontrol, however, offered no crumbs of optimism, especially as a computer simulation conducted by experts had confirmed the agency's belief that any attempt at flying would end in tragedy. The flight ban remained in place for eight days, and it was April 23 before the first planes were allowed to taxi out onto runways. Not long after, Eurocontrol was accused of having taken draconian measures and overestimating the real level of risk. The main argument leveled against Eurocontrol was that several airlines (including Lufthansa, KLM, and Air France) had conducted more than twenty test flights along the ash-filled air corridors in the real world, not a simulated one. The planes flew with only skeleton crews and, of course, no passengers. Not a single irregularity in the functioning of the craft was observed during any of these flights, and all the aircraft landed safely. Final estimates put the cost of the ban to carriers at around $1.7 billion.

NO ONE knew it at the time, of course, but much more would be lost as a result of the Daimler-Benz and Chrysler merger. On May 7, 1998, everything looked rosy. That day, a press conference was held, with the CEOs of each company, Robert J. Eaton and Jürgen E. Schrempp, basking in the glow of the cameras as they announced a "merger of equals." And so the world's third-largest car maker was created, with annual earnings of over $150 billion. Automotive industry analysts were ecstatic, stressing the excellent synergy between the two organizations. For Chrysler, the deal provided the opportunity to break into the European market; for Daimler, renowned for its Mercedes limousines, it meant broadening its range to include the minivans, off-roaders, and pickups that its US partner, the owner of brands such as Dodge and Jeep, was famed for. Both firms would make massive savings by integrating their purchasing operations as well as research and development. Costs were projected to fall by $1.7 billion within twelve months of the merger, and by $3 billion annually after seven years. Few eyebrows were raised, therefore, when one of the oldest and most influential magazines in the sector, *Automotive Industries (AI)*, published in the USA since 1895, called it the "deal of the century." For Daimler, which paid the dizzying sum of $36 billion for Chrysler, it was definitely the expenditure of the century. It was also a move that ended in tears for both firms.

ALL THE events described above occurred in totally unrelated worlds, but they share a common denominator: mistakes that were made during the decision-making process. The road to each unfortunate event was paved with the good intentions of those responsible, all of whom had significant experience and numerous past successes to their credit. Their errors can be traced to a combination of numerous interrelated reasons: relying on past successes, ignoring significant information, conducting superficial analysis, yielding to outside pressure, putting too much faith in luck, or misinterpreting important data, for example.

All of the errors could have been avoided.

The book that you are holding in your hands will challenge your current beliefs about decision-making and possibly change some of them forever. In this single volume I attempt to examine the most prevalent weak spots in decision-making processes, not only in business but in life in general; during crises and in calmer times; in both individual and group decisions. I try to answer the question of how to make decisions that are simultaneously rational, effective, and wise.

CHAPTER 1 contains a description of some of the startling changes that have occurred in the last couple of decades, as well as their influence on decision-making. The technological and information revolution taking place before our eyes, the new trends in consumer behavior, backed by the boom in social media, crowdsourcing mechanisms, open innovation, and the sharing economy, as well as ongoing globalization, have radically altered the factors behind success. Previously tried and trusted methods often fail nowadays, leading even competent, experienced people into spectacular failure. Chapters 2 and 3 are devoted to this paradox and analyze the traps set by our own minds, which are conditioned to accommodate somewhat different realities than those presented in our dynamically changing world. In these chapters I also examine a highly dangerous paradox in which today's success sows the seeds of tomorrow's failure. Chapter 4 looks at decision-making as a process, discussing three modes we can apply to it. A deeper understanding of these three approaches is essential for perfecting the way we make choices. This is the subject of Chapter 5—enriching the story with improvement tools developed in operational management. Chapters 6 and 7 look at the Kaizen approach to decision-making in the context of organizational culture, developing a truly fascinating perspective: the one on the role of leaders. Chapter 8 focuses on the world of neuroscience and social psychology and on the power of emotion and illusion, all of which affect even the greatest leaders and decision-makers. I also discuss some practical tools that can offer at least a degree of protection from these traps. The final chapter romps into the future, outlining the most important trends that are likely to shape decision-making in the years to come.

This is not a theoretical work. I drew on my first-hand experience of numerous case studies that I have encountered in over twenty years of working as a CEO, a business consultant, collaborating with *Harvard Business Review Polska*, and leading coaching projects, training sessions, or workshops for company owners and senior managers. I learned from the world's foremost thought leaders, as in 2016, I was selected to join the first cohort of the 100 Coaches project, launched by Dr. Marshall Goldsmith. I also drew on source materials documenting the events I reference in which the decision-making process had played a central role—either positively or negatively. In doing so, I discovered that it is not only the business world that can teach us how to make good decisions (although there's no shortage of such cases); interesting lessons can also be learned from such disparate worlds as high-altitude mountaineering, space travel, military operations, and . . . organized crime syndicates. I hope that this tour of decision-making in very different realities will be both inspirational and practical.

Thanking everyone without whom this work would never have been created is my mission impossible. Everyone around me, in both a professional and personal capacity, has contributed in some way to this book. I would like to thank them all.

KOYAANISQATSI

ONE OF THE most colorful, yet little-known figures in world cinema is director Godfrey Reggio. Born in 1940, he has had a varied life, to say the least. At age fourteen he became a monk in an enclosed monastery. When he left the monastery twelve years later, he became involved with various community organizations in New Mexico, where his work ranged from helping disaffected youths in street gangs to promoting civil liberties. He drew on his experiences and what he'd learned from them when he moved into movies, and, in 1982, he directed *Koyaanisqatsi*, an experimental film lauded for its innovative use of images and music to highlight the clash between the urban and natural worlds.

"*Koyaanisqatsi*" is a Hopi word that translates as "life out of balance." The word is more than just an ideal title for Godfrey Reggio's work, it also sums up the reality of modern life. We really do live in a world where everything is out of whack and everything we thought we knew is being called into question.

ALVIN TOFFLER'S third wave phenomenon was like a powerful uppercut, albeit delivered in a velvet glove. Most of us probably regard the current ongoing technological changes and accompanying information and communications revolutions as progressing gradually. We might feel that although we're living faster than ever before, evolution is still progressing in a linear, predictable fashion. However, a mere glance at a handful of figures is enough to confirm that a large proportion of the processes we're living through are happening violently and exponentially. Take, for example, Moore's Law, which states that the economically viable number of transistors in a dense integrated circuit will double approximately every eighteen months (and thus will grow exponentially and not linearly). A similar phenomenon is occurring with the volume of information surrounding us. Between the dawn of history and the end of 2003, humanity generated a total of 5 exabytes of data (5 × 1,018 bytes). While that figure might seem dizzying, it doesn't compare with the fact that in 2012 we generated that same 5 exabytes of information... in barely forty-eight hours. While seemingly incredible, the phenomenon is fairly easy to explain. The dramatic increase is down to the three major revolutions taking place before our very eyes: technological (enabling us to gather, store, and process ever-greater quantities of data), social media (creating new communications platforms and multiplying the amount of information available), and mobile (guaranteeing access to the other two revolutions from practically anywhere on the planet,

24/7). The result? According to various estimates, the digital world today contains from 2.7 to 4.4 zettabytes of data. Facebook alone is used by over 2 billion people (of whom half access it exclusively via mobile devices), bombarding our senses by generating fresh information every millisecond. In 2017, it was estimated that 50 percent of the world's population had Internet access, a previously unimaginable figure; and it is widely expected that by 2024-25, it will be 100 percent. This apparent gift to humanity has a darker side, though: it's getting harder and harder to sift out the relevant information needed to make a decision from all the background noise.

It also means that the information world is awash with black swan events—unpleasant surprises and events that we cannot predict from prior experience. The black swan theory was the creation of Nassim Nicholas Taleb, who expanded on it in his book, *The Black Swan: The Impact of the Highly Improbable*, in which he draws on a true story from many years ago that created shock waves through the ornithological community. Ornithologists had long believed that swans had only white feathers. In the world of birds, this was really quite an anomaly, and it attracted considerable interest from scientists. Much research was conducted, academic articles and reports were written, and the phenomenon of white swans was increasingly better documented and explained, until one day... a black swan was spotted in Australia. The astonished ornithologists couldn't believe it. In a fraction of a second, all the knowledge amassed about the color of swans' feathers, all the concepts and explanations developed through thousands of hours of work were relegated to the garbage pile.

The crazy new reality surrounding us is replete with just such "black swans," events that take us totally by surprise and for which we were not only unprepared but also unable to prepare. A classic example of a black swan is the attack on the World Trade Center in New York, carried out by al-Qaeda in 2001. Had this been a business transaction, it would have been lauded as a breakthrough innovation, as no other terrorist organization had ever launched— or, as far as we know, even considered—such an attack. There's no disputing that it took the North American Aerospace Defense Command (NORAD) totally by surprise. They had been perfectly well-prepared for any conventional air-to-land attack, and had also prepared and practiced procedures for how to behave in the event of a passenger plane hijacking over US territory. They hadn't predicted, though, that a hijacked plane could be used as a weapon to carry out an air-to-land attack with both terrorists and passengers still on board. In the face of just such a black swan, NORAD was helpless. Its commanders were not only unable to decide whether or not to shoot the hijacked planes down, they couldn't even decide who had the authority to make such a decision. For over ninety minutes virtually no effective action was taken.

IT HAS been noted that black swans like this, events that challenge our hitherto adequate knowledge and solutions, are on the increase. One reason for this is the information overload (and the associated ever-increasing risk of our missing vital information) noted above; another is globalization. We are more connected than ever, literally and figuratively. A disruptive event in one place can cause problems in another place entirely.

In March 2011, a powerful earthquake in Japan generated a tsunami and caused the deaths of more than fifteen thousand people. In addition to the human toll, there was an economic one, one that extended beyond Japan: global car production was impacted. In many cases, this came as a complete surprise. How could a natural disaster in one corner of the world affect people on the other side of the world? It turns out that, in the era of globalization and extended supply chains, the concept of "other side of the world" has changed. On March 11, 2011, it wasn't only Japan's auto sector that was shaken—the entire auto sector suffered from the aftershocks. With hindsight, it's not quite so surprising: 60 percent of the world market for motor vehicle airflow sensors was held by Hitachi, and its Japanese plants had to severely limit production. Leading car producers, battling to increase efficiency over many years, had enthusiastically adopted the Japanese just-in-time inventory management system. This allowed them to maintain the lowest-possible stock levels—but it also narrowed their safety margins. Due to the multitude of components and co-producers involved, they couldn't build alternative supply chains, especially as in some cases suppliers' suppliers were affected. One prime example of this concerned the pigment Xirallic, produced by the German company Merck KGaA, which is a crucial component in the metallic paints used on many automobiles. The tsunami destroyed a factory belonging to the company in Onahama, which led to a break in the supply chain of one of the ingredients of the pigment. Barely two weeks later, car producers around the world were facing a serious problem: they couldn't deliver cars in the most popular colors to their customers. And so a black swan emerged: in this case, a seemingly geographically remote event that suddenly disrupted the functioning of businesses around the world.

However, black swans can also be a positive force, especially when we create them deliberately, as with disruptive innovation. Where there's a loser, there's also a winner somewhere. Every breakthrough innovation that takes a rival unawares gives the innovator the upper hand.

Toward the end of the twentieth century, Google demolished its rivals when it introduced the PageRank algorithm developed by Larry Page and Sergey Brin. PageRank was a breakthrough in indexing and ranking search results; in a departure from the prevailing use of keywords, it used the number and quality of links to a given page in its algorithm. This mechanism gave higher-quality and more accurate search results, which Google's rivals simply couldn't match. In a little over a year, the world of Internet search engines was turned on its head. The former market leader—AltaVista—began to dramatically lose market share, and second-placed Yahoo! fared little better. Google's search engine became stronger and stronger, and Google consequently became one of the biggest companies in the world.

BLACK SWANS can appear in any of five areas.

The rarest are those with a worldwide influence, although global crises, technological breakthroughs, and catastrophic events (such as pandemics) do occasionally surprise us. Global black swans affect everyone, or almost everyone, both directly and indirectly, regardless of sex, age, location, education, race, sexual orientation, or business sector. An example of a global black swan could be the financial crisis of 2008, the scale of which no one foresaw, and which affected almost every single country and the entire business world.

Next, we have sectoral black swans, which affect only a certain group of people or companies. An obvious example of this would be the imposition of new rules by an industry regulator. This type of sectoral swan can be illustrated nicely by the sudden, and wholly unexpected, ban on taking more than 3.4 ounces of fluids on board a plane. This exclusively affected airline passengers, and in particular those who didn't read about the change in the rules and didn't adapt their packing accordingly. Being sectoral, of course, doesn't diminish the level of pain inflicted by a black swan. With deep regret and sadness, I bade farewell to a bottle of excellent wine at Frankfurt Airport, which I'd placed in my hand baggage only a day before the ban came into effect.

From a business perspective, organizational black swans affecting a single company are the biggest threat. And to make it more interesting, these are often the result of events occurring within an organization, whereby the company is responsible for its own ornithological nightmare, usually due to poor decision-making. An example of a particularly vicious black swan was the *Deepwater Horizon* offshore oil rig explosion, whose tragic consequences were several deaths and a massive ecological disaster, as well as enormous damage to the company's image and finances. It's estimated that the tragedy cost BP over $61 billion.

The fourth subspecies of black swans are those that affect a small group of people—say, a team in a company, a family, or a group of friends. A friend's unexpected illness, a bad financial decision that has consequences for the whole family, or a key employee suddenly quitting are all examples of such black swans.

The fifth group comprises events that affect individuals—they take only one person by surprise. I suspect this is the kind of black swan we subconsciously fear the most. In all the other categories, the problem affects groups; in this case, we're left to deal with the black swan ourselves. There are myriad examples of the careers of competent, high-ranking, successful people in a range of fields collapsing due to something that was blindingly obvious to everyone else around the person affected.

RULE #1

Prepare for a black swan, because one thing is certain: sooner or later you will meet one.

IN THE world of black swans, it becomes more and more difficult to predict how a given situation will develop. Mohamed A. El-Erian, the former CEO of the Pacific Investment Management Company, and his colleagues even proposed a term for it in an economics context—the "new normal"—which over time became more and more popular and used in a more general sense.

The new normal defines a reality in which change and surprise are constant features and where nobody really knows what might happen, even in the immediate future. The new normal by itself is fairly unpleasant. It's human nature to like to have a relatively clear view of what might happen, and when we don't have such certainty we can feel psychologically uncomfortable. What's worse, though, is that in the new normal, the traditional methods of decision-making fail, mechanisms that worked perfectly well for years suddenly become useless. The traditional approach to risk management is no longer a fundamental tool to support decision-making processes. It has become unreliable. However, it's difficult to abandon tried and tested tools and approaches, even if we can see that they're no longer fit for purpose and no longer provide us with reliable data, thus undermining our ability to make good decisions. The power of habit is so strong that we often stumble on, making more and more errors, despite its being plain as day that we're heading in the wrong direction.

Look at the period 2008–12. The financial crisis and ensuing economic collapse were essentially the global sum of the combined decision-making errors by investors, entrepreneurs, managers, regulators, and even customers and consumers, all operating in an interdependent, interconnected system. It was an archetypal Catch-22 situation: the gradually deepening crisis made it increasingly difficult for the decision-makers to properly assess the situation, and the bad choices they made destabilized the environment even further, which in turn led to even more misguided decisions. Meanwhile, amid the rising chaos, people held on ever tighter to their tried and trusted management methods—and in so doing perfectly implemented all their wrong choices.

Once the world recovered from the shock, of course, the billion-dollar question was asked: Whose fault was it? Among all the hundreds of macroeconomic conspiracy theories, relatively little time was devoted to the actual decision-making mechanisms behind the crisis and the numerous traps that the new normal had set for the decision-makers.

The traditional approach to decision-making rested on a simple assumption that both the quality and the accuracy of decisions were based on the competence and experience of the decision-maker in tandem with the quality and completeness of the information at their disposal. That approach was highly effective for many years. If a decision was made by a professional acting in good faith and drawing on information from trusted sources, the decision was pretty likely to be the correct one. All you had to do was develop good systems for gathering and analyzing data and entrust key decisions to the most competent personnel to be guaranteed relative peace of mind. Recent years, though, have turned the situation on its head. During the crisis, it was precisely those people who were most experienced, with the greatest successes behind them, relying on tried and tested, reliable sources of information who made the most dramatically awful decisions. Suddenly the skies were filled with falling business stars, who despite their glittering careers and prior successes came crashing down, often not only dragging entire organizations down with them but also wiping out the fortunes of thousands of individuals. The cause of these dramas was not solely greed, though many diagnosed this as the source of the problem.

NO, THE main culprit was ... the turkey.

TURKEY 2

TROUBLE

ONCE UPON A time, there was a turkey living the good life on a farm. He passed his days in blissful peace, each day as lovely as the one before. Three times a day a nice farmworker brought him a bucket of feed, which the turkey gobbled down in ever-greater quantities. His pen was cleaned regularly. Time drifted by, 50 days, 100 days, 150 days, then 200 days. Every day the same: feeding and cleaning. If we'd asked that turkey to comment on life on that 200th day, he would have been full of positivity. This is the life! And if we'd asked him what the 201st was going to look like, he would have been puzzled: What else *could* it look like? The same as before! Three meals a day and a clean pen. Sadly, the turkey didn't know that Thanksgiving was just around the corner and that on day 201 he would be meeting

the first and last black swan in his life—something he was unable
to predict based on his previous experience and for which he
couldn't prepare.[1]

Here's the bad news: We're no different to the turkey. We have
a tendency to extrapolate positive trends. If something has developed over a reasonably long period in a predictable and ordered
fashion, we subconsciously assume that it will continue that way.
This is a trap that our cognitive system sets for us. It affects the
way we absorb and process information from our environment,
and then draw conclusions based on that information. We are particularly susceptible to positive trends because it's comforting to
assume (consciously or not) that our current successes will follow us into the future. This assumption is typically accompanied
by our ignoring important signals from the world around us that
the trend is about to change—just like the turkey, who, after 200
days of pampering, failed to notice that the farmer was sharpening
his knife.

This extrapolating of trends in a new normal world, replete with
black swans, is potentially lethal. The appearance of a black swan
typically flies in the face of trends and destroys the status quo, surprising the decision-makers, who were fully convinced that the
situation was stable. Here are a few examples.

AN ACQUAINTANCE of mine—let's call him Mr. Turkey—was an
active investor in the stock market. He invested over many years
in the financial sector, and his portfolio brought consistently high
returns. Mr. Turkey always thought of himself as a low-risk investor. For example, he avoided tech shares like the plague, which
in 2001 saved him from painful losses when the dot-com bubble
burst. I recall how, after this particular crash, he argued that come
what may, nothing like that would ever happen to the banking

world—one or two firms might go under due to poor decision-making, but a radical, global crash across the entire sector was simply impossible.

Then came January 2008, which was the best January ever for Mr. Turkey who, seeing how bank shares were rising, was ecstatic. He repeatedly explained to me how a thorough analysis of trends was the key to accurate decision-making. He showed me dozens of graphs and simulations that confirmed his arguments and of which, I'm ashamed to admit, I understood little.

There's a classic trick that film directors often use: after an emotional, life-changing event, a caption appears on the screen saying "one year later," and in this way, we jump forward to see how the lives of the protagonists have changed.

I wouldn't recommend doing that for Mr. Turkey. Jump one year ahead and, rather unsurprisingly, you'd find an embittered man, angry at the world. Mr. Turkey had to watch as his portfolio, based on a few stable and respectable banks (or so he thought), crumbled to dust before his eyes.

After a time, Mr. Turkey came clean (with the help of a little tequila) and admitted he'd been completely taken in by the positive trend. I remember his words well: "I saw reality the way I wanted it to be. I accepted any information that confirmed my assumptions were right, and anything that called them into question was tossed in the garbage, the more so because the situation over the previous few years had been so good." That's it in a nutshell. These words of Mr. Turkey should be a kind of business memento mori for investors.

Just look at Nokia.

The beginning of the twenty-first century was a great period for Nokia. The Finnish cell phone manufacturer had crushed its rivals, taking an amazing 50.9 percent of market share and giving Symbian, the operating system installed in its equipment, an even bigger advantage: up to 62.5 percent of the phones sold in 2007 used it. Nokia had left its rivals trailing way behind as it rushed toward a glittering future. The various innovations that were emerging, like touch screens, which consumers were slow to take up, or the weird operating system launched on November 12, 2007, called Android SDK, weren't perceived as threats in any way. It was more than a year before the HTC Dream, the first smartphone to use the Android operating system, even appeared. Drunk on its enormous successes, Nokia, despite many and varied warnings and criticisms of Symbian, continued to back the system, sticking with phones fitted with traditional keyboards or, at best, combining a keyboard with a smallish touch screen.

Time to use that filmmaker's trick . . .

"Six years later."

Nokia's share of the cell phone market was 2.8 percent (data from Q1, 2013), and nobody could even remember what Symbian was. According to a report from "Worldwide Quarterly Mobile Phone Tracker," published by the International Data Corporation, at the end of 2013, 81 percent of all mobile appliances sold came with the Android operating system, the same system dismissed and ignored by Nokia. Meanwhile, the Finns had almost totally dropped out of the cell phone game, becoming one of the most surprising business failures of the twenty-first century. In 2014, Nokia was acquired by Microsoft, which in 2016 sold it to HMD Global and FIH Mobile. It re-entered the game in 2017, launching new smartphone models using—shock, horror—the Android system, but the company does not seem likely to regain its position as market leader any time soon.

Nokia fell prey to the same mistakes as the turkey. Years of success dulled its edge and led it to, very conveniently, extrapolate the prevailing trend—everything had gone swimmingly yesterday, so tomorrow would be just as good. This mind-set meant it was easy to overlook the warnings coming from all around, which, it later turned out, were absolutely worth paying attention to. It was also easier to stick to the same old routines and ignore new ideas. During this period, the Finns put countless new models onto the market, few of which sold well. The market turned away from traditional keyboards, seduced by the allure of touch screens. The biggest irony, as Frank Nuovo, a former chief designer at Nokia, recalled, was that the first prototypes of a smartphone and tablet using touch screens were developed by Nokia at the end of the 1990s, years before Apple's iPhone appeared. Sadly, Nokia, which spent a total of $40 billion on research and development (four times the amount Apple spent!), failed to implement its own solutions and monetize them. Should we be surprised? As the industry portal gizmodo.com reported, Anssi Vanjoki, Nokia's chief strategist, said at the end of 2009 that "Apple has attracted much attention [...], but they have still remained a niche manufacturer."[2]

RULE #2

The better it's going, and the more successful you are, the more you are at risk of turkey syndrome.
    The deeper you fall into turkey syndrome, the nastier your black swan will be.

OTHERS WHO clearly forgot Rule #2 were the aforementioned Robert C. Merton and Wendelin Wiedeking. In both cases, the fundamental reason for their poor decisions was their conviction that past successes were proof of the correctness and effectiveness of the solutions applied, so it made no sense to change anything. Unfortunately for both men, the arrival of a black swan destroyed that theory.

In business, this phenomenon has been observed on a much grander scale. Jim Collins, renowned author of the bestseller *Good to Great*, spent four years researching the reasons behind the collapse of companies that had previously been market leaders. He published his findings in 2009, in a book whose title requires no further comment: *How the Mighty Fall*. Collins divided the process of collapse into five phases, which ideally fit the cases described above.

Phase 1: Hubris born of success. A series of wins breeds arrogance and, with it, the disappearance of the desire to understand the reasons for the ongoing success. The commonest symptom of this phase is the increasing conviction that we are successful because we are special.

Phase 2: Undisciplined pursuit of more. The certainty of being right and of having a guaranteed recipe for success leads to reckless diving into uncharted waters, frequently with no real reason to do so. This phase isn't accompanied by deeper analysis. Why analyze anything when you're sure you're going to win?

Phase 3: Denial of risk and peril. This phase is key and heralds the beginning of the death spiral. Early warning signals of impending doom are repeatedly ignored, and the decision-makers focus on the most positive fragments of reality, no matter how minuscule, that confirm their assumptions. (I suspect Mr. Turkey would relate to this.) All the decisions that follow are entirely misguided.

Phase 4: Grasping for salvation. When the scale of the threat suddenly hits home, many decision-makers react in a chaotic, unconsidered fashion, hoping to save the situation with a single shot. However, instead of drawing on analysis or discipline to help them focus their aim, they're shooting in the dark. It isn't difficult to spend a fortune launching a new product; it does, however, take skill to make money doing it—and that's the only way to save a company caught in phase 4.

Phase 5: Capitulation to irrelevance or death. Phase 5 marks the point where a deteriorating financial situation and successive poor decisions extinguish an organization's internal energy and undermine the positions of its leaders and morale of employees. A company that capitulates internally has only two options: to vegetate long-term and struggle to survive, or to shut up shop completely.[3]

Andy Grove, past CEO of the Intel Corporation (1987–98), often said that success leads to complacency, and complacency leads to failure. The better things are going, the less willing we are to change and the more likely we are to ignore warning signals that all is not well.

THE PUBLISHER of the *Encyclopædia Britannica* certainly ignored the warning signs. The *Encyclopædia Britannica*, originally published in three volumes between 1768 and 1771, became synonymous with quality in encyclopedias, achieving enormous market success. It dominated the world of reference publishing for decades, undergoing constant improvements and simultaneously strengthening its position as an unchallenged leader. Nobody could compete with *Encyclopædia Britannica*. A legendary brand, years of history, a renowned academic board taking care of the facts, and the end product itself made it not only an academic aid but also an object of desire for collectors the world over. A business model like this couldn't fail. And for 230 years, it didn't.

Then, toward the end of the twentieth century, the publisher heard from one of their managers about a strange idea. A group of enthusiasts had decided to create an online encyclopedia, entrusting the definitions and developments of the entries to the users themselves. From the point of view of the publisher, whose work was based on the highest academic rigor and factual accuracy, the idea was absurd—there was no way it could work. But Nupedia, which launched in 2000 and was renamed Wikipedia a year later, was a smash hit. Its lightning development in multiple languages gave people easy access to almost 4 million entries (that's about forty times the number in *Britannica*), which may not have been as perfectly defined as in the legendary encyclopedia, but appeared to be good enough for the majority of users. Customers began to ebb away from *Britannica*, and the publisher, which only a decade earlier had been able to sell over 100,000 copies annually, saw its sales shrink by 2010 to a paltry 8,500. In 2012, the company took the painful decision to abandon traditional publishing and concentrate instead on a digital version, as well as developing its educational programming. More than two hundred years of unbroken business success were abruptly halted by a seemingly benign black swan, which revolutionized the field the publisher operated in.

IT'S ONE of the greatest paradoxes to have appeared in decision-making in recent years: The better we are, the bigger the risk, because the less keen we are to change. Meanwhile, the speed at which the world around us evolves makes the business stability and long-term planning we fought so hard to achieve extremely risky.

Today, not being prepared to instantly modify your behavior can translate into an equally instant disaster.

There's a quote from the world of sport that goes along the following lines:

> My biggest enemy isn't my rival, it isn't injury. I'm most worried about my past successes, because every day I spend in first place, in the leader's position, means my motivation to train and to invest extra energy in training drops.

While I am not sure who said these words, they've stuck in my mind because they perfectly describe the deadly trap of the new normal. They also lead us back to a classic dilemma in managing change, one familiar to anyone who has tried to modify their company's operational procedures, or their team's, or even that of a group of buddies who go skiing together. People like stability, they create rituals, and they will, consciously or otherwise, favor decisions that preserve the status quo. They will look for arguments to justify rejecting a proposed change, or at the very least delaying it. Breaking that mind-set, shaking people out of their comfort zones, and initiating a process of change is one of the biggest challenges faced by business leaders. (This is examined in Chapter 7.)

IF YOU'RE now concerned at how easy it is to become a turkey, fasten your seat belt—you're in for a bumpy ride.

3

IN THIS CHAPTER, THERE IS NO GOOD NEWS...

THERE ARE, THOUGH, three extremely dangerous advisors. In 1961, Stanley Milgram, a well-known, although somewhat controversial psychologist from Yale University, was closely following the trial of senior Nazi Adolf Eichmann, who had been captured by Mossad in Argentina and flown to Jerusalem to face charges of war crimes. During his trial, Eichmann maintained a consistent line of defense and stubbornly rejected the charges, claiming that as a soldier he had to obey the orders of his superiors, who were authority figures to him. He portrayed himself as a helpless pawn on a chessboard, toyed with by vastly more powerful people than he. As a result of this, he argued, he shouldn't even be on trial; instead, the chiefs of staff who made the decisions should be on trial. This strategy was of no help at all to Eichmann.

On December 12, 1961, he was found guilty and sentenced to death by hanging; he was executed six months later.

Eichmann's testimony inspired Milgram to conduct a series of experiments, using some of his students, aimed at verifying just how susceptible to blind obedience humans are when they are in the grip of power and authority. In one of the better-known versions of the experiment, Milgram informed his student participants that the aim of the research they were helping with was to measure the influence of punishment on the ability to memorize. The participants' task was to deliver that punishment (in the form of electric shocks varying from 15 to 450 volts) to the "learner," played by an actor who was in cahoots with Milgram and knew all about the real purposes of the experiment. The switches for each successive level of current were very clearly marked—from "slight shock" for 15 volts, to "danger: severe shock" for 375 volts, and "xxx" for 450 volts. The earlier prepared responses of the "learner" were highly suggestive: at 150 volts the learner would ask to be released from the experiment; at 285 volts, they would scream in pain. When the students hesitated over switching to the next level, to an even higher voltage, the "teacher" would step in (another actor, clad in a lab coat and specially chosen for his bearing and appearance so as to command the students' respect). The "teacher" would inform the students in a firm, confident voice that, regardless of the reactions of the "learner," they should continue the experiment. Horrifically, up to 65 percent of the participants reached the end of the scale and subjected the actor to a potentially fatal 450-volt shock.[1]

This, and further experiments by Stanley Milgram, illustrate how readily we accept the opinions and views of those we regard as experts. We assess the views of such people less critically and are generally prepared to agree with whatever they say. We can also fall into this trap if someone we are meeting for the first time is presented to us as an authority figure. In fact, numerous studies have shown that symbols unrelated to knowledge or experience can influence our perception of someone as an expert. For example, people are assessed as being more credible if they display symbols of wealth, like an expensive watch or high-end car, or are wearing a suit rather than sportswear (hence the white lab coat worn by the "teacher" in Milgram's experiment).[2] And as absurd as it may sound, an equally influential factor is . . . height. Studies have also shown that taller people are perceived as more trustworthy—even in politics.[3] All this means that if someone deliberately and skillfully puts us in an authority trap, our chances of remaining objective are minimal. In the process of decision-making, somebody's authority may turn out to be a very bad guide.

In *Obedience to Authority*, Milgram commented on the results of his experiments:

> Stark authority was pitted against the subjects' [participants'] strongest moral imperatives against hurting others, and, with the subjects' [participants'] ears ringing with the screams of the victims, authority won more often than not. The extreme willingness of adults to go to almost any lengths on the command of an authority constitutes the chief finding of the study and the fact most urgently demanding explanation.[4]

We can see this danger everywhere in the world around us. In its mildest form, we see it in the actors chosen to appear in adverts (thanks to a range of consumer research, we know that a tall, graying man in a lab coat, with a blue shirt underneath, will be perceived as more credible in, say, an advert for painkillers, than someone from the emo youth subculture sporting eyebrow rings and a torn leather jacket, even if in reality they know more about a given pharmaceutical—being, for example, a pharmacy student— than the actor). In its more brutal form, organized crime groups, based on strict hierarchies and numerous rituals, unconsciously take advantage of a similar mechanism to reinforce the subservience of their inferiors.

In the business world, the authority trap is known as ... charismatic leadership.

CHARISMA IS difficult to define. We most often hear it described as that "something" in a person that moves and inspires others, but historically, it was defined a little more precisely, admittedly, though, in the New Testament, where the charismatic gifts of the Holy Spirit—including prophecy, miracles, and healing—are described. Over time, great rulers, or religious or military leaders, began to be described as charismatic, gifted with great authority and the associated glow of success. Thus evolved the modern definition of charisma as particular personality traits that enable the person in possession of them to acquire unquestioned authority and influence over others.

Charisma in this sense entered the corporate world at the beginning of the 1990s, when it became one of the most sought-after features in candidates for high-level positions in an organization. In addition to being quizzed about their formal qualifications, job skills, and accumulated experience, candidates had to show how convincing they were when speaking, how effective their verbal and nonverbal communication was, and how they handled pressure. Recruiters were looking for strong, distinct personalities with the ability to rouse a crowd.

Over time, though, it became clear that not all these charismatic CEOs were leading their companies to success—and in many cases they were the direct catalyst for spectacular disasters. The fundamental problem was that others were placing blind trust in the charismatic leader and uncritically, and unquestioningly, following their chosen course. This meant that the need for internal discussion in an organization gradually disappeared, and when the chairperson eventually made a bad decision, there was no one around who knew how to rescue them and the company from the consequences of that decision. When we're in thrall to charisma, we don't challenge the decision-makers or the integrity of their decisions. We probably should.

Shareholders in the French company Vivendi learned this the hard way when the unusually charismatic Jean-Marie Messier was at the helm. In 1996, Messier was appointed chairman of Compagnie Générale des Eaux (CGE), a company founded in 1853 following a decree by Napoleon III. CGE supplied water to the city of Lyon and in 1860 won the concessions to supply water to Paris; in the following decades, it consistently expanded its operations in this sector. In the 1980s, it invested in public services, energy, and public transport. Messier, though, had an entirely different vision, and he decided to transform CGE into ... a global media group. He succeeded in inspiring the owners of CGE and convincing them of the wisdom of this innovative decision, and, in 1998, CGE changed its name to Vivendi and began selling the companies that had hitherto comprised its core activities. At the same time, it went on a massive shopping spree, buying up, among others, Maroc Telecom and the Havas Media Agency, and merging with Pathé, a leading French film production company. Events really took a revolutionary turn in December 2000, when Messier announced a merger with cable television channel Canal+ and the simultaneous takeover of the Canadian Seagram Company, which owned Universal Studios, among other assets, at the time. Messier had even greater ambitions, and he was willing to spend the company's money like there was no tomorrow to achieve them. After launching numerous takeovers, Vivendi Universal, as it was now called, was around

€37.1 billion in debt—with no plan in place to rapidly generate profits from its acquisitions. On top of all this came the bursting of the dot-com bubble and stock market crash of 2001. This led to a major slump in Vivendi's share price on the Paris stock exchange (from almost €150 in 2000 to €10 two and a half years later) and the sacking of Messier in 2002. Vivendi's annual losses peaked at €23.3 billion, which was at the time the largest financial loss ever recorded by a French company, and the business fought for a long time to get back on track. Jean-Marie Messier found he couldn't just walk away from the mess he'd made; he was taken to court and charged with fraud and share price manipulation. Vivendi Universal is a classic example of how dangerous a charismatic leader can be when he chooses an inappropriate strategy and manages to persuade his entourage to blindly follow him.

The majority of charismatic leaders possess strong, distinct personalities, extreme self-confidence, above-average ambition, and frequently an inflated ego. Jean-Marie Messier was no exception. Though he usually shortened his name to "J2M," those around him began to call him "J6M," which stood for "Jean-Marie Messier, Moi-Même, Maître du Monde" (Jean-Marie Messier, myself, master of the world).[5]

EXCESSIVE AMBITION can blind us to the reality of a situation and render us more likely to make poor, frequently irrational decisions. Look at Groupon, which in 2010 epitomized masterly use of new technologies and social media. Founded in 2009 by Andrew Mason, Groupon was a breakthrough concept for Internet purchasing, connecting large groups of customers interested in exceptionally generous discounts with retailers ready to offer them. For the sellers, being on Groupon brought a number of benefits: a sudden jump in sales volumes, warehouse clearance, and, of course, the ability to promote new enterprises or services, as many consumers attracted by, for example, good prices at their local dentist or hairdressing salon, became repeat customers. Mason's concept worked, and Groupon very quickly became one of the icons of the Internet, like Facebook or YouTube, demonstrating that on the Web, there's nothing more valuable than a good idea. In the fall of 2010, Groupon received an exceptionally generous offer: Google expressed an interest in buying the company for the dizzying sum of close to $6 billion. It seemed an attractive offer for a company that had hit peak growth and was battling with more and more competitors. However, Mason unequivocally rejected the offer, stating that he planned to float the company on the stock market. He kept his word. On November 4, 2011, Groupon debuted on the stock market, with the share price jumping 31 percent on the first day of trading and bringing massive profits to investors dazzled by Andrew Mason's amazing ideas and vision.

Remember the old filmmaker's trick?

"One year later."

In November 2012, Groupon shares stood at $2.50, and the company was valued at $2.7 billion, less than half the amount offered by Google. In his annual rankings, Herb Greenberg of CNBC rated Andrew Mason "Worst CEO of 2012." On February 28, 2013, the board and shareholders came to the same conclusion and dismissed the company founder from his post. In leaving, Mason displayed a great deal of honesty and a sense of humor, and in a farewell letter to employees, he wrote:

> After four and a half intense and wonderful years as CEO of Groupon, I've decided that I'd like to spend more time with my family. Just kidding—I was fired today. If you're wondering why... you haven't been paying attention. [...] As CEO, I am accountable.[6]

Eric Lefkofsky, who had collaborated closely with Mason, was made CEO after Mason's departure. He admitted that Mason's rejection of the Google offer was rooted in a firm conviction that the company could still grow considerably and that its value was several times that offered by the giant from Mountain View.

An equally interesting story unfolded with another corporate giant, this time the one headquartered in Redmond. Between 2000 and 2014, Microsoft shareholders were not exactly happy campers. Though Steve Ballmer, their charismatic head of the business was something of a media darling (just check out the videos on YouTube), he was attracting significantly fewer accolades for his efforts to increase the value of the company he'd been leading since January 2000. Microsoft shares had been at their peak at the time—a single share was worth nearly $60—and the market capitalization stood at over $500 billion. While the prospects for continued growth were positive, instead there followed an almost unbroken fall in the share value, worsened by the economic crises in 2001 and 2008. At the end of 2012, Microsoft shares were going for $26 each, giving a market cap of $300 billion, which itself was a recovery from the historic low of three years earlier, when Microsoft was valued by the markets at barely $160 billion. From the point of view of investors, the picture was even more depressing when Microsoft was compared with the other giants of new technologies. Between 2000 and 2012 (when Microsoft shares halved in value), the share price of Oracle almost doubled, rising from $17 to $32, Google went from $108 to over $400, and Apple shares increased from $25 to... $530.

In August 2013, Ballmer announced that he would step down within twelve months. On February 4, 2014, he was replaced by Satya Nadella, the former executive vice president, who had been with the company for twenty-two years. After Ballmer's successor was announced, the share price of the Redmond giant spiked, and the new CEO met the expectations of investors to a large extent: over the following three years, the share price doubled, adding a further $300 billion to the company's value. Importantly, Nadella's actions, regardless of the financial successes, rekindled the company's somewhat forgotten spirit of innovation.

Charismatic leadership can also lead to far more serious troubles. One of the most convincing business leaders in the last couple of decades was the head of Enron, Jeffrey Skilling, a graduate of Harvard Business School. Rakesh Khurana, a professor at Harvard Business School who conducted a detailed analysis of Enron's management culture in an article published in the *Harvard Business Review*, wrote:

> One former Enron executive has described the upper managerial ranks of the company as a "yes-man culture." CFO Andrew Fastow [...] was so enamored of Skilling that he reportedly named one of his children after him and hired the architect who designed the CEO's Houston mansion to design his house.[7]

Skilling possessed extraordinary inner energy and an ability to convince others that his ideas were good ones. For example, he persuaded the board of directors to—are you ready for this?—abandon the requirement to adhere to the internal code of ethics for the most senior managers. He was equally effective at persuading the auditors to take a more creative perspective when reviewing the company's financial statements. It all ended in the resounding collapse of Enron in 2001, with Jeffrey Skilling being sentenced to fourteen years in prison. Andrew Fastow spent more than five years behind bars, until his release in 2011.

RULE #3

The more you admire someone, the more critically you should examine their opinions.

The more exciting somebody's vision seems, the more closely you should test its foundations in reality.

CHARISMATIC LEADERSHIP has one more major drawback. Even if a company is currently being led by an apparently infallible leader who only makes correct, and ethical, decisions, a surprising trap is being set for the future: succession. Many firms have failed simply because, having enjoyed the benefits of a great leader, they were unable to find another, equally great leader to take their place. It is incredibly difficult to replace a truly charismatic person, as Apple found out following the death of Steve Jobs.

THE SECOND bad advisor is connected to a phenomenon as old as the world: conformity.

At many business training sessions and conferences, you will hear an apocryphal story in which the protagonists are some monkeys, bananas, and exceptionally nasty researchers: In the 1960s, an experiment is rumored to have been conducted in which a ladder was placed in a laboratory cage with bananas dangling temptingly from the top. Several monkeys were released into the cage and, predictably, threw themselves onto the ladder, fighting for the prize. But when the fastest monkey reached out for its reward, it, and all the other monkeys, instead received an unpleasant surprise.

You see, as it reached for the fruit, it set off a sprinkler system that caused icy water to rain down across the whole cage, meaning that all the monkeys were punished, not just the one that achieved the goal. The monkeys soon learned that going on the ladder and reaching for the bananas was a bad idea, and so they sat idly on the floor of the cage. Then the scientists did something interesting. They took one of the passive monkeys out of the cage and introduced a new individual. The newbie, of course, set off enthusiastically up the ladder, somewhat surprised that its companions were sitting around and not trying to eat the bananas. The reaction of the remaining monkeys was, again, fairly predictable: when the newcomer got on the ladder, they all jumped on him and aggressively chased him away from the fruit, while not trying to reach for it themselves. The newcomer didn't understand the cause for their aggressive behavior but did learn that it was not a wise move to get on the ladder. The researchers kept changing the monkeys in the cage, removing those from the initial group and replacing them with new individuals; each time, the same situation occurred, with the animal that went for the prize being attacked. The surprising finding is that the exact same thing happened even when none of the original monkeys were left in the cage, only monkeys that had never experienced the cold shower. It seems that the lesson learned—not to get on the ladder—had become an imperative and influenced the behavior of the monkeys toward new individuals. They attacked every new monkey that tried to get on the ladder, despite not knowing why they were doing so.

There is some dispute over whether or not this experiment ever actually took place, and the source most often cited in support of it is, in fact, about something else entirely.[8] However, as sixteenth-century philosopher Giordano Bruno so beautifully expressed it, *se non è vero, è molto ben trovato.*[9] Even if the experiment with the monkeys and the ladder never happened, the actual learning mechanism for specific group behaviors is widely applicable and affects every single one of us.

The underlying phenomenon is called *acculturation*—or the assimilation of a new model of behavior. In a business context, this means a new employee must quickly learn and adopt the typical behaviors, attitudes, and beliefs of their colleagues in order to fit in and be accepted.

While the topic of organizational culture modeling has been popular in recent years and genuinely translates into more effective functioning of a company, it can have a dark side when it comes to decision-making. It involves unifying not only behaviors and attitudes, but also the manner of thinking of a team or organization. Such unification can be a truly bad advisor in the decision-making process for the same reason as the authority trap: it hinders the objective assessment of a situation.

The problem of conformity frequently begins at the recruitment stage. How so, you might ask? Imagine you're looking for a new person for your team. The final shortlist comprises four candidates, all of whom have an impressive résumé and relevant experience and are equally competent and highly professional. During the interview, though, you realize that while you get on fine with three of the candidates, you seem to be on the same wavelength as the fourth one. You get on like a house on fire, think alike, and even use similar expressions.

So who should you employ?

The fourth person seems the obvious choice, and the majority of recruiters fall into this trap—known as *cloning*—of employing someone who matches their own cognitive mechanisms, who views reality similarly, processes data in the same way, and draws similar conclusions to themselves. Companies enhance the trap of conformity by encouraging employees to conform and become a cohesive group. All this comes from a fundamental misunderstanding that

a harmonious group = a tight group = an effective group

The smoother the discussion, the quicker the conclusion, the more satisfied the company is, even though the price of that harmony is poorer decisions.

RULE #4

The more everyone around insists something is impossible, the more you should check it yourself. Several times.

THESE TWO bad advisors together make one of the worst (and most commonly met) decision-making combinations. Namely, facing a black swan event that we are trying to deal with while being led by a charismatic leader of a conformist team that has recently enjoyed numerous successes (and so is highly respected and regarded within the company). For such a group, breaking away from the status quo is incredibly difficult. Above all, there seems no justification for changing the existing vision and modus operandi, because it's been laid out by an exceptional authority and is backed up by the team's achievements to date—a team that is additionally characterized by unanimity, where everyone agrees with everyone else. In such a setup, you won't find constructive disagreement and the open discussion that results from it anywhere. There's only one way the situation could be worse—if the sunk cost effect is added to the mix.

Please let me introduce our third bad advisor.

DESPITE WHAT most people commonly think, Concorde wasn't the world's first supersonic passenger aircraft to take flight. On December 31, 1968—more than two months before the maiden flight of the Anglo-French version—the TU-144, designed by Andrei Tupolev and produced by the Voronezh Aircraft Production Association of the USSR, took to the air. The Soviets can also take credit for the first passenger aircraft to go through the sound barrier, in June 1969, four months before Concorde did the same.

Despite losing that particular race, though, Concorde ultimately won the fame, completely eclipsing the TU-144, which, despite all its initial success, was rapidly withdrawn from the commercial market. There were many reasons behind this decision, not least that the aircraft was seriously underdeveloped and therefore unreliable, which led to two catastrophes, the first of which occurred during the 1973 Paris Air Show and resulted in long-term damage to the aircraft's public image. Furthermore, the Soviets, basking in the propagandistic success of having beaten two countries from the capitalist bloc, were aware of the high costs of maintaining and commercially exploiting the plane. They therefore waved goodbye to the TU-144 in 1978 with few regrets, after barely three years' operation and only fifty-five scheduled flights completed.

The situation with Concorde was totally different. Lavishly financed by the governments of the UK and France, the manufacturers—the British Aircraft Corporation and Sud Aviation—consistently promoted their aircraft as heralding a breakthrough in transatlantic flight and rapidly attracted around seventy orders from over a dozen airlines. In addition to Air France and BOAC

(British Overseas Airways Corporation, renamed British Airways in the 1970s), Lufthansa, Japan Airlines, American Airlines, Air Canada, and Singapore Airlines, among others, wanted Concorde in their colors. However, the 1973 oil crisis sent fuel prices rocketing. That, combined with the cost of Concorde and the ever-increasing environmental concerns about its exhaust emissions and the noise created by the engines, meant that almost all the potential buyers withdrew from their options to buy.

The collapse in demand brought into question the rationale for the entire enterprise, and costs spiraled. In the mid-1970s, they were already six times the figure initially estimated, and pressure mounted in both France and the UK for the suspension of the Concorde program. Giving up at this point, though, would have meant losing the money already invested and, worse still, would have inflicted a severe blow to the image of both countries and their governments. So, work continued and the aircraft finally joined the fleets of the French and British airlines, thanks in part to generous subsidies via public funding. Regular passenger flights commenced in 1976.

In later years Concorde was the source of both admiration and controversy. On the one hand, the airplane was a symbol of outstanding technical achievement;[10] on the other, it was an example of spending enormous sums of taxpayers' money with no chance of recovering the investment. The flames of controversy were further fanned by the constant discussions about environmental issues— one country or another was always either banning Concorde from flying through its airspace or restricting it to subsonic flight because of the excessive noise it produced. Many airports refused to accept it on their runways, for fear of lawsuits from local residents.

Yet Concorde remained in operation until the beginning of the twenty-first century. The proverbial nail in its coffin was delivered by the catastrophe in Paris on July 25, 2000, in which all one hundred passengers, nine crew, and four people on the ground were killed. Flights were halted for several months, and in 2003 both airlines retired the beautiful, ingenious, but extravagantly costly beast, which ended up in aviation museums around the world.

However, its legacy lives on, not only in museums but also in social psychology, where the term *Concorde fallacy* is a colloquialism for the phenomenon more formally known as sunk costs effect.

The sunk costs effect rests on the irrational continuation of an action that has no chance of success, but in which we have invested significant finances, time, or effort. A person caught in this trap thinks that, because they have already incurred serious costs, they can't withdraw, as this would essentially confirm their losses to them. We've all encountered numerous examples of this behavior. Someone who's invested money in a bad business is prepared to continue investing, keeping their illusory hopes of success alive. A gambler in a casino who's lost all his money will think nothing of pawning his watch in hopes of recouping his losses. A car that keeps breaking down despite countless repairs (and that you should really sell as quickly as you can) continues to be a drain on your finances, much to your mechanic's delight. We find it hard to make a decision that is tantamount to admitting we were wrong, and we therefore continue to throw good money after bad.

A particularly dangerous form of sunk costs is the image trap, as our reputation is also a kind of investment. The more we've backed a venture, the more we feel emotionally tied to it. The more emotionally engaged we are, the harder it is to remain neutral about it. One of my friends from the high-tech sector observed many years ago that there's nothing more difficult than dropping a project you've put your name to.

It's no accident, then, that the sunk costs effect acquired its colloquial name from the Concorde story. This groundbreaking project became increasingly difficult to justify in economic terms, and at a certain point it really should have been shelved, set aside until better times or technological advances made it possible to reduce its operating costs and noise levels, and so on. Unfortunately, the costs already incurred, together with the earlier enthusiastic declarations of support from not only the airlines but also the governments of France and the UK, left the decision-makers in a sunk costs trap, which they couldn't get out of. Irrational economic decisions were taken to continue the work and introduce the aircraft into the fleets of both carriers.

Other examples abound in the world around us.

Surprisingly, even the Germans, consistently held up as models of solidity and scrupulous business sense, are struggling with a project whose financial dimension bears an uncanny resemblance to a bottomless pit. Berlin used to be served by three airports, Schönefeld, Tegel, and Tempelhof. With the reunification of Germany came the idea of building a large airport to accommodate a significant portion of the passengers from the existing ones and serve not only the German capital, but the whole of Brandenburg. After much squabbling, construction of the new Berlin Brandenburg Airport, slated to serve close to 30 million passengers annually, began in 2006. Costs were estimated at over €2 billion, and the airfield was to open to passengers and airlines in 2010. The deadline wasn't met—even though Tempelhof ceased operations in 2008 in anticipation of the planned opening of the new airport. Very soon, it appeared that nobody could realistically set a completion date for the project. By 2010, the sole achievement of the project team was to have chosen a patron for the airport (Willy Brandt, who beat out Albert Einstein, Marlene Dietrich, and Claus von Stauffenberg, among others). It was finally announced that the airport would open on June 3, 2012. In May 2012, this was amended to March 17, 2013. When September 2012 came around, a new opening date was given: October 27, 2013. As I'm sure you've guessed by now, that date also turned out to be unrealistic, so, at the beginning of 2013, the authorities announced that the Berlin Brandenburg Airport would open in 2014. This, however, was still a highly optimistic prognosis, because at the beginning of 2014 we were informed that an accurate prediction for the opening date of the airport was simply not possible, especially as a fundamental problem had arisen: the only airline that was considering using Berlin Brandenburg as its main hub was the financially unstable Air Berlin (which ultimately went bust at the end of 2017, even further complicating the situation). It's worth adding that, to date, close to €7 billion have been sunk into the project—and that's certain not to be the final figure. Klaus Wowereit, the mayor of Berlin and head of the team supervising the Berlin Brandenburg Airport project, resigned from his role as team lead in recognition of his involvement in the ongoing debacle. Despite this "heroic" gesture, nobody can say whether the new airport will ever be ready, and if so, at what cost.

LOOK AROUND you. Many companies have a great number of projects which, looked at objectively, have no hope of success, but which are allowed to continue, because they've already swallowed a lot of money and time, and nobody has the courage to point out that the emperor is naked. While hosting a conference for one of my clients, I heard a very good expression for this phenomenon. The CEO of a large technology firm liked to call inefficient business projects, of which his company had many, "Titanics." He compared them to the situation in which it was already clear the ship was sinking and couldn't be saved, but some people were still manning the pumps and trying to bail out the water, instead of dealing with more important matters.

Having the courage to abandon such Titanics pays off, because it allows us to free up employees' time and energy for other, more constructive tasks, which gives a much better return on our money. In a world where time is constantly in short supply, that's a massive advantage.

We rarely realize the scale of the savings we could make. For example, the board of a large service sector company twice refused the suggestion that it review its project portfolio, saying it didn't make economic sense. The third time the idea was presented to the board, it was persuaded to go ahead with it—and subsequently introduced a system for the rapid elimination of ineffective projects, based on an accurate assessment of the key performance indicators (KPIs). In only six months, the company cut the number of its projects by 18 percent, which reduced the number of employees engaged in them by 24 percent. The savings didn't affect the income from the portfolio of projects, because they were achieved solely by eliminating those projects that had no chance of success and, consequently, no prospect of generating income.

RULE #5

The greater the investment of time, effort, money, and our own reputation, the harder it is to objectively assess a situation and make the right decision.

COLIN POWELL, when asked what he understood by leadership, is quoted as saying that "it's the art of accomplishing more than the science of management says is possible." Very often, then, the authentic leader in an organization becomes the person who is able to persuade those around them to engage in deep discussion on a relevant matter, even if those same people are convinced that the solution is obvious and safe and has been tested many times over, thus making the discussion pointless. In the world of black swans, that is a very dangerous approach.

The combination of our unconscious extrapolation of positive trends with the ease with which we succumb to real, or presumed, authority, together with our natural tendency to match our behavior to meet the expectations of a group lies at the root of both the smaller and the larger mistakes we make every day. In the last twenty years, I have frequently encountered very good managers who stared dumbfounded at an unexpected failure, with not the remotest idea about how it happened.

"That business process had been developed to perfection and had never let me down before."

"I went with the opinions of the best consultants on the market."

"I didn't fight for this project a year ago and then work over twelve hours a day on it to give up on it now. I put everything into it."

"Everyone was convinced it was the right decision."

"There's no way that should have happened."

Once we started to talk about these basic decision-making traps, which our cognitive mechanisms and social psychology set for us, we soon discovered the source of the mistakes. The next question the managers asked themselves had little educational merit—"How could I have been so stupid?"—but it did lead to a more fundamental and productive one: "How do I not make such an idiot of myself in future?"

THE ANSWER to that will be revealed in the following two chapters.

PROCESS 4

ONE OF THE most valuable guidelines I've encountered for making good decisions is astonishingly simple: Always treat making a good decision as a process, not an event. In other words, don't reduce deciding to a single act, a single point in time; treat it as a process that demands an appropriate approach, careful consideration of your options, a choice, and timely follow-up. And don't forget to pay close attention to the time requirements. Most of our decision-related mistakes come from underestimating not only the preparation required before we make a decision, but also the implementation requirements. This results in either, less than perfect decisions (faulty approach), or decisions which, even if they were perfect, didn't bring the expected result (faulty implementation).

There are three fundamental approaches to the decision-making process, each with its own particular advantages depending on circumstances.

THE FIRST approach is called *routinized decision-making*—essentially an intuitive approach in which we make a decision unconsciously, drawing on repeated experiences and ingrained habits and decision-making mechanisms without thinking too much about them. It sounds dangerous, but the routinized approach is the one that we naturally use for making recurring decisions in known conditions (i.e., when we know exactly what the effects of an action will be). In such conditions, routinized decision-making not only works, but thanks to the extra automaticity of this method of deciding, it also saves our brains the time and energy needed for more important, conscious choices. A simple example of gradually routinized decision-making is driving a car with a manual transmission. When you're learning to drive a car with a manual transmission, every gear change is a conscious, thought-out decision in which you run the whole sequence of actions through your mind as you carry them out. When you want to shift up a gear, for example, you check that the revs are high enough, you press down on the clutch while taking your foot slowly off the accelerator until your clutch bites, select a higher gear, and then slowly release the clutch while gently pressing on the accelerator, so as not to stall the engine. The years pass, you drive hundreds of thousands of miles, and, with your increasing experience, your driving becomes more and more routinized and automatic. While you're driving, you think about a thousand other decisions—but none of them concerns which gear to select.

Routinized decision-making is therefore the natural and appropriate approach when you're dealing with fixed conditions, and the decision itself is repeatable and has been tested on numerous occasions. One way or another, this mode kicks in without our conscious participation, which can be risky when we treat a less than obvious problem, requiring somewhat deeper analysis, as routine.

The other two decision-making approaches are called *advocacy* and *inquiry*;[1] they each involve a conscious process and rational consideration, but are otherwise significantly different from one another.

In *advocacy mode*, when we encounter a problem that requires us to make a decision, we rely on our prior experience, knowledge, and sense of the situation to point us toward an appropriate solution. Once we find a starting point, we look for information to confirm that our idea is a good one, and if we find that information, we make our decision and then act on it. In this mode, decision-makers and teams operate quickly and effectively, looking for key pieces of information that are pertinent to the choice to be made. Advocacy therefore works in numerous situations where we are dealing with classically understood risk management—that is, when we know what the consequences of a decision will be and how likely it is that they will occur. It is enough, in such circumstances, to analyze whether the assumed approach is confirmed by concrete, tested data. The vast majority of business decisions are made in this mode, as it enables us to save one of our most precious resources: time.

A weakness of the advocacy mode is that it offers a superficial, incomplete analysis of the available information, especially in conformist teams operating under tight deadlines. In some cases, information can even be filtered in such a way that only data that support a particular choice are presented, so as not to arouse any doubts or extend the discussion of the problem. This kind of mistake may be forgivable in a fraught situation, but in an uncertain one—such as a black swan—where we are unable to assess the likelihood of certain consequences of a decision, or even what those consequences might be, the advocacy approach can be literally fatal. Eurocontrol's response to the eruption of the Eyjafjallajökull volcano (discussed in the Introduction) is a classic example of such a mistake. While the initial decisions taken were correct (halt air traffic, as we've never been in such a situation before and we don't know what the actual risk to flights is), the later ones were equally wrong. Eurocontrol went into advocacy mode, only accepting arguments that demonstrated that flying in such conditions would end in disaster and that, as a result, their decision had been correct. Data that disagreed with this thinking, data presented by the airlines, who were testing their machines in the real world, were either ignored or rejected by the organization.

A VERY similar error was made in 1998 by the decision-makers at Daimler-Benz and Chrysler as they prepared to merge the two companies. On the surface, everything looked great: they'd done their due diligence, and so had a detailed analysis of the prospects for the merged company, which clearly demonstrated the real benefits of the decision. The further work progressed on the merger, the more enthusiastic about it the two CEOs, Jürgen Schrempp of Daimler and Robert James "Bob" Eaton from Chrysler, became, and the more their optimism was shared by the other executives. So, the CEOs were passed more information confirming that this was a match made in heaven—analyses showed opportunities not only for increased sales, but also for significant cost reductions in the newly created company. When the merger finally took place, no one doubted how sensible a deal it was. And yet, almost at once, obstacles to daily collaboration and communication arose, and open conflicts between managers and teams occurred with great regularity, resulting in a lot of poor business decisions being made. The result of all this? The share price for DaimlerChrysler AG, $100 on the day of the merger, plummeted to less than half of that in the course of two years.

Despite the efforts of the company's bosses and innumerable internal projects supporting integration, the problems couldn't be resolved, and in 2007, Daimler opted to legally separate from Chrysler. It sold its shares for just under $7.5 billion to Cerberus Capital Management, but received less than $1.5 billion from that sum as the remainder had to be handed over to support Chrysler. That wasn't the end of the bad news. Before the separation agreement came into force, Daimler also had to cover ongoing losses, which came to $1.6 billion. The Germans ended up paying out about $600 million. In business terms, though, the decision to split wasn't a bad one—not least because Daimler had extricated itself from future pension liabilities included in the contracts of Chrysler employees. For Chrysler, the story ended much worse. In 2009, their suffering exacerbated by the economic crisis in the USA, the company filed for Chapter 11 bankruptcy.

The cause of the unexpected collapse of what was widely referred to as "the deal of the century" lay in the over-selective analyses of both firms prior to their merger. In the course of their due diligence they examined only business factors—which, to be fair, did look positive (product portfolios, markets and customer segmentation, financial and operational perspectives, etc.)—and ignored the enormous cultural incompatibilities not only between the two firms but, worse still, between the two nations they called home. Daimler was a conservative organization, quite hierarchical and dominated by a culture of thorough, methodical operations and decision-making based on solid figures. Chrysler was heavily decentralized, and emphasized freedom of operation to the point where it expected its employees to make their own decisions, be creative, and even take risks. It will probably come as little surprise that these differences dealt a body blow to the merger, generating all sorts of conflicts, hampering everyday work, and negatively affecting morale in the company. The potential problem of cultural differences, which probably seems obvious to anyone reading this, was missed, because the information was provided and analyzed in a way that would support the merger.

In the context of a black swan event, which is the situation Daimler and Eurocontrol found themselves in, the third decision-making approach—inquiry—should be the only option. With *inquiry mode*, the decision-maker tries to analyze all the available data, to review the evidence from all angles, involving as many people and perspectives as possible. This leads to open, constructive discussion and an intellectual battle of ideas (detailed discussion of different options, actions, and possible scenarios), but without affective (personal) conflicts. The crucial factor in inquiry-based decision-making is diversity: people from different positions within an organization and with a variety of experiences should be involved in the analysis and preparation stages before a decision is made. The more cognitively diverse a team is, the deeper and more multifaceted the discussions will be, and the more meticulously the decision-making process will be conducted. Inquiry is certainly the most time-consuming approach, but it helps anyone using it to make the best possible decisions, based on a thorough analysis of the data and assessment of possible scenarios.

THE CONSISTENT application of the inquiry approach helped John F. Kennedy resolve the most serious problem that arose between the superpowers during the Cold War: the 1962 Cuban Missile Crisis. Paradoxically, it was a success whose beginnings lay in the failure of the Bay of Pigs operation.

After Fidel Castro took power in Cuba in 1959, socialism was perceived to have come dangerously close to US soil. One of his first decisions—to nationalize private property in Cuba—enraged Americans, who lost around $2 billion in assets as a result of the decision. In response, in October 1960, the US government imposed a trade embargo on the island. But that wasn't all. While Eisenhower was still in office, the CIA set up Brigade 2506 in Guatemala, composed mainly of Cubans who opposed Fidel Castro and who had immigrated to the USA after his victory. The aim of the brigade, which comprised almost fifteen hundred people, was to attack Havana and overthrow the authorities. The CIA presented the outline for the operation, as well as a range of arguments and figures confirming it would be a guaranteed success, to Eisenhower's successor, JFK, who ultimately signed the order. So, on April 17, 1961, five divisions of Brigade 2506 landed on the beach at Girón in the Bay of Pigs, and within forty-eight hours . . . it was all over. The Cuban army, led personally by Fidel Castro, rapidly took control of the situation. Over a hundred members of Brigade 2506 were killed, and several hundred more (the figures vary according to which source you consult) were arrested and either sentenced to thirty years' imprisonment or sent back to the USA in exchange for $30 million worth of tractors. Many, if not most, people immediately began to speculate that the CIA was behind the entire operation, provoking an enormous scandal which resulted in its leader at the time, Allen Welsh Dulles, being forced to resign.

The mistakes made in preparing the Bay of Pigs operation can be summed up as a typical error of process: a highly complex decision, played out in a context of uncertainty, was made using advocacy instead of inquiry, in an environment dominated by a group hell-bent on military conflict. But that's not the worst part. It later transpired that the army and CIA representatives had deliberately excluded from the discussion any experts from the US Department of State who were well informed about the local situation and the realities of Latin America and who did not support the operation. As a result, the discussion and analysis were rendered positively skeletal, with a whole range of critical assumptions—for example, the time needed to transport Brigade 2506 from the beach at the Bay of Pigs to the mountains, almost 19 miles from the coast and how the Cubans actually felt about things—were left unchecked. It was assumed that any strike against Fidel Castro would be supported by the local people, a presumption that turned out to be totally unsubstantiated.

Kennedy took responsibility for the disaster and decided to radically change how decisions of key importance to the nation were made, with the aim of forcing his advisors to operate via the inquiry mode.

His chance came barely a year later, when escalating tensions had the world teetering on the brink of nuclear war. Directly after the Bay of Pigs debacle, the Soviets had decided to take advantage of the situation in Cuba, placing missiles capable of carrying nuclear warheads on the island. This gave them a chance of catching up in the arms race, as in 1961 the Americans had managed to place Jupiter missiles on territory belonging to Turkey, which had joined NATO a decade earlier. The operation to deliver forty-two SS-4 and twenty-four SS-5 missiles to Cuba began in the first half of 1962, and was soon detected by US intelligence. On August 15, 1962, a US Lockheed P-2 Neptune surveillance plane spotted the Soviet ship *Omsk* heading for Cuba, and on October 14, Colonel Richard S. Heyser, after seven hours' piloting a U-2 spy plane, captured film footage confirming Washington's worst fears: in Cuba, barely 90 miles from the Florida coast, Soviet missile launchers capable of delivering nuclear warheads had been installed. JFK reacted instantly. Wiser now, thanks to his Bay of Pigs experience, on October 16, he convened a meeting of EXCOMM (the Executive Committee of the National Security Council), which was composed not only of top-level representatives of the army and intelligence services, but also people outside of military circles. The Committee's actions were accompanied by several principles. First, all EXCOMM meetings had to involve not just experts in the field, but also representatives from other disciplines (e.g., military decisions were made not only by army and intelligence services personnel, but also by people from the worlds of business, diplomacy, academia, and so on). Second, committee members were told to be skeptical at all times and to dig deeper to understand everything under discussion, no matter how little they knew about certain topics. Third, all formalities and notions of hierarchy were set aside during the meetings, and Robert Kennedy and Theodore Sorensen, a long-standing friend and advisor to the president, made sure this rule was obeyed. The most important principle, though, concerned the head of state himself: aware of just how much his opinion might affect the opinions of other people in the meeting (the authority trap!), he decided not to take part in the group's initial sessions.

The situation was extraordinarily grave and demanded the detailed analysis of a range of options. The two extreme scenarios (do nothing or launch a massed assault on Cuba) were unbelievably risky, as they each introduced a black swan—nobody knew how the Soviets would react, given that successfully placing nuclear warheads on Cuba along with launching a large-scale American invasion could constitute a justification for embarking on an all-out nuclear war.[2] Two working groups were set up within EXCOMM. One had the task of drawing up a detailed plan of attack, which the army was pushing for, while the other was to look for solutions that might prevent the installation of nuclear warheads on the island. After much discussion, the second group proposed a compromise solution in the form of a sea blockade of Cuba by the US Navy to make it physically impossible to supply the warheads. On October 22, President Kennedy opted to back the compromise option, much to the chagrin of the generals, who had already announced the mobilization of 180,000 soldiers and planned over 1,000 air sorties on the first day of the operation. A total of forty vessels were sent to the area of the blockade, led by the heavy cruiser USS *Newport News*. This move bought the Americans some time.

However, the sea blockade didn't resolve the problem, and in the days that followed the situation continued to escalate, with warning shots being fired from US ships. As the end of the month grew closer, one outcome seemed increasingly inevitable: direct confrontation between the two superpowers. On October 26, 1962, for the first time ever, the United States was put on DEFCON 2.

One of the EXCOMM members was Llewellyn "Tommy" Thompson, a former US ambassador to Moscow who knew Nikita Khrushchev and his wife very well. Thompson reckoned from the very beginning that Khrushchev had been trapped in an increasingly dangerous game. Following the death of Stalin, Khrushchev had come to power by ruthlessly eliminating his rivals, Lavrentiy Beria—who was sentenced to death for what *Pravda*, the hugely popular government-backed newspaper of the time, reported as "criminal activities against the Party and the State"—and Georgy Malenkov—a former prime minister who was exiled—and the Central Committee of the Communist Party still included many supporters of the two deposed dignitaries, hawkishly waiting for the slightest show of weakness in the General Secretary. According to Thompson, Khrushchev absolutely had to emerge from the Cuban missile crisis with a simple message: I saved Cuban socialism from US aggression. The business of locating warheads faded into the background. In terms of image, it was more important to preserve Fidel Castro and the political system on the island. On October 27, 1962, during the decisive EXCOMM meeting regarding the eventual attack on Cuba, there was an extraordinary exchange of opinions between President Kennedy and Thompson. The president, convinced that attack was the only option, had decided to take that route. He stated firmly and authoritatively: "We're not gonna get the weapons out of Cuba probably anyway through negotiation." Thompson's reply surprised everyone: "Afraid I don't agree, Mr. President. I think there is still a chance. The important thing is for Khrushchev to be able to say 'I saved Cuba, I stopped the invasion.'" Such direct, public disagreement with the president simply didn't happen in those days. The EXCOMM members at the meeting were dumbfounded. Robert S. McNamara, then Secretary of Defense, said many years later: "That takes a lot of guts." [3]

As a result of Thompson's declaration, Kennedy, despite his earlier convictions and the enormous pressure being placed on him by the military, and in particular by General Curtis Emerson LeMay, Chief of Staff of the USAAF, decided to halt the attack. Negotiations took place behind the scenes, which offered some hope of resolving the problem. The decisive moment occurred on October 27. In the course of a few hours, two messages came from Moscow. The first was signed by Khrushchev and sounded distinctly conciliatory. In it, the Soviets demanded a declaration from the USA that Cuba would not be attacked; in return, they offered to remove their missiles. Before a response could be drafted, another message arrived, this one obviously from a group of hard-liners. Its tone was distinctly harsher and it contained a direct threat that if the USA attacked Cuba, the USSR would respond with all the military means it possessed. It said nothing about removing the missiles. A startled EXCOMM assessed the situation. Yet again, Thompson proved invaluable, as he suggested to the president that he should respond to the first message and say nothing about the second one. Kennedy once more agreed with his advisor's opinion and publicly announced that the United States did not intend to attack Cuba, and that they were waiting for Khrushchev to withdraw the missiles as he had declared. Kennedy adopted a positive approach toward the General Secretary in his official statements to the media, declaring him to be a great statesman. Unsurprisingly, Khrushchev did the only thing he could in that situation: accept the USA's position and withdraw the missiles.[4] Though a nuclear conflict between the superpowers had been avoided, Khrushchev paid a heavy price. Barely two years later, in October 1964, he was removed from power in a conspiracy led by Mikhail Suslov, Alexei Kosygin, and Leonid Brezhnev, who became the new General Secretary of the Communist Party. One of the official reasons for Khrushchev's removal was diplomatic failures in the international arena.

Another extraordinary example of applying an inquiry approach to a black swan situation took place a few years later, but in an entirely different environment.

MOST OF you have probably seen the 1995 Oscar-winning *Apollo 13*, based on the mission of the same name. The movie, based on the dramatic events that took place during the mission, was directed by Ron Howard, and the lead roles were played by a host of brilliant actors, including Tom Hanks, Gary Sinise, Kevin Bacon, Kathleen Quinlan, and Ed Harris, who played Gene Kranz, the flight director of *Apollo 13* and chief architect of the rescue operation.

Kranz was an extraordinary figure. Fascinated by aviation from a young age, he later developed a passionate interest in the conquest of space. He studied at St. Louis University, where he specialized in aviation and technology, after which he went to the Lackland Air Force Base in Texas, where he trained as a fighter pilot. He served in South Korea as an F-86 Sabre pilot and on his return home began working for the McDonnell Aircraft Corporation. In 1960, he joined NASA.

NASA was created in 1958 by President Dwight Eisenhower, one of a range of initiatives to respond to the USSR's growing dominance of the competition to conquer space. The Soviets were way ahead of the Americans, not only in the race to be first in space (they had launched *Sputnik*, the first artificial Earth satellite, and put the first man into orbit around the planet), but also in the arms race, where an important element of nuclear dominance was an ongoing increase in the quality and quantity of ballistic missiles.[5] Organizations such as NASA, while important for national prestige and self-image, were also crucial to national defense systems. NASA's first undertaking was the Mercury project, the goal of which was to send the first American into space. It was partially successful in 1961, when Alan Shepard, flying the *Freedom 7* spacecraft, completed a fifteen-minute suborbital flight, making him the first US citizen in space. Less than a year later, John Glenn, onboard *Friendship 7*, made history when he became the first American to make a complete orbital flight. These successes were reflected in the unusually bold vision set out by President Kennedy. On May 25, 1961, speaking before a joint session of Congress, he said:

> This nation should commit itself to achieving the goal, before this decade is out, of landing a man on the moon and returning him safely to the earth. No single space project in this period will be more impressive to mankind, or more important for the long-range exploration of space; and none will be so difficult or expensive to accomplish.

His words fired the starting gun for the race to win the greatest trophy in the global space conquest tournament: landing man on the Moon.

The Americans set up the Gemini program to build up knowledge and experience that would help them in their later, decisive undertaking, the Apollo series of missions. But while successive Gemini flights were successful, the very first Apollo mission ended in tragedy. A fire broke out in the capsule on January 27, 1967, during a launch rehearsal test, killing the three-man crew. The following five Apollo missions, in which the Saturn V delivery rocket was tested, were unmanned, and it was a full two years, at the end of 1968, before people were once again sent into space—the astronauts onboard *Apollo 7*. Further missions managed to go into orbit around the Moon (*Apollo 10* got positively up close and personal, coming within almost 9 miles of our planet's natural satellite) and finally the great day arrived. On July 20, 1969, two of the three astronauts in the crew of *Apollo 11*, Neil Armstrong and Buzz Aldrin, stood on the surface of the Moon. President Kennedy's bold vision had become a reality.

Less than a year later, NASA unexpectedly faced one of the most serious problems in its history. On April 11, 1970, punctually at 13:13 the *Apollo 13* mission began (anyone feeling superstitious?). Despite the triptych of thirteens, the liftoff from Launch Complex 39 (LC-39) pad A at the Kennedy Space Center went smoothly and the three-man crew—James A. Lovell, Fred Haise Jr., and John Leonard "Jack" Swigert—took off according to plan on a flight whose mission was to be the third US landing on the Moon. The *Apollo 13* crew was not a random assortment of colleagues. Commander James Lovell, an experienced US Navy fighter pilot and a graduate of Harvard Business School, was a leading US astronaut and had three flights under his belt—on *Gemini 7*, *Gemini 12*, and *Apollo 8*. In 1969, he was the leader of the backup crew for *Apollo 11*, so had Neil Armstrong been unable for some reason to participate in the mission, Lovell would have been the first man on the Moon. Although Fred Haise (another graduate of Harvard

Business School) and Jack Swigert were on their first space flight, both were highly experienced military pilots. Haise's task was to fly the *Aquarius* lunar module, while Swigert was in charge of the *Odyssey* command module.[6]

On April 14, 1970, fifty-five hours and fifty-four minutes into the mission, at 03:08 universal time, a damaged electrical cable caused an explosion in one of the oxygen tanks, which led James Lovell to send back to Earth the famous, albeit frequently misquoted, message "Houston, we've had a problem." The explosion resulted in a dramatic series of consequences that not only put an immediate end to their chances of landing on the Moon, but also put the ability of the crew to return safely in jeopardy. The story of the following eighty-seven hours became one of the most fascinating rescue missions in human history, and it remains a superb example of a practical application of an inquiry approach.

The mission director, Gene Kranz, was in the Mission Operations Control Room in Houston when those on the ground heard Lovell's fateful words. Immediately after receiving the information about the problems onboard, the leader of *Apollo 13* clarified that the explosion had caused the craft to lose power on the main B bus, one of the two main electrical circuits onboard. A moment later the telemetry came back on, and on Earth, a steady flow of automatically generated reports of new malfunctions began arriving: two of the three fuel cells failed, one of the oxygen tanks was completely destroyed, and the pressure was rapidly dropping in the other. The scale of the problems was difficult to imagine. Seymour Liebergot, the mission's EECOM (Electrical, Environmental, and Consumables Manager), said in an interview that "It was not a single or a double or a triple failure I was looking at. It was a quadruple failure. That was impossible, it just couldn't happen on that craft,"[7] thus classifying the situation as a black swan. Of course, there was no way the mission could continue, and instead the battle to save the crew began.

Apollo 13 was composed of two independent craft: a command module (CSM), connected to the service module where the explosion occurred, and a lunar module (LM), named *Aquarius*. Kranz's team, analyzing the possible scenarios, very quickly came to the conclusion that, as a result of the damage sustained by the command module, the only way to save the crew was to use the LM as a life boat. The LM was equipped with its own power source, as well as oxygen tanks independent of the command module and life support systems for the crew. Houston therefore ordered the astronauts to get into the landing module and to switch off the power in the command module to save power for the return journey—the CSM was the only part of *Apollo 13* suited to enter Earth's atmosphere. If the command module totally ran out of power in the ensuing hours, or if it mechanically failed, the crew would have no chance.

Kranz's team were faced with making another key decision: how to get the seriously damaged spacecraft to Earth. When *Apollo 13* hit problems, it was almost 200,000 miles from Earth and almost 43,000 miles from the Moon. Houston's challenge was how to plan a flight trajectory when the shortest route (i.e., turning the spacecraft round using its rockets) wasn't necessarily the best. First of all, it meant dumping the LM; secondly, there was a risk that the command module engine wouldn't work, as it was beside the site of the explosion. Neither the crew nor mission control had reliable information about the condition of the rocket, so if the CSM turned out to be inoperable after the lunar module was dumped, the crew would be certain to die. A second option, which involved continuing the flight toward the Moon, seemed utterly absurd, but only at first glance. In this scenario, NASA planned to use the Moon's gravity to jump-start *Apollo 13* and to turn it around and send it on its way home. The spacecraft would have to make a controlled flight around the Moon and then, after a brief blast of the engines, head back to Earth. Two pluses of that option were that it allowed for some emergency alternatives if the engine in the command module failed and it saved fuel; a minus was that it significantly extended the timeline of the whole operation—according to the estimates of Kranz's team, it would take about forty-eight hours more than the direct return option, which in light of the meager supplies of oxygen in the lander constituted a genuine risk to the astronauts' lives. A further minus was that this scenario also required those involved to work out a set of totally original solutions and take absolutely nonstandard, previously untested actions.

Kranz brought all the mission control staff together in the main hall and spoke the words that have passed into history as an example of authentic leadership in crisis conditions, at the same time providing a superb example of initiating an inquiry process:

> Okay, team, we have a hell of a problem. There has been some type of explosion on board the spacecraft. We still don't know what happened. We are on the long return around the Moon and it is our job to find out how to get them home. [...] The odds are damned long, but we're damned good.

He then named his team leads and gave a detailed breakdown of what he expected of everyone involved—making clear that communication across the board was crucial to success, that instructions from the team leads were to be followed to the letter, and that if anyone felt they were not the right person for a task assigned to them, they should suggest someone more suitable. His closing words were nothing short of inspirational:

> Okay, listen up. When you leave this room, you must leave believing that *this crew is coming home.* I don't give a damn about the

odds and I don't give a damn that we've never done anything like this before. Flight control will *never* lose an American in space. You've got to believe, your people have got to believe, that this crew is coming home. Now let's get going![8]

Kranz was in an extremely difficult situation—he had to balance the demands of two opposing forces. On the one hand, as he was dealing with a black swan, it was essential to carry out the most thorough and detailed analysis of the data possible, and to then generate the maximum number of potential scenarios. On the other hand, time was of the essence, as every second that passed sucked up the dwindling oxygen supplies.

Stuck in this dichotomy, Kranz was nonetheless certain about a few points. He knew that this was a mission impossible—a rescue operation without parallel in human history. He also knew that any error would be fatal, so he had to make use of every available second to check the data he was going to have to base his decision on. He knew that without involving a broad group of experts in the discussion, from both within NASA and outside the organization, he would have no chance of saving *Apollo 13* and its crew. He knew that although the final decision was his to make, success hinged on very precisely defining the responsibilities of the key personnel in the decision-making process and involving them every step of the way.

He was also aware that there wasn't enough time, resources were limited, and there was absolutely no margin for error.

Kranz recognized that it was fundamental that he involve the largest possible number of experts, from the widest possible range of fields in an open discussion. Every second had to be dedicated to understanding the essence of the problems Houston was struggling with and to generate the maximum number of action scenarios to then be further tested and analyzed. The team instantly abandoned any options that had even a whiff of not being implementable in the time available. All work was constantly checked by the designated leaders, Arnold Aldrich, John Aaron, and William Peters, so that the solutions chosen didn't threaten to waste the time available for the critical resources on the spacecraft and the entire operation.

Later, Kranz explained that by creating an environment in which everyone believed in their collective ability to save the crew and felt able to speak out for the greater good without worrying about the reactions of their colleagues, the team was able to push forward and focus solely on addressing the crisis.

> With a team working in this fashion, not concerned with voicing their opinions freely and without worrying about hurting anyone's feelings, we saved time. Everyone became a part of the solution.[9]

Kranz's instant decision to deepen the inquiry approach meant inviting engineers from NASA's subcontractors to join the discussions—the Apollo program was carried out by over five hundred companies, which were responsible for designing and manufacturing various elements of the craft. Among the most important subcontractors were MIT's Draper Labs, Grumman Aerospace Corporation, and North American Rockwell, whose experts were literally pulled from their beds and catapulted into the work for Kranz's team. They had to deal with a range of doubts and questions that they had never previously encountered.

The problems with the engines on *Apollo 13* required switching off all the spacecraft's systems until it was time to prepare for re-entry. That gave them a chance of saving the energy that would be required later. The navigational system used the most energy onboard, being essential for the proper administration of all maneuvers during the mission and while landing, making it the prime candidate to be switched off. However, the engineers from Draper Labs, who built the system, were concerned because no one had ever powered down and then restarted the equipment during a flight. The matter was escalated, and a row, albeit a highly constructive one, broke out among the most important personnel. They debated the facts and concrete data that made it clear that leaving the navigational system powered on meant that the electrics would surely fail before the crew made it back home. If they turned the navigation off, however, there was no guarantee that they would be able to restart it successfully, and without it, there would be no return trip. After lengthy analysis and testing, a surprising solution was put forward: leave the navigation on, but turn off the heating and lighting in the module the astronauts were in, which meant a drastic reduction in the temperature inside the *Apollo 13* capsule. The idea was put into action, and from that moment on the crew continued the flight in darkness and bitter cold, which was an enormous test of their physical and mental endurance.

Another black swan dealt with in inquiry mode was the matter of the carbon dioxide filters onboard the craft. Increasing concentrations of carbon dioxide during a mission was a relatively routine occurrence, and there were two distinctive square filters, like two large boxes, for cleaning the air on the command module. The unexpected problem stemmed from the crew's being in the landing module, which enriched the air using its own filters—which were cylindrical. Typical air use in the LM was meant to be at much lower levels (only two people, not three, and for two days, not four), so there were no spare filters, and it rapidly became clear that if they didn't change the filters, the crew would slowly suffocate. In an unfortunate twist on the old adage about trying to fit a square peg into a round hole, they were faced with trying to make the available square filters fit the canister sockets in the landing module, which could only take round filters. And as if that weren't enough, they had to do it only using objects already on *Apollo 13* and that weren't required for any other vital tasks. After a whole night of fevered work and endless brainstorming, Ed Smylie's team in the Johnson Space Center discovered they could use the cardboard covers of the pilot's manual, some plastic bags, a piece of tubing borrowed from a spare space suit, and large amounts of gaffer tape. Transmitting the idea to *Apollo 13* was no easy task in itself, and the crew needed to use a great deal of spatial imagination. The solution worked, though, and two hours later, the concentration of carbon dioxide in the landing module started falling back to safe levels.

All these actions, though, didn't solve the fundamental dilemma of the increased flight time leading to the power supplies and oxygen running out. Mission Control therefore decided to switch on the module's engines, so as to increase *Apollo*'s speed and reduce the return trip by about ten hours. This decision also came at a cost. Re-entering Earth's atmosphere in a craft hurtling along at over 25,000 miles an hour was an operation requiring almost surgical precision. The tiniest error could have catastrophic consequences. If they re-entered at too shallow an angle, the module would bounce off the outer layers of the atmosphere, like a skipping stone off water. Too steep an angle would lead to a sudden slowing and the capsule burning up. The safe zone was barely 2 degrees across, which—bearing in mind the massive speed and the still unknown levels of damage sustained by the CSM—posed an extraordinarily difficult challenge.

Before powering up again and starting the re-entry maneuver, the entire procedure was analyzed for hours and simulated on Earth, with the backup crew of *Apollo 13* playing an essential role in the process. The final checklist contained over four hundred steps and ran to thirty-nine pages. The job of transmitting it to the CSM

fell to Joseph Kerwin, the communications officer, who was super-
vised throughout by the entire team, including Arnold Aldrich.
Dictating the checklist took over two hours, and Jack Swigert used
up, among other things, every single cover from the onboard man-
uals to write it all down.

On April 17, 1970, the crew managed to restore the power
on the CSM and the three astronauts left *Aquarius* to prepare for
splashdown. At 1:40 pm, 138 hours after liftoff, the crew detached
the service module in which the explosion had taken place from
the command module. Photos of the ditched section, which were
sent to Houston, showed massive damage, arousing fears about
the state of the command module itself. If its outer surface had
been even slightly damaged in the explosion, the CSM would never
survive re-entry. Three and a half hours later, it was time to say
farewell to the LM. The lander was detached and *Apollo 13* began
its final, decisive maneuver.

The most stressful time in mission control is the *blackout*, the
period in which there is silence as the capsule passes through the
upper layers of the atmosphere. In these minutes there is no contact
between the astronauts and mission control, and no data from the
onboard instruments get through. In this case, the blackout lasted
three minutes. What it was like in the Mission Operations Control
Room during that period is best expressed by Gene Kranz:

> Everything now was irreversible. [...] The control room was
> absolutely silent. [...] All eyes were on the clocks counting down
> to the end of blackout. Blackout was an eternity. [...] Quietly, in
> hushed tones, I called Deiterich, my RETRO: "Chuck, were the
> clocks good?" In a whisper he responded, "They're good, Flight."
> We waited. The world waited. We were 1:28 past the expected
> acquisition time when a crackly report from a downrange aircraft

broke the tension: "ARIA4 has acquisition." I pounded the edge of the console; the room erupted [...] Kerwin called again and a few seconds later we heard, "Okay Joe." Just two words, but the intensity of the relief was overwhelming. In the control room, each controller has his moment of emotional climax. [...] I was standing at the console crying.[10]

For his achievement, Gene Kranz received the Presidential Medal of Freedom, and in the months that followed, he and the other heroes of the rescue mission became celebrities and the story of *Apollo 13* became a synonym for successful completion of a "mission impossible."

Kranz's team's working methods are still held up as a model application of the inquiry mode in practice. The Herculean engagement of all those involved in the operation and their unshakeable faith that it would succeed are also seen as a model for best practices in such circumstances.

Gene Kranz worked for NASA until he retired in 1994. That same year, he took part in the documentary film *Apollo 13: To the Edge and Back*. When he began describing the mission's final minutes, he was unable to hold back the tears, despite the dramatic events having unfolded over a quarter of a century before. The scene survived the cutting room and is part of the final film.

RULE #6

If you find yourself in a black swan situation, go into inquiry mode. Whatever your intuition or experience is telling you may be wrong.

THIS IS one of the most important, but hardest rules to apply. First, it requires you to realize that the situation you're in is a black swan. Considering our natural tendency to categorize problems, automatically looking for analogies with past situations, it's easy to tell yourself, "Ah, it's nothing new, I know what to do." Second, black swans frequently arise in situations requiring fast, decisive action to address the problem (e.g., Eurocontrol's situation, where a lightning reaction was required to address the risk posed to flights). And here's the rub—again, like Eurocontrol—we side with our initial assessment and then, instead of switching on inquiry mode, we start cherry-picking the data that confirm this initial assessment is right. I like to call this "decision narcissism." Once our knowledge and experience tell us which decision to make, we will look far more positively at information confirming our intuition. After all, it's screaming at us, "You were right!" By the same token, if the data starts showing that our initial assessment was wrong, we don't feel good. Here is somebody demonstrating to us quite clearly that our intuition, be it general or business, is faulty. Research has demonstrated that in extreme situations, decision-makers take a very dim view of those who bring them information that doesn't confirm their initial assumptions, often completely unrelated to the actual decision. "Johnson has brought me an analysis that suggests that my decision to reject the offer was wrong. I always thought Johnson was pretty average. Definitely not a star. He has family problems, too, I hear. Crashed his car a while back, as well. I reckon that report of his should probably be filed in the bin."

Sound familiar? Even if we avoid that pitfall ourselves, is someone out there treating you like poor old Johnson?

The vast majority of the time, we are working in an environment where inquiry mode is unnatural, because it involves ongoing mental conflict—and its associated stress—and what's worse, it demands a lot of time (and who has a lot of time these days?). In a highly conformist and hurried business world, lack of time is the fundamental enemy of applying inquiry mode, which further explains why black swans are so horribly effective at what they do.

RULE #7

Set up your own EXCOMM. Surround yourself with people who don't think like you. Value those who disagree with you, and who aren't afraid to say it.

IT'S THEREFORE worth having your very own Executive Committee, a group of trusted people you can involve in decision-making processes. This isn't so easy in business, not least because of the tendency of groups to aim for unanimity and the cloning trap, whereby we tend to employ people who share our view of the world. It's a vicious cycle: the more uniform the group is, the more strongly those who think differently are rejected, even though they are the group's scarcest and therefore most valuable resource. Those who openly question the group's view are generally disliked, and in extreme cases, they may be ignored or even ostracized. It's yet another paradox.

So if you find yourself surrounded by competent, professional, experienced people but you find them awkward to talk to, don't reject them. They may be your best bet when it comes to making decisions. If you face a problem together, looking at it from different, but complementary perspectives, you have a chance of going into inquiry mode, analyzing the problem thoroughly and making the right choice. I am always saying that when I was the CEO with ICAN Institute, *Harvard Business Review Polska*'s publishing house, my closest ally in making business decisions was someone with whom I almost never agreed. Not only that, he was really irritating and often drove me crazy, dragging the issue out when I thought it was done and dusted. And yet, despite that (or probably because of it), he was incredibly valuable and saved me several times from making serious mistakes that neither I nor anyone else around me had noticed I was in danger of making.

To put it bluntly, I didn't like the guy, but he was an absolute diamond when it came to making business decisions.

The quality of discussion and analysis is closely correlated with the degree of psychological safety sensed by team members. A mentally secure team generates an environment in which its members aren't afraid of taking risks and openly expressing their opinions. The higher the degree of mental security, the more energetic the discussions are and the more people engage in them, without fear of being ostracized or suffering other consequences as a result of articulating dissenting opinions. Of course, mental security doesn't happen by itself; it becomes a feature of a group whose members have been given enough time to establish the right interrelations and have learned to trust one another. The important thing is shared goals—if a team really is all pulling in the same direction and everyone wants the same thing, open debate naturally ensues. We mustn't forget about the authority trap, though, because it also influences the sense of mental security. The more uniform the status and rank of team members are, the easier it is for open discussion to take place. To put that in practical terms, it's worth not only investing time and effort in improving internal communications but also promoting those who are introverted, but might disagree with the official line. If there's a real star in your group, though, exclude them from the initial meetings, just like JFK excluded himself.

Some of the companies I've worked with decided at some stage to take the bull by the horns. Realizing that black swans are unavoidable, even for the most competent decision-makers, they decided to prepare for the unexpected. The only certainty in a black swan situation is that reacting quickly—understanding the problem and responding nimbly to the new rules of the game—is crucial for survival. An organization that reacts faster than its competitors can not only not lose in a black swan situation, but may even gain. At the same time, truly unexpected situations typically create chaos in an organization, and too much time passes before the key people recover from the shock and set in action the appropriate mechanisms. For this reason, more and more organizations are setting up rapid response teams (sometimes even calling them the *black swan response team*), made up of people from a number of departments, with varying competencies and a range of experiences, whose task is to shorten the time is takes to react to a crisis. These teams meet often and rehearse reacting to different types of black swans. They analyze how to respond to events on a global, sectoral, organizational, team, and individual level, looking for weak points in the company that require immediate action. They also force others to discuss new solutions and promote the inquiry mode.

Rapid response teams have four highly effective weapons in their armory.

The first one is *positive paranoia*. This somewhat surprising term means looking at reality not from the perspective of the most likely scenario, but from that of the most negative option. It requires assuming that if something can go wrong, then it probably will (also known, of course, as Murphy's Law). Taking this approach enables us to test various systems in an organization in test crisis situations, and as a consequence, to find flaws in contingency plans that are not immediately obvious. Stress-tests, which banks were subjected to in 2010-11, are an example of this. A side effect of simulating black swans is that it takes people out of their comfort zones, away from the equilibrium and self-satisfaction that sets in when everything seems fine. An interesting form of this exercise is a technique the military uses—"accumulating experiences within experiences"—which I learned about from General Bernard B. Banks, Associate Dean for Leadership Development at Northwestern University's Kellogg School of Management, in 2017. Every military exercise for the army is an opportunity to test the effectiveness of an individual, a team, or an organization by introducing unplanned (but controlled and safe) changes in a given operation. In terms of business, a possible scenario could be a sudden shortage of production line staff and the exercise would involve testing a range of possible solutions in this artificially created situation. This kind of activity not only teaches us to prepare for the unexpected, but also sparks the creativity of employees in addressing the challenges posed by a black swan.

The second weapon is *process audits*, but interpreted in a less orthodox way. Process audits are nothing new in business—almost every organization carries them out regularly. They are used to identify the gap between planned parameters and the real world. So, in process audits, we look for mistakes and faults in order to eliminate them. Teams responding to a black swan, though, should regularly look at the results of these audits from another perspective: to look for those processes that work so well that the company has never had to correct them. Everyone assumes they are a strong point and cannot fail, thinking "it's always worked perfectly, so it will keep working perfectly" (the turkey syndrome). The problem with this is that black swans don't distinguish between weak and strong processes—they're kind of versatile in that respect. The most painful shocks are felt when something that was a characteristic strong point suddenly fails. An extreme example of this is the story of *Encyclopædia Britannica*, whose fact-checking and accuracy were its strongest selling points. While the arrival of Wikipedia didn't make this process worse, it did make it irrelevant.

RULE #8

When improving an organization, also pay attention to the best and most efficient processes.

In a black swan situation, they can fail. Do you have a back-up plan?

RAPID RESPONSE teams also practice shooting down "Concordes"—that's the third weapon, as it were, in the arsenal. Every organization hoards projects that are going nowhere fast, despite the effect on sunk costs and decision-making inertia. So, when you're initiating a project, it's worth identifying the KPIs that must be achieved at every phase for the project to move into the next stage.[11] Establishing measurable, objective indicators here is absolutely essential because it means that at a later stage, you can focus discussions on the facts, minimizing the emotional input of those involved in the project and thus avoiding an affective conflict. One of the tasks of response teams is to regularly review the portfolio of ongoing projects in a company, and to eliminate those that don't meet the criteria established for them and have no chance of achieving success.

The fourth weapon is to hunt for monkey habits—attitudes and behaviors that might once have been justified, but are now anachronistic and reduce an organization's flexibility and efficiency. This is the most difficult of the four weapons to wield, as it requires you to take a step back and look at your organization with fresh eyes, being as critical and objective as you can. The longer you've been with a company, the harder it is to adopt such an attitude. So, it's worth inviting some of those who've been with the company for the shortest time to get involved in the exercise, because they can still see the inefficiencies that others have become inured to, simply treating them as part of the game. A rapid response team should proactively include such people as members, as very few of them will express a critical opinion right off the bat. Most newly employed staff will adopt the stance of cautious observers in their first few weeks and months: "I want to see how it all works, and for now, I'll keep my doubts to myself, so as not to be a laughingstock. Once I see how everything works, then I'll ask questions." Unfortunately, by then it's too late—the new person has learned that it doesn't pay to climb on the ladder.

RULE #9

Shoot down Concordes and hunt for monkey habits.
Eliminating loss-making projects and ineffective practices frees up time for other things, increasing a company's agility and flexibility.

JUST HOW ingrained such habits of many years' standing are can be shown by the example of a European financial sector company whose board I advised for many years. In this seemingly very modern, well-managed organization, a "high potentials" group operated—forty-five middle managers who had been identified as talented and possessing real potential to advance rapidly through the company. In 2011, the board planned to include this group in the process of operational improvement and scheduled a day-long workshop, which I had the pleasure of facilitating. The aim of the workshop was simple: the managers, divided into groups, had to analyze the functioning of the organization in various fields and find as many minor inefficiencies, accrued over years of habit, as they could. They had to look for things they could eliminate quickly, cheaply, and without involving lots of people. At the end of the day, each group submitted their list of "monkeys" (the session was called "Monkey Hunting," for which metaphor I extend my sincere apologies to any ecologists reading). We eventually identified a grand total of eighty-two inefficiencies that could easily be eliminated! It's worth looking at one of them, as it was particularly eye-catching. On the 28th of each month, in each of the company's dozens of branches, a designated employee printed out a report, several pages long, from the IT system, which they then sent to the head office—by Priority Mail! What was especially surprising was that the company had an integrated IT system, which meant all the data could be consolidated at head office with just a few clicks of a mouse. On closer analysis, the origin of this paper trail was identified: it was a procedure implemented by the CEO in 1995. At the time, it was an appropriate solution. Over the years, the responsibility for preparing and sending the report was delegated to people lower and lower down the hierarchy, so by 2011, the report was being submitted by a worker who had been programmed to remember that the report must be sent on the 28th. At head office, another low-ranking employee received the reports, put them in a file, and sat them on a shelf—because that's how it had always been done. For fifteen years, nobody asked why they were printing and sending these reports. Strange but true. That's how strong monkey habits can be in an organization.

Rapid response teams act so that any eventual black swan attacks with less force. They relentlessly test an organization and its components from the point of view of the unexpected. They optimize processes, structures, resources, and working practices. They free up time and energy. An effect of their work is a kind of decisional *Kaizen*, constantly seeking minimal gains that make a firm more agile and thus better prepared for a surprise scenario.

改 善

 : THAT is how the Japanese write *Kaizen*—one of the most important and effective techniques of continuous improvement, and one of the fundamental principles of Total Quality Management (TQM). Although *Kaizen* originated in the manufacturing sector and is still predominantly identified with it, it has far wider applications and can be an excellent tool for improving decision-making processes. As a set of methods involving all employees in an organization, it is also an interesting tool for shaping an organization's culture, creating an environment within which everyone is expected to constantly seek opportunities and make suggestions for improvements.

At its simplest, *Kaizen* means the critical appraisal of tasks and of the processes associated with them, identifying things that aren't right or that deviate from the norm, introducing changes, and increasing efficiency and quality. The process is a continuous one, so once we've introduced improvements, we go back to research and analysis, looking for further refinements. Often the sequence PDSA (Plan-Do-Study-Act), devised by William Edwards Deming, is used to describe it. The key point in the cycle, of course, is analysis (= Study), which makes it possible to discover things that are wrong. However, as more businesses began to adopt the PDSA approach, it soon became apparent that a problem commonly encountered in the world of medicine—focusing on the symptoms, instead of the underlying causes of the disease—was becoming equally common in the business world and, as a result, it was impossible to effectively and permanently solve problems. Thus, one of the crucial elements of *Kaizen* is the analysis of the source of the problems, or RCA (root cause analysis). RCA is ideal if your aim is to draw profound conclusions from events in which the actual decision-making process played a role. Understanding the root cause of a bad decision provides the opportunity to make corrections and avoid falling into the same trap in the future. You could say that thanks to RCA, we don't get rid of only the pain, but also the cause of the pain.

An excellent example of how easy it is to get fixated on the symptoms, and so not take the appropriate action, comes again from the world of medicine. For many years, it was considered that the trigger for stomach ulcers was excess acid, caused by having too much spicy food or being too stressed. The treatment of ulcers was therefore to give sufferers drugs to reduce acidity and to tell them to take things easy. From the perspective of the pharmaceutical companies, the prescription of antacids was great news because it created a market that was valued in the second half of the 1990s at over $8 billion. From the patients' perspective, things weren't quite as rosy, as the treatment recommended to them wasn't very effective and often ended in their needing surgery. But nobody questioned the treatment method and nobody looked for an alternative cause of the problem, because it was widely believed at the time that it was impossible for bacteria to survive in such a strongly acidic environment as the human stomach, so they couldn't possibly be a cause of stomach ulcers.

The breakthrough only came at the beginning of the new millennium, although its origins can be traced back to Australia, almost twenty years earlier. In 1981, two doctors from the gastroenterology ward of a Perth hospital, thirty-year-old Dr. Barry James Marshall, a clinical fellow, and forty-four-year-old Dr. John Robin Warren, discovered something unexpected in the stomachs of twenty patients suffering from ulcers: bacteria resembling *Campylobacter*. For many months, the astonished scientists tried to isolate it in the lining of the stomach and then grow it in laboratory conditions to subject it to further testing, but to no avail. Then they had a lucky accident: after one of the biopsies they'd been conducting, a test tube was left in an incubator for three days longer than it should have been, but this mistake turned out to be the missing link, as the extra time gave the bacteria time to grow. As a consequence of their oversight, the Australians discovered *Helicobacter pylori* and, in 1983, they put forward the thesis that the bacteria could be the main cause of ulcers in the stomach and duodenum. Marshall even demonstrated it in a somewhat drastic manner, deliberately infecting himself with the bacteria and observing an inflammation develop in his own digestive tract. Although the researchers faced a great deal of resistance not only from their peers, but also, not surprisingly, the pharmaceutical companies, their tenacity and dedication were finally recognized when they were awarded the Nobel Prize in Physiology or Medicine for 2005. Today, ulcers are treated with antibiotics to destroy the bacteria that cause them.

Our concentration on looking at symptoms and natural reluctance to search for root causes are a result of several factors. First, in business, we operate constantly under time constraints, and RCA is quite time-consuming, as it demands thorough testing of numerous aspects of a problem and frequently involves many people. Second, we don't like to analyze failures, because they demand that we face up to something we'd much rather forget about. This leads to the trap of denial—we push away unpleasant memories and focus on more positive things instead. Third, we have a natural tendency to blame people, not processes, so we try to identify the specific person responsible for a mistake. This means that, even though the underlying cause of a failure was someone's poor decision, we tend not to consider the factors that led to that bad decision being made. Finding a scapegoat usually ends the discussion, and we focus more on punishing than on drawing conclusions and learning lessons. These three factors lead to our not making use of one of the most important tools in improving decision-making processes, one that helps us draw in-depth conclusions from the mistakes we and others make.

RCA is an extremely straightforward method. The analysis aspect is governed by a set of rules known as the 5 Whys, a series of questions to ask to get beyond the symptoms to the root cause of a problem. The first Why questions the cause of, or reason for, an error; the second Why is asked to analyze the underlying causes of the immediate cause. Then it's the turn of the causes of the causes of the immediate cause (the third Why) and so on. (The "five" in the name of the approach is arbitrary. We could equally stop the analysis at the fourth Why, having found the root cause, or continue on to a twenty-fourth.) Such an approach creates a kind of logic tree whose branches hold successive links in a chain of cause and effect. RCA therefore makes it possible to discover dozens of underlying causes of a problem, and consequently effectively prevent it from recurring.

A thorough RCA reveals the chain of events leading up to an event, which gives you the information you need to reject false (although frequently obvious-looking) conclusions that could result in bad decisions being made again in future. To paraphrase Mark Twain, a cat that sits on a hot stove lid not only won't sit on one again, it won't sit on a cold stove again, either. RCA enables us to identify such misleading simplifications before they do any harm.

It's worth looking at how the RCA approach works in the context of a specific event that was caused by a tangle of causes and the kinds of mental traps I've described in the preceding pages. Let's take a look at the infamous 1996 tragedy that hit two commercial expeditions on Mount Everest.[1]

CLIMBING HAS always aroused strong emotions, from admiration for the bravery of the daredevils, heading up the highest peaks on Earth, to disdain for the risk-takers and disapproval of the unnecessary risks involved. Every death in the high mountains is followed by harsh commentary, generally suggesting that climbers are all to a greater or lesser degree quite mad, seeing that they are prepared to risk their lives in the pursuit of adrenaline and glory.[2]

No matter how you feel about the climbers, the events that played out on Mount Everest in 1996 rocked the world of Himalayan climbing, and inspired numerous books and films. The disastrous outcomes for the Rob Hall and Scott Fischer commercial expeditions up the highest peak on Earth had a common denominator: bad decisions were made during the planning and execution of the entire undertaking. None of the participants died from an act of God, like a sudden avalanche, falling into a crevasse, or the sudden breaking of a fixed rope. All the victims were the result of mental traps that led to poor choices and the direst consequences imaginable.

PEAK XV in Nepal didn't immediately spark much excitement. It was only in 1856, when the Great Trigonometrical Survey conducted by the government of India estimated its height, by using theodolites, at approximately 29,000 feet, that it became apparent that the mountain known to the locals as Chomolungma ("Goddess Mother of the Land" is just one of its English translations) was the highest point on our planet. In honor of the British surveyor Sir George Everest, one of the leading surveyors of India between 1830 and 1843, the mountain was given his name, and from then on, the race to become the first to climb the world's highest peak began in earnest.

In the first half of the twentieth century, the authorities in Nepal were not amicably disposed toward climbers, so all the teams attacked from the Tibetan side, the North Face. The ascent from the Nepalese side, also known today as the classic route, is far less technical, so we can probably risk saying that if the brave souls back in those early days had been able to attack from the South, they would have had a far greater chance of success. The first two significant attempts to conquer the peak took place in 1921 and 1922, with the second breaking the 26,000 feet barrier for the first time ever.[3] The team, led by Charles Granville Bruce, had no chance of reaching the peak, yet its achievements were lauded resoundingly by the European press.

In both cases, the expeditions included George Herbert Leigh Mallory, born in 1886, a British history teacher and, in my opinion, the greatest hero in the many years of attempts to climb Mount Everest. Mallory was an experienced traveler and alpinist who had climbed Mont Blanc in 1911, hence trying his hand at the world's highest mountain was, to him, a natural evolution. He joined the 1921 expedition and ended his first encounter with Everest on the North Ridge, at an altitude above 23,000 feet. The following year he did even better, reaching a then-record height on the North Ridge of 27,000 feet. While both attempts ended with the team's turning back before reaching the summit, Mallory analyzed the experience he had accumulated and decided to make a third attempt in 1924, setting off with Andrew "Sandy" Irvine, a twenty-two-year-old member of the Oxford University Mountaineering Club. According to Noel Odell, who observed their efforts from base camp, the two climbers were making good time and were close to the so-called First Step on the ridge at an altitude of almost 28,000 feet when they vanished into cloud. That, sadly, was the last contact anyone had with the two climbers. Neither Mallory nor Irvine returned to base camp, and for many years no one knew whether they had died on the way to the summit or on the way back down. Mallory's body was finally discovered in 1999, by a US expedition led by Eric Simonson; a little above the frozen remains, close to the Second Step and spread out at a height of 28,000 feet, were the two men's oxygen tanks. Irvine's body still hasn't been found. Neither has the camera that the Englishmen were using, and which could have provided evidence of them reaching the summit. Most experts therefore consider that Mallory didn't conquer Everest, but some point out that in the intact wallet found on Mallory's frozen remains, the photo of his wife, Ruth, which he had intended to place on the summit, was nowhere to be found.

In 1950 and 1951, two British expeditions explored the possibility of attacking the summit from the South Side, in Nepal. A year later, a very well-prepared Swiss expedition led by physician and alpinist Edouard Wyss-Dunant, and which included the Sherpa Namgyal Wangdi, generally known as Tenzing Norgay, arrived on the mountain. While Norgay and the experienced Swiss mountaineer Raymond Lambert managed to set an altitude record of 28,000 feet, the pair didn't reach the peak.

The following year was a breakthrough one in the history of Everest. In March 1953, a well-equipped British expedition led by Colonel John Hunt and comprising over four hundred people, mostly porters, had begun operating in Nepal. The expedition set up a series of camps on the massif, and finally, on May 26, the first attempt to reach the summit began. Two British climbers from Hunt's expedition, Tom Bourdillon and Charles Evans, were selected for this honor. In the opinion of many, this was not the best decision Hunt could have made, as they were not seen as either the strongest or the best prepared of the group. Hunt, though, felt that the British should have the first crack of the whip, and so up they went. Bourdillon and Evans almost made it, however, as they were merely 300 feet below the summit when they were forced to turn back due to Evans's faulty breathing apparatus. On May 28 another attempt was made, this one led by the pair considered to be the strongest: twenty-eight-year-old New Zealander Edmund Hillary and thirty-eight-year-old Tenzing Norgay, who had returned to Everest following the failed Swiss expedition of 1952. On May 29, 1953, at 11:30, the two men stood on the summit of Chomolungma, the highest peak on the planet; fifteen minutes later, they began their descent. They made it back safely to camp and immediately became heroes. The leader of the expedition, John Hunt, also basked in his share of the glory, as the newly crowned Queen Elizabeth II made him a life peer.[4]

In the years that followed, Everest was conquered by successive expeditions. In 1978, the legendary Reinhold Messner, the first to complete the Crown of the Himalaya, reached the summit without the use of supplemental oxygen, and two years later he completed the first solo ascent. That same year, Everest was conquered in winter by two Polish climbers, Leszek Cichy and Krzysztof Wielicki.

In 1985, the next frontier—one not entirely connected with alpinism—was pushed back in no uncertain terms. Top US climber David Breashears guided the Texan oil baron Richard Bass to the top of Everest, with Bass covering most of the costs of the expedition in return for being taken along for the ride. Bass, despite having no experience of being at such extreme altitudes, was very well-prepared for the expedition both mentally and physically and made it to the top with Breashears. The event was reported widely, among both business people and mountain climbers, with the latter seeing a chance to earn some cash. And that is how commercial expeditions on Mount Everest became a new and lucrative business involving ever more people. In the following years, it was often decided to include one or two wealthy adrenaline junkies in the expedition teams.

At the beginning of the 1990s, two New Zealanders, Rob Hall and Gary Ball, decided to go a step further and set up a firm organizing commercial expeditions to the top of the Earth. They named their company Adventure Consultants. They decided it was worth starting ambitiously, so their first expedition for commercial customers was an ascent of Everest in 1992. The undertaking was an unarguable success: on a single day six people, not counting the guides, stood on the summit. The following year, seven customers went up, following in the footsteps of an expedition up Aconcagua and Mount Vinson in Antarctica that had ended successfully. These successes brought Adventure Consultants a lot of publicity. Its reputation survived the death of Gary Ball on Dhaulagiri in 1993, and over time Rob Hall became a legend in the world of commercial expeditions. Within three years of Ball's death, Hall could boast of having guided thirty-nine clients to the top of Mount Everest. No other company or guide could come close to such a score.

Hall was highly valued by customers for his extraordinary attention to detail and precise planning, as well as his obsession with safety, which came from a genuine humility in the face of the mountains. He was a strong leader type, imposing strict rules of behavior on his teams. The combination of these factors meant that there was enormous interest in expeditions run by Adventure Consultants, who charged much more than their competitors did. For the 1996 expedition, Hall recruited eight customers, including Jon Krakauer, a very talented rock climber and a contributor to *Outside* magazine. His role, therefore, was a double one, as the publicity generated by the article about his experience would increase the likelihood of the company's getting even more customers the following year.

At the same time, a team led by the American Scott Fischer, owner of Mountain Madness, arrived at base camp. Fischer was six years older than Hall but came across as much younger at heart. His approach to organization was much more relaxed, and he didn't set out much in the way of rules or defined procedures. This approach had worked on earlier sporting expeditions, ultimately giving Fischer the first US ascent of Lhotse (27,940 feet) and helping him to conquer Everest and K2 (28,250), considered the toughest eight-thousander. On both Everest and K2, Fischer climbed without oxygen. Like Hall, he had attracted eight people to join his party for this particular expedition, including his own media presence, Sandy Hill Pittman. Pittman was a New York socialite who was breaking new communications ground by blogging about her attempt to complete the Seven Summits (to climb the highest peak on each of the continents), a feat that required a great deal of equipment in addition to her climbing gear. Everest was the last one on her list.

In the case of both teams, a vital role was played by the professional guides who were hired to help the amateurs throughout the entire climb. Hall's team included Andy Harris and Mike Groom, while Fischer's team had the excellent Kazakh climber Anatoli Boukreev (who was against using supplemental oxygen on ascents) and Neal Beidleman. Both expeditions also included several Sherpas, led by a sirdar named Ang Dorje, who climbed with Hall. Another sirdar, Lopsang Jangbu, accompanied Fischer. The Sherpas were there not only to carry heavy equipment and food to the higher camps, but also to prepare the fixed ropes securing the especially dangerous sections of climbing. Throughout April, the Sherpas prepared the camps, and the clients of both companies acclimatized themselves to the increased physical demands of higher altitudes. Lopsang took up the heavy electronic equipment that Pittman needed to relay the course of the expedition live on NBC's website.

It's worth mentioning that in May 1996, Hall's and Fischer's expeditions were not the only ones on Everest. There was also a poorly prepared team from Taiwan, led by Makalu Gau; a South African team, led by the controversial Ian Woodall;[5] Todd Burleson's commercial expedition; and an IMAX team that included David Breashears and that was planning to film a documentary about the realities of climbing the highest peak on Earth. This meant that there were dozens of people on the South slopes of the mountain all at the same time, and the majority of them had little experience of climbing at such an altitude. Taking this into consideration, Hall and Fischer decided to join forces and lead their clients together, so as not to get in each other's way during the most critical stages of the climb.

After analyzing the weather data from previous years, as well as the current forecasts, the leaders decided that May 10 would be the best time to push for the summit. The combined teams set off on May 5 from a base camp at 17,600 feet, crossed the dangerous Khumbu Icefall, and reached Camp I, at an altitude of 20,000 feet. On May 6, they attempted to reach Camp II, during which one of the Mountain Madness customers, Dale Kruse, began to feel sick and was taken back to base camp by Fischer, who rejoined the remaining climbers at Camp II the following day. During the following two days, the teams pressed on higher, and by May 9 they had reached the fourth and last camp, just beneath the South Col at almost 26,000 feet. From that camp, the climbers would set off on the final assault. So far, though, the weather conditions had been very difficult, with winds of up to 60 mph, which persuaded the IMAX team, among others, to descend to base camp and wait it out.

The Adventure Consultants' customers had been given cast-iron instructions by Rob Hall. Regardless of how the assault on the summit was going, there was a 2:00 pm time limit. No matter what happened, at 2:00 pm, they had to turn around and head back to Camp IV so that they had a good chance of returning safely and their oxygen wouldn't run out. Those in Scott Fischer's team had no such rule, because their leader worked on the principle that during an eighteen-hour assault, everyone should make their own decision about turning back.

Late in the evening of May 9, the weather began to improve, and the two leaders decided to set off. At 11:30 pm, the two teams left their tents and made their way onto the South Col, where the ridge leading to the summit begins. Soon after, four of the Adventure Consultants team took ill, and Hall decided they should return to Camp IV. The remainder continued their offensive. At about 5:30 am, the climbers got an unpleasant surprise: an extended section of the route had not had ropes fixed, even though both leaders had earlier been absolutely sure that the entire route had been prepared. The necessity of attaching the lines seriously delayed the push, and in the following hours, the two teams spread out, with the stronger climbers making brisk progress and the weaker ones lagging behind. Around noon, the first of the group arrived at the Hillary Step, a roughly 39-foot-high, vertical rock face, the toughest technical obstacle along the route and a spot where lineups had a habit of forming.[6] At almost precisely 1:00 pm, the first three climbers—Krakauer, Harris, and Boukreev—reached the summit. Less than an hour later, they were joined by Neal Beidleman, Martin Adams, and Klev Schoening. They were the only ones who managed to reach the summit before the 2:00 pm deadline imposed by Rob Hall.

Meanwhile, in the area below the summit, a dramatic scene was playing out. Rob Hall, who was personally assisting his good friend Doug Hansen, suddenly realized the time and ordered Hansen to return to Camp IV. Hansen, who had been on the Adventure Consultants expedition the year before and had been sent back a mere 300 feet from the summit, refused. He wanted to carry on at all costs, even if that increased the risk of running out of oxygen and putting himself in danger. Hall was ultimately swayed and continued the ascent, his friend following some way behind. Hall reached the top at about 2:30 pm as part of a group of six, and waited for Hansen, who ultimately achieved his dream of conquering Everest—at 4:15 pm. Half an hour earlier, an extremely exhausted Scott Fischer had reached the top and then almost immediately begun his descent, supported by Lopsang. The others also set off down the mountain.

First to reach the relative safety of Camp IV, at 5:00 pm, was Anatoli Boukreev, one of the guides. Boukreev—in accordance with his years-long principle—had earlier refused Fischer's request to take supplemental oxygen with him on the climb. He argued that he had to descend quickly, recover in his tent, and then set off back up the mountain to take oxygen bottles to the group to help them on their way down. Many experts later criticized the decision, saying Boukreev should have stayed with the group the whole time and absolutely should have had oxygen with him to give immediate help to any of the tired climbers whose bottles were empty.[7]

At about 5:00 pm, the weather suddenly took a turn for the worse. The upper parts of the massif were enveloped in cloud, visibility fell to only a few feet, and worst of all, a brutal wind whipped up, meaning the temperature with wind chill plummeted to a mind-numbing −100°F in the following hours. In such appalling conditions, both the paying customers and their guides got totally lost. By 8:00 pm, only Jon Krakauer and Martin Adams had made it back to camp. A large group of the climbers in their party, accompanied by two of the guides, Neal Beidleman and Mike Groom, were stuck a little way above the camp—and oblivious to how close to shelter they were. Realizing how hopeless the situation was, the four strongest people in the group (including both guides) set off to find a way down, finally making it back to the tents just before midnight. Anatoli Boukreev set off into the area above the camp three times in total. His bravery saved three people from the Mountain Madness team, Sandy Hill Pittman, Tim Madsen, and Charlotte Fox. Suffering from hypothermia, they reached the tents at 4:30 am.

Neither of the two leaders made it back, as they were stuck in different places on the upper reaches of the mountain. Rob Hall twice made contact with the climbers in Camp IV, the first time informing them about the deaths of Andy Harris and Doug Hansen, and asking for oxygen. The Sherpas tried, but the dreadful conditions meant they couldn't reach the New Zealander. Despite this, Rob Hall survived the entire day, and at 6:20 pm, the second time he made contact, he asked for a satellite connection to his wife. That was his last conversation.

The following days revealed the true scale of the disaster. Five people from the two teams died on the mountain, including both leaders, and one of the Sherpas contracted HACE (high-altitude cerebral edema) and died a few days later in hospital.

A discussion about the causes of the tragedy ensued in the media, which led to several books being written by those involved, either directly or indirectly, in the tragedy. Despite the differences in opinion and different points of view presented in the books, there was agreement on two things: first, the tragedy was a result of numerous poor decisions and not an unforeseeable incident (like, say, an avalanche). Second, many of these errors occurred during the early stages of the operation, and their accumulated negative consequences manifested in those last, desperate stages of the assault on the summit.

If we apply the logic of an RCA to this, together with the 5 Whys method, it's quite easy to identify the most serious groups of errors. For the sake of clarity, I shall present them in chronological order, although an RCA is most often carried out in reverse order, starting from the final mistake, which led to the failure, and then going back, looking for the cause of that event, then the cause of that cause, and so on. In a chronological approach, there is another question alongside "why?": "and what were the consequences?"

THE FIRST group of causes were related to the approach to organizing the expedition. Both leaders went about organizing their expeditions in a startlingly routine manner, making light of the risks associated with it. The project they were intending to carry out was extremely difficult: it meant taking amateurs, who had never experienced comparative conditions or altitudes, into a highly dangerous and unpredictable world. The situation demanded a thorough, robust inquiry approach, risk reduction and buffers for unexpected situations, preparation of several alternative scenarios, and the testing of processes against potential black swans. However, the leaders did the exact opposite. They sold their expeditions in a way that made light of the risks. The famous claims of Hall and Fischer in conversation with clients and the slogans from their brochures left no doubts: "100% success!"[8] "We've built a yellow brick road to the summit,"[9] "We've got the big Everest figured out, we've got it totally wired," "Experience is overrated"[10]... My impression is that the tragedy was set in motion the instant the leaders began to believe their own publicity. Unconsciously, they began to regard climbing Mount Everest with an unfamiliar bunch of amateurs as a pretty straightforward thing. They viewed it as a simple, routine project in a predictable environment.

Here is where the next "why?" should appear. How is it possible that experienced Himalayan climbers like Hall and Fischer could make such a fundamental error? They were perfectly acquainted with the risks involved in expeditions on the highest peaks on the planet. In my opinion, two things lay at the root of their misjudgment: first, Hall's earlier expeditions were (mostly) spectacular successes, creating a dangerous turkey effect, gradually making the approach to organizing and running the expeditions routine. Krakauer recalled a moment in which he expressed his uncertainties and concerns, and Hall made light of them, saying, "It's worked 39 times so far, pal."[11] Second, the prospect of celebrating yet another success, especially in light of the PR machine in the form of Krakauer and Pittman, had become a priority, putting the two decision-makers under additional pressure. The entire world would be informed in real time of their victory (or failure), which clearly affected the decisions they made.

The heart of the problem lay in shifting the level of acceptable risk to a point that turned out to be deadly. In the name of increased profits, the leaders accepted numerous risks that simply would not have been considered acceptable if the venture had been properly assessed. They applied a purely commercial, routine approach to a quest being conducted in the realm of the black swan.

Organization and logistics also played a role. The commercial approach meant that profit margins were the key motivator. This means maximizing income and cutting costs, which in this case meant the protagonists agreeing to increased risk. The end result was whole series of mistakes, which only emerged too late to circumvent.

Both expeditions had to deal with a range of problems relating to supplies and logistics. Negotiations with Poisk, the company that was supplying the oxygen, dragged on. The Sherpas went on strike for higher wages. Finally, the truck bringing in the equipment was delayed at the Nepalese border. Each of these events was caused by the decision to take a commercial approach: the oxygen, vital for the safety of the amateur climbers, was treated as an expensive resource that needed to be economized on, like the Sherpas' wages. Even more curious was the transport situation. It turned out that Scott Fischer had tried to cut back on expenses by having the expedition equipment transported in a truck traveling the same route with other goods, rather than paying for a truck of his own. The truck got stopped at customs because of its main load, not the climbing equipment, but of course, it couldn't continue its journey.

Even worse, Fischer sorted these problems out personally, disrupting his acclimatization procedure, which later had lethal consequences. Why did he deal with it himself? In another cost-saving measure, he didn't have a logistics team or expedition manager to carry out those types of preparations before the team set off up the mountain.

Many people on the mountain at that time also commented on the insufficient equipment carried by the leaders and guides. The radiotelephones were old, heavy, and highly unreliable, and there were far too few of them. In extreme situations, and in an inquiry mode, the flow of information between those involved in making decisions is vital; in the case of both 1996 Everest expeditions, there was no chance of this, because the vast majority of the decision-makers didn't have access to the necessary equipment. Why? Because of cost cutting and underestimating the risks. *(Why do we need expensive equipment on an expedition that is easy, straightforward, and safe?)*

In addition, the media coverage of the expeditions also had consequences. Although the required radiotelephones weren't taken, there was a place found for the heavy electronic equipment needed to help Sandy Hill Pittman get her live reports to NBC. That equipment was carried by Lopsang, who also literally supported the socialite during the summit, short-roped to her.

That short-roping also triggered a series of events that nobody anticipated. The leaders assumed that in the unlikely event of their having to fix ropes on a section of the route, Lopsang and Ang Dorje would be the ones to do it. When it turned out, to everyone's surprise, that a very long section of the route hadn't been secured, there was an ensuing period of confusion—Lopsang, who should have set about fixing the ropes, was still a long way away, helping a rapidly tiring Pittman. The guides therefore set about the task, losing precious time and energy.

And that brings us to another cause: the participants. The routine, commercialized approach to organizing the expeditions was also applied to the process of selecting who could participate in the expeditions. The two most significant qualifying criteria were to have both $65,000 (although some of the climbers got special discounts) and enough free time. There were no intensive fitness tests, and the clients' medical history wasn't checked. Why? Well, Hall already had numerous commercial successes under his belt, and it was only Everest, after all, so why bother with all that extra effort and expense? The case of Beck Weathers, a member of Rob Hall's expedition who was fifty at the time of the climb, proved the flawed logic of this line of thinking.

Weathers, a wealthy pathologist from Texas, was trying to achieve his dream by conquering Everest. He had been working toward it for years. His application to join the Adventure Consultants trip was accepted unconditionally and he thus became part of Hall's team. During the climb, the pathologist felt excellent, he was very fit and operating on the lower sections of the mountain didn't cause him any difficulties. At Camp IV, just before the final push for the summit, he was still in good shape. He set off with the group and kept pace. At a certain point, though, his eyesight suddenly deteriorated; he could see less and less, and then, a little way above the South Col, he went totally blind. He couldn't go on. Weathers admitted to the stunned leader, who immediately went to his aid, that he'd had an eye operation called a radial keratotomy eighteen months or so prior to the expedition. A combination of the enormous physical demands of the climb and the shortage of oxygen had rendered him temporarily blind. As Jon Krakauer recalls, this led to a highly illuminating exchange between Hall and Weathers. When the angered guide asked why Weathers (a doctor, after all!) hadn't told him about the surgery beforehand, Weathers replied, "Well, you never asked." Such unexpected consequences arise when we don't use an inquiry mode, leaving us vulnerable to the prospect of lacking vital information at key moments in an undertaking.

Beck Weathers himself suffered severe consequences from this. Hall decided that the pathologist, whose lack of vision meant he couldn't move by this point, should remain on the ascent route and wait for his eyesight to improve. The leader promised to take

Weathers back to the camp on the descent from the summit. Placing enormous trust in Hall (the authority trap!), the client waited. Many hours later, his eyesight began to return. The first people heading down the mountain from the summit passed him, but Weathers declined to descend with them, because he had it fixed in his head that he should wait for his leader. A leader who—it later turned out—never made it back.

Beck Weathers survived, and his story has since become one of the most startling to have played out on Everest. The doctor spent the night high above Camp IV, waiting for Hall and slowly losing grip on reality due to advancing hypothermia. He survived the night and was discovered on the morning of May 11 by Stuart Hutchinson. However, he was in a hypothermic coma at the time— he was covered in a layer of snow 4 inches thick, his coat was open, and he had lost one of his gloves, so his hand was totally frozen. He was still breathing, but he didn't react to anything, and Hutchinson made the assessment that Weathers, like Yasuko Namba, who had been found nearby, had no chance of surviving, so he went back to the camp to relay the news about the death of both the Adventure Consultants climbers he had found. Over a dozen hours later, Beck Weathers came to and managed to stand. How he managed to descend to Camp IV, nobody knows. We do know, though, that Todd Burleson, an American climber on another expedition, came face-to-face with an apparition upon stepping out of his tent. In an interview given later, he says this:

> I couldn't believe what I saw. This man had no face. It was completely black, solid black, like he had a crust over him. His jacket was unzipped down to his waist, full of snow. His right arm was bare and frozen over his head. We could not lower it. His skin looked like marble. White stone. There was no blood in it.[12]

The doctor's condition was so serious that everyone expected him to die that night. The next morning, Weathers surprised everyone by leaving his tent and asking others to help him put on his crampons, ready to descend via the South Face of Lhotse. He was accompanied on this dangerous journey by Todd Burleson and Pete Athans, both excellent American climbers. On the way, they met the IMAX team, who, having heard about the drama engulfing the Hall and Fischer teams, had halted their own attempt and come to help. David Breashears, Ed Viesturs, and the Austrian Robert Schauer helped take the utterly exhausted Weathers all the way to Camp I.

Here, though, the rescuers faced an insurmountable obstacle. There was less than no chance of Weathers crossing the Khumbu Icefall under his own steam, and the technical difficulties of the area made it impossible to carry him as they had higher up. And they couldn't organize a helicopter to rescue him, because the upper edge of the icefall was way above the maximum altitude for landing one.

Colonel Madan Khatri Chhetri of the Royal Nepal Air Force, though, took an enormous risk. Flying a severely stripped-out Eurocopter AH350 Squirrel, he managed to reach approximately 19,600 feet, a record altitude for helicopter flight at the time, and on only his second attempt, he managed to keep the machine stable long enough to get Weathers onboard. The colonel's skill enabled Beck Weathers to make it safely to hospital in Kathmandu, from where he flew a few days later to the United States.

Let's go back a few months now and look at how the teams prepared before setting off.

Another problem that later led to a number of bad decisions, in addition to those we've already looked at, was the lack of any team integration, in both Adventure Consultants and Mountain

Madness. Members of both expeditions only met in Nepal, so there was no opportunity to develop relationships or trust.

It's worth recalling here a distinction introduced into the business world by Jon Katzenbach. In an article published in 1993 in the *Harvard Business Review*, he introduced the concept of a *workgroup*, defined as a group of people who come together at the same time and in the same place to perform a similar task. However, for a workgroup to become a *team*, time must pass, trust must develop between group members, an awareness of shared goals and a sense of joint responsibility must appear, a feeling of psychological safety must be created, and there must be open communication. It's important to bear in mind that in business, we frequently come across workgroups (e.g., workers in a call center) rather than teams, and there's absolutely nothing wrong with that. Some workgroups should remain just that, as investing the time, money, and resources required to turn them into a team won't provide any returns. Every manager, though, should be able to assess a situation and understand what kind of group they're leading. Treating a workgroup as you would a team can turn out just as badly as treating a team like a workgroup.

On Everest, then, there were two typical workgroups whose members were only just getting to know one another. These groups, unfortunately, were treated right from the start by their leaders as if they were teams, which later resulted in numerous negative consequences.

If we look at the merging of the two expeditions from a business perspective (after all, they were commercial undertakings), we get a great manual on what not to do.

First, the joining of the two differently managed groups took place at a brief meeting in a tent at base camp, where the participants were simply informed that the leaders had decided to integrate the two teams for safety purposes. The intention was to gain greater control over a challenging situation (remember, there were many climbers on Everest at the time). Alas, that was where the integration ended. No new leader of the combined group was appointed. Why? Hall, as the more experienced commercial operator, couldn't possibly imagine a situation in which he would cede authority to Fischer; in turn, Fischer, who had ambitions to catch up with Hall's achievements, had no intention of backing down. The lack of clear leadership led to inconsistent rules of operation. For example, Rob Hall's expedition had a precisely established turnaround time, whereas Scott Fischer's didn't.

The merging of the two teams wasn't a merger in any real sense of the term. Two discrete workgroups became one in a chaotic environment of where unclear principles of operation reigned.

THIS BRINGS us to the question of the design, alignment, and communication of the guides' roles. An RCA shows that a curious, yet understandable mistake was made in relation to the roles and responsibilities of the guides who had been hired.

The professional climbers employed by each of the two teams had very different levels of experience. Boukreev was one of the best in the business. He was renowned for his ascent of Kangchenjunga (28,170 feet) by a new route and in Alpine style (without Sherpas or supplemental oxygen). He had climbed Mount Everest twice and stood on the tops of Makalu, Manaslu, and Dhaulagiri. On Dhaulagiri, he not only climbed a new route, but also set a record for the fastest ascent. In 1993, he added a true diamond to his collection: K2. His partner, Neal Beidleman, had no such achievements in his résumé, and counted only Makalu among his eight-thousanders. Furthermore, Fischer had offered him far less pay, which meant Beidleman classified himself as the number three in the team, taking orders not only from the leader, but also from Boukreev. There was a similar discrepancy in experience in Hall's team. Michael Groom had, by 1996, built a solid reputation as a climber, being the fourth person in the world to conquer the four highest peaks on Earth without oxygen: Everest, K2, Kangchenjunga, and Lhotse, adding Makalu in 1999. Andy Harris's experience was much less extensive.

Despite these differences, all the guides were excellent sports climbers. Importantly, though, they had little prior experience in the world of commercial expeditions. They had never previously filled the roles that Hall and Fischer expected them to, and Hall and Fischer did virtually nothing to teach them their roles. The situation can be summed up by Anatoli Boukreev, who didn't climb with oxygen on principle, refusing his boss's instruction to take bottles on the summit assault and not understanding that it wasn't about him but the safety of the clients. Fischer, too, made a fundamental mistake by agreeing that Boukreev could leave the bottles at the camp.

And this brings us to another "why?" Why did Scott Fischer, as leader of the group, allow his subordinate, whom he was paying $25,000, to ignore his instruction? Why did he let Boukreev do what he wanted? There were two reasons. First, I'm not convinced that Boukreev saw the somewhat less experienced Fischer as his actual leader. If I'm right about this, I wonder if he therefore didn't take the American's rules seriously, didn't regard them as something a man of his experience needed to heed. It's worth recalling that Boukreev repeatedly emphasized that, in his opinion, the clients should be as independent as possible and were responsible for their own safety. The second, less immediately obvious reason can be traced not only to Scott Fischer, but also, although indirectly, to the other professional climbers.

One of the most startling phenomena in the business world is the deeply held conviction that a renowned specialist in a field is automatically the best candidate for a manager. Think about it. Who is typically chosen as the new regional manager from among twenty sales reps? In the vast majority of cases, it's the people with the best sales figures. Unfortunately, as numerous studies and business practice shows, this is shooting yourself in both feet. The traits of a true expert have little in common with those of a manager or leader. In one fell swoop, you lose a brilliant salesperson and probably don't acquire a great manager.

I learned this lesson myself a few years ago. I employed a very young, but unbelievably talented guy, a typical Millennial (we even called him Neo). Neo was a top expert in social media, moving through the medium even better than a fish through water. At the age of twenty-five, he had more important social media campaigns under his belt than most people of my generation will manage during their next twelve incarnations. Neo brought a lot to the company, not only creating a comprehensive strategy for our social media presence, but also successfully implementing it.

You're probably picturing Neo right now as a long-haired, skinny geek, wearing a threadbare jumper covered in stains, chained to the computer monitor, and barely visible behind a massive pile of empty pizza boxes.

Well, you'd be wrong. Neo is a snappy dresser, genuinely well read, and with wide-ranging interests beyond the virtual world. In the real world he communicates just as clearly and interestingly as he does via the Internet. Admittedly, I don't know if he's partial to the occasional pizza, but even if he is, I suspect the empty boxes are regularly cleared from his work station.

My mistake lay in assuming that because Neo not only excelled in the use of new technology but also, in stark contrast to the majority of keyboard wizards I've encountered, possessed effective interpersonal skills, he would be the ideal person to manage the digital marketing team (a management function with four subordinate positions).

I know I've done this before, but bear with me: "Twelve months later."

The history of those twelve months can be summed up as a succession of increasingly frustrating errors and outright catastrophes. Despite his outstanding abilities, Neo never got to grips with the role of manager; instead, he did most of the work himself and didn't engage with his team, whom he couldn't motivate enough, thanks to his assumption that they were all as motivated as he was. He also coped poorly with tricky situations—for example, if there was conflict in the group, Neo wouldn't intervene, assuming things would sort themselves out. What was worse, although he learned from these failures, he wasn't able to put those lessons into practice and change anything. His nature was stronger than his will and, even if he knew that he shouldn't do everything himself and that micromanaging was a bad idea, ultimately his expert tendencies took over and he went back to his old ways. The only good news is that I managed to retain Neo in the business, despite his misadventures as a manager. He's proven to be something of a phoenix, and is currently flourishing in a role that is ideally suited to his skills and personality. He is progressing along a path typical for specialists, because we both faced facts and openly acknowledged that management was not his forte.

LET'S RETURN to 1996 and the hostile slopes of Mount Everest to look at the leaders of the two expeditions, as well as the decisions they made. Both Scott Fischer and Rob Hall were very experienced climbers who had been in the Death Zone on several occasions and had learned first-hand about the effects of high altitudes on the human body, as well as its impact on a person's ability to assess situations and make rational decisions. Rob Hall also had a lot of experience in leading amateurs, the majority of whom had never been above 26,000 feet before, in such environments.

Both leaders adopted very discrete styles of managing their teams. Rob Hall behaved as he had on his earlier expeditions. Strict, authoritative, imposing his opinion on others, and—while climbing—tolerating no dissent in the ranks. As he said, he was always ready to explain the reasons for a particular decision, but only back at the camp, and not halfway up an eight-thousander. He set up numerous detailed procedures and rules for the clients to observe. Those joining his expedition accepted them because they were designed to protect their safety and ensured that the key decisions were taken by a recognized expert.

Scott Fischer saw himself more as a coordinator of the expeditions. Those who knew him say that he believed in improvisation, and that each of his customers had to follow their own rules of the game. Procedures would have restricted that freedom, so he gave his people far greater room to make decisions. He also placed less attention than Hall on the roles and duties of his guides—he treated them more like partners than employees or contractors.

Given the nature of the undertaking, Hall's approach was appropriate—managing a workgroup in a high-risk situation requires a leader to ensure that clearly defined rules be consistently applied, almost like a benign dictator. The way Fischer led his team can be a great approach for a close-knit, competent, experienced team, but not so much for a group of amateurs who are all focused on their own goals.

And yet, as it turned out later, apart from the two leaders, everyone who died was on Rob Hall's team: Andy Harris, Yasuko

Namba, and Doug Hansen. This was because the New Zealander unwittingly placed his people in a highly dangerous authority trap. Imagine you were on that trip. You're being led by one of the best climbers in the world running the best commercial operation. He's a hard man, decisive, and right from the beginning, he drills the idea into you that what the leader says, goes. He imposes a vital rule: at precisely 2:00 pm, you must begin descending, regardless of where you are on the mountain. You're attacking the summit; 2:00 pm comes around—and the leader keeps climbing. What is a client, caught in an authority trap, supposed to think in this situation? You'll start rationalizing the leader's decision, placing faith in his vast experience and expertise in assessing the risks. "He knows what he's doing," "The weather must be better than usual, and we've got a bit more time," "We're clearly a stronger group than the previous ones and the leader knows we can make it back down in time," "The time limit is probably 4:00 pm and he just told us 2:00 pm to make sure we had time to spare." And so on.

Why did Hall make such a fundamental and ultimately tragic mistake? Why did he make a decision that destroyed the established and oft-repeated rule of ascent? The answer partly lies in the relationship between Hall and Hansen. Hall, who had sent his clients, including Hansen, back down the mountain just short of the summit in 1995, had to work incredibly hard to persuade his close friend to have another go at climbing Everest. In this way, he created a dangerous version of the sunk costs trap: in an environment of close relationships, he essentially promised (consciously or otherwise) that this time they would succeed, which made it far more difficult to make the right decision at the key moment. Rob Hall, the famous leader of Adventure Consultants, gave into his friend and broke the central principle that he himself had established, and this is what led to the tragic consequences in the hours to come.

Scott Fischer was caught out by the exact same mechanism. One of the members of his expedition was Dale Kruse, a friend of his for many years. When Kruse's condition deteriorated rapidly as he climbed to Camp III, all while exhibiting the symptoms of high-altitude edema, the leader made the right decision by taking the patient back to base camp. Unfortunately, he decided to take on this task himself instead of delegating, despite the disruption to his acclimatization plan and the enormous effort demanded from him during the assault on the summit. He justified his decision succinctly: "[Kruse] was in tears and I couldn't send him with anyone else ... I didn't want Anatoly or Neal or one of the Sherpas [to do it]. He's my friend."[13] It was several hours before an exhausted Fischer finally made it back to camp.

Emotional ties can be a terrible advisor when it comes to making choices. I always feared making decisions most when they affected people I found it hard to remain neutral toward—not only those I particularly liked, but also those for whom I felt some sort of antipathy. Any emotion, positive or negative, renders us subjective when we need to be objective. There's a reason they say you should never do business with friends, and surgeons shouldn't operate on family. As the cases of Hall and Fischer show, taking close friends on a high mountain climbing expedition brings an additional substantial risk that needs to be taken into account.

If you look at this analysis in graphic form (overleaf), it's easy to see the chain of cause and effect, and find the underlying causes of the tragedy.[14]

The first "why": the direct causes of death of five climbers in May 1996.

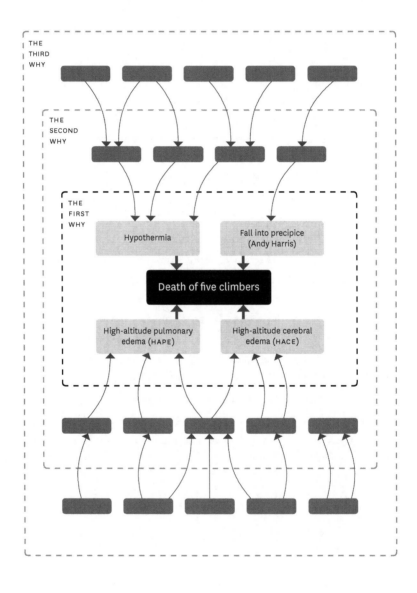

Example of a detailed analysis: the underlying reasons for breaking Rob Hall's turnaround time rule.

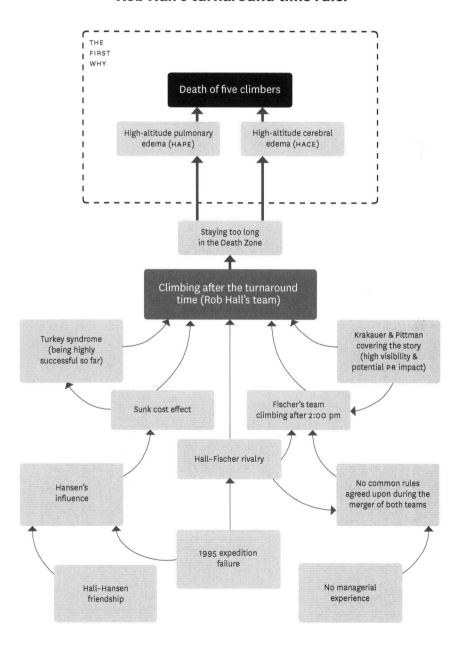

RULE #10

Recognize the value of your failures (and those of others).
　Thoroughly analyze your past failures and draw in-depth, objective, and actionable conclusions for the future.

IT'S AMAZING how easily we forget this rule. Obviously, upset by failure, we ask ourselves questions like, "How did that happen?!" but rarely do we manage to put our emotions to one side and examine the real causes of the failure. Our judgment is most probably clouded by anger, disappointment, and frustration. Even if we change something in our behavior, approach, procedures, or processes, we mostly deal with the visible symptoms (whatever upset us), and not the deeper causes of the problem.

For this reason, an RCA, while being a technically simple operation, is difficult emotionally. It involves looking into things we generally prefer not to speak about: the mistakes we made at various stages that led to our making the wrong decision. On top of that, in many modern, dynamically growing companies, I have noticed a trap in the organizational and management culture that makes it harder to initiate an RCA. The imperative of positive thinking is a trap that often leads to our hearing a high-ranking manager say, "Okay, that's enough crying over spilt milk; let's focus on the future and fight for success." Everyone is relieved to hear these words, because who wants to talk about unpleasant matters . . . ? In business, analyzing failure too often comes down to quickly identifying the "guilty party," who all too often is merely a scapegoat whose eventual dismissal doesn't fix the source of the problem.

There's an old joke about corporations that involves two rowing teams—the Greens and the Blues. There was an annual eights race between the teams for a Very Important Cup awarded by a Very Important Person, and it was certainly a Very Important Event for the two teams who prepared for it in minute detail. Come the day, emotions were running high and the teams' supporters lined the banks of the river. The two teams took their places and the starting gun was fired. What happened next was an outright disaster for one of the teams. The Greens reached the line ten minutes behind the Blues! The Greens were in uproar—how could this possibly have happened!? They called in consultants from a Very Important Consultancy Company who, after many days of hard work (reflected in the billable hours and the invoices), found the reason for the failure. The eight of the winning Blue team was a cox and seven rowers, while the Greens had seven coxes and a rower. The consultants from the Very Important Consultancy Company pointed out the obvious problem: poor management structure. So, the Greens made the appropriate changes. They decided four coxes were enough and that they should report to two Supercoxes who in turn would be managed by a Cox of All Coxes to create the necessary accountability that was obviously hitherto lacking. They introduced the changes and an entirely new team was entered for the next competition. This time they lost by twenty minutes. The angry Greens management team fired the consultants, checked the results of the regattas once more, and decided to summarily fire the rower, who was clearly the source of the problem.

It's probably best all round if you don't ask about the times of the Greens in the ensuing races.

A perfect real-world example of this approach was illustrated in a series of events I witnessed not long ago in a company from the tech sector (let's call it The GREENS). So, The GREENS, finding itself the leader in its field, was boxing clever to maintain its position against ever smaller, more aggressive rivals. Its strategy was to keep ahead of the competition by rapidly introducing innovations into its range (both in terms of improved products and services, as well as in terms of pricing policy and customer service models). The strategy was effective, and The GREENS organization was frequently presented on the pages of business magazines as a good example of a competitive strategy. Everything went smoothly until one of its new product launches bombed. Not only were sales way below expectations, but the actual product was riddled with faults, which only became apparent after a few weeks of use. The GREENS lost a lot of money introducing modifications and upgrades until—in response to the still poor sales volume—it withdrew the product and started looking for the guilty parties (seriously, those were the precise words—I heard them myself: "guilty parties," and not "source of the problem"). Of course, there could only be one guilty party: the manager in charge of the team that developed and introduced the product. They decided to fire the manager, and several other employees followed suit soon after.

After this, a member of The GREENS board sent an emotional letter to all employees, stating that they were deeply convinced their strategy was the right one and the company should focus on replacing the failed product with a range of new solutions as soon as possible, adding that there was no point in debating the failed venture. The person responsible no longer worked at the company, and so the problem had been resolved.

Less than a year later, it turned out that the problem hadn't actually been solved at all. A new version of the product hit the shelves, developed by a new group, led by a new manager. Within two months it became clear that the nightmare was recurring. Angry customers were contacting the company about faults appearing several weeks after purchase. Fortunately, this time, The GREENS board displayed more curiosity and, instead of firing another manager and half the design team, they carried out an RCA. It transpired that the cause of the problems was that two years earlier, there had been a change in the IT system used by the HR department. When the new system was implemented, some of the data on technical training completed by employees had been lost. For this reason, no one realized that four people in one of the analytics teams hadn't been trained in the changes made to a different computer system. These alterations, while seemingly small, were significant enough to require the analysts to make minor changes in the way they entered the data to be analyzed. The result was disaster: the analysts, acting in good faith and blissfully unaware of the changes, created key reports for the development of new products which were faulty. Based on the bad data, programs were created for the new devices that were never going to work as intended. The extended operation tests carried out prior to the product launch were too short to identify the faults in the program, which only emerged once the customers had been using the equipment for several weeks.

AN OBVIOUS trap in the inquiry mode and RCA methods lies in finding a happy medium between the thoroughness and depth of the analysis and the time available—and time is always the most precious resource in business. We'd all like to have the time to calmly analyze something from all sides, go through all the data, and grill all the experts. Unfortunately, we have schedules, timetables, meetings, and deadlines. We often have to choose the lesser of two evils, as any decision can often be seen as better than no decision at all.

Time will always be a key factor when seeking a competitive advantage, so it's a problem that will never go away. The sooner we launch our product, the better our chances of beating our rivals and cornering the market. The faster we decide, the more agile and flexible we are as an organization. The more agile we are, the better our chances in the world of black swans. We must therefore find a compromise option to keep the decision wolf from the door and the business lamb safe and sound.

The good news is, there is a range of things we can do to achieve this. One option is to accelerate and improve the decision-making process for standard decisions that don't entail major risks to the business. The more we automate and delegate down the management ladder, the more time we have to look into things that demand an inquiry mode. Our second option is to free up time by shooting down "Concordes," eliminating projects that are doomed to fail and that only continue because of the accumulated momentum and because we're in a sunk costs trap. A third method is to set up a rapid response team, which in a black swan situation will be prepared and primed in terms of at least certain actions and procedures in order to act quickly and save time. A fourth method is something I call "decision salami." In negotiations, the salami tactic involves gaining ground incrementally, so as to not arouse your opponent's suspicions. You gradually gain small concessions and your stunned opponent sees too late that they have swallowed your proposal whole. Decision salami works in much the same way: we win time by making small moves all while securing the key issues. An example of that approach is the sea blockade of Cuba by JFK. It bought time for further analysis, and simultaneously stopped the warheads being placed on the island, which would have irreversibly changed the balance of power. Likewise, when Eurocontrol decided to close the skies after the eruption of the volcano in Iceland, it bought itself sufficient time to conduct an inquiry approach, while eradicating the chances of an aviation catastrophe. However, in this case, the time wasn't well used, as the experts at Eurocontrol chose instead to go into advocacy mode.

So, the decision salami should be guided by two factors: winning extra time and simultaneously securing the fundamental issues. From the perspective of effective decision-making in a world of black swans, every organization should identify critical processes: the people, resources, or tasks that are crucial to the effectiveness of the entire organization. In short, it's about identifying those issues that will destroy us, not make us stronger, if they go wrong. Once we know what they are, we have to create a set of decisions that will secure the short-term future of the organization and give us additional time to research the black swan. If such an approach is accompanied by the decision-making *Kaizen* described earlier, based on an intelligent, thorough RCA, we have a chance of creating a winning organization that is permanently focused on continuous improvement in terms of both the attitude and the behavior of individual employees.

This won't happen, though, if the organization lacks authentic leaders, people whose fundamental role in shaping effective decision-making we shall discuss in detail later. In the case of improvements based on RCAs, authentic leaders play a major role in moderating discussions, ensuring that they don't become another battleground for power and influence in the company. An old corporate truism states that nothing improves your chances of promotion like a colleague's failure. But if a group is led by an authentic leader, and not just your typical nominal manager, the chances that the problem, and not one of the employees, will be attacked is much greater. This doesn't imply that using an RCA means we shouldn't draw negative conclusions about people who commit cardinal errors; it's important, though, that the analysis doesn't turn into a witch hunt looking for guilty parties.

It's also worth bearing in mind that the basic problem that arises when we're managing innovative processes in the real world doesn't concern creation, it concerns implementation. It's easy to generate hundreds of innovative ideas; the problems begin when we start putting them into practice. Sometimes, the problems get blown out of proportion and brilliant ideas get shelved because the decision-makers conclude they just won't work. For example, look at the Palo Alto Research Center (PARC), set up in 1970 by Xerox. PARC's job was to constantly seek out technological innovations that could form the basis of new products for Xerox (then famous for their photocopiers) to sell. The PARC team performed their tasks excellently, creating such concepts and prototypes as the computer mouse, local area networks, email servers, graphical user interfaces, and the WYSIWYG word processor. The management of Xerox was regularly informed about each of these breakthrough inventions developed by the engineers, and each time they concluded that the market wouldn't like it, or it couldn't be monetized. Idea after idea was shelved and left to gather dust. This happened with the Xerox Alto, a personal computer with a graphical user interface and QWERTY keyboard. In 1979, PARC was visited by a man whose vision and imagination were far greater than those of the board of Xerox at the time. That man was Steve Jobs, and he was looking for inspiration for Lisa, the personal computer Apple was working on at the time. Jobs loved the engineers' ideas, so he bought some of them—he also copied some, which many criticized him for—and poached several employees. One way or another, the ideas developed by PARC were used in the personal computer that Apple launched in 1984—and that proved to be an enormous success. The Xerox board must have gasped in amazement. They had had the winning lottery ticket and somehow had never managed to cash it in. (Another PARC breakthrough was the XEROX 8010

STAR, an innovative combination of local networks and email that was essentially the first mass email server. It also never got approval from the bigwigs at Xerox.)

Lack of innovation in such a competitive area can mean only one thing: problems on the horizon. By the end of the 1990s, Xerox was suffering serious losses and fighting for survival. The mission to sort out the company was accepted by Anne Mulcahy, who in 2002 made PARC independent of the structures in Xerox, enabling the unit to look for other customers. Today, although a significant proportion of PARC's revenue comes from Xerox, the center also works for Samsung, Fujitsu, and NEC, to name but three.

So, innovation dies not at the creation stage, but during implementation. It's the same with RCAs: even if we reach profound, justified, precise conclusions, in many cases they don't lead to concrete changes in the functioning of a team or company (in the next chapter, we shall encounter just such a tale of decision-making inertia at NASA). Authentic leaders, then, are also responsible for ensuring that the root causes of problems are eliminated, and that new solutions have been thoroughly tested before becoming standard. Their task is not only to initiate intelligent discussion, but also to oversee the process of implementing change.

The role of leaders in improving the decision-making infrastructure, though, goes beyond the actual analysis of failures and successes, or introducing improvements; we shall explore this in more detail in Chapter 7.

Before that, though, we have to face a business hurricane.

RCA in Decision-Making:
A Step-by-Step Guide

1. Prepare a robust "opening account": Identify the problem and the effectiveness criteria that failed (why did they fail? which factors were crucial?), draw up a list of personnel, and gather all the available data about the project. Try to be as objective as possible. Present the resulting report to two or three people with whom you frequently disagree and ask for their opinions. Is the report neutral or tendentious?

2. Select the people for the RCA team: Don't use only people who were involved in the failed undertaking; bring in people whose experience will allow them to compare the project with earlier ones. Aim for variety: alongside experienced people, include more recent employees, as they may see faults that you've become blind to (the monkey and banana syndrome). Engage people with different roles and from different departments in the company. If you can justify it, and it's possible, look outside the organization—it's often customers, suppliers, or partners who can see the broader picture.

3. Set out the rules for conducting an RCA to the team (e.g., brainstorming, 5 Whys) and set a timeline for the work. Ask if the team thinks anyone else should be included in the team.

4. Present the opening account, emphasizing the starting point for the analysis. Allow for a discussion examining the account.

5. Divide the RCA team into subgroups (ideally four to eight people). Try to choose members so that each team contains people who don't work together daily. The greater the variety, the greater the chances that the discussion will be thorough. Allow the subgroups to conduct the analysis independently. Don't rule out areas, don't appoint group leaders, don't suggest how they should work.

6. Once the work in subgroups has been completed, bring together the whole team and carry out a chronological analysis, or use reverse chronology (starting from the failure and working backward) if that's more appropriate. The subgroups then present their opinions about the causes of the mistakes. Moderate the debate, making an effort to engage and involve less active participants. Express your opinions, but be careful not to impose them, especially if your direct subordinates are part of the RCA team.

7. After you've written down the results of the analysis, end the meeting. Leave all the materials and notes from the meeting behind. Bring the group together the next day and return to the room where the results are. Look at them again, individually, with fresh eyes. Take into account any remarks made by the team following this review. Make sure the final "Why?" really is final.

8. Bring the results together in a "closing account." Present that to someone who didn't participate in the work of the RCA team. Ask them to assess the clarity of the material and the justification of the causes and effects—is it all clearly documented, credible, and convincing?

9. Set out the priorities for change, looking first for simple improvements that can be implemented relatively quickly and cheaply. In each process of change, *quick wins* are important, as they further motivate people to act. Also define the changes needed in the medium and longer terms. Make someone responsible for each initiative and don't forget to set deadlines, milestones, or indicators. An RCA mustn't end with diagnosing the problem, it must constitute a starting point for further action.

10. Thank the RCA team for its energy and engagement.

6

SOMETHING

IN THE AIR

THINK BACK TO the controversial experiment with the monkeys and the bananas. The animals gradually learned a certain behavior, and the group accepted not climbing the ladder to reach the bananas as the norm. Like it or not, we're no different from those monkeys. We yield to pressure, overt or otherwise, from our cultural environment, which forces us to conform to the behavioral norms and standards of the group. This process is frequently unconscious, and over time, like the monkeys, we stop wondering about the reasons behind our actions. When we apply the banana experiment to entire countries, we call such emergent behavior *national culture*; in the case of individual businesses, the phenomenon of groups of employees adopting similar behaviors is called *organizational culture*.

Culture is the set of norms and beliefs that are shared by a specific group of people and that affect their attitudes and behavior, although they may be oblivious to its influence. Culture is, in short, the way in which we behave. In many cases, the principles of behavior that govern us are so deeply ingrained that we don't even realize they exist; stereotypes emerge in a similar manner, as they're instilled in us throughout our lives by the representativeness heuristic. It's no accident that Geert Hofstede described culture as "the collective programming of the mind" that creates the discrete set of values, attitudes, and behaviors typical of a given set of people. Linda Smircich, of the University of Massachusetts Amherst, called culture "social glue," a set of attitudes and unwritten rules that contribute to a feeling of belonging within a particular group. From this perspective, an organization's culture becomes an identifying trait that enables its members to feel like they're playing on the same team, one that stands out from the rest.

Every social group creates a specific culture, even if it's not a conscious, managed process. Culture, then, is a little like air. We can't see it (though it certainly exists) and we easily forget its importance—until there's a hurricane. At which point, this invisible force shows its destructive side. In business, this kind of hurricane might take the form of a merger of two companies that leads to a culture clash between two groups with totally different social glues. In those situations, the formerly inconspicuous cultures collide, generate conflicts, and create a significant problem. Just think about the problems that followed the merger of the German company Daimler with the US firm Chrysler. Failure to carry out a cultural due diligence prior to the merger led to a hurricane, with a clash not just between organizational cultures, but between national ones, too. The behavior of the two groups that came into conflict with each other was a result not only of conscious adherence to rules and procedures (which would have been relatively easy to resolve), but above all, from deep-rooted, partially unconscious convictions about how (not) to behave.

Intercultural differences can also lead to a multitude of tragi-comic incidents, from the trivial to the spectacular.

A very good friend of mine is extremely well-traveled. He is passionate about discovering and exploring new places. Organized trips are not for him; he's only happy when he takes his seat in a local restaurant that has never seen a tourist before. It's an approach that once went badly wrong. It all began in the Laran-jeiras district of Rio de Janeiro, which he was visiting for the first time. While my friend was eating supper in one of the local restau-rants, the waiter asked how he was enjoying his meal. As his mouth was full, my friend decided to answer the question with a classic European and North American A-OK gesture, raising his hand and forming his index finger and thumb into an O shape to explain that everything was splendid. Unhappily for him, the Brazilian waiter, it later turned out, had only been working four days and this was his first experience of a foreign customer. From my friend's point of view, it could have been worse. On the plus side, the waiter didn't actually kill him, and the traumatized owner didn't charge him for his meal. On the downside, though, his khakis and light blue shirt were unequivocally ruined by the dark gravy of the *feijoada* tipped over him. My friend had been blissfully unaware that the gesture, regarded so positively in Europe and the USA, has an unpleasant, even insulting connotation in Brazil and so enraged the waiter.

The influence of cultural differences in decision-making can result in way more than the odd conflict or amusing anecdote. Social psychologist Professor Geert Hofstede, the guru of cultural anthropology and the true precursor of its business application, is best known for his breakthrough research, which dates back to 1975, in this area. That year, Hofstede, fascinated by organizational culture, spent time observing IBM, which was regarded at the time as monolithic in terms of its working environment. Wherever it set up a new division, the rules of behavior and company values developed over decades by the legendary Thomas Watson, one of the company's first directors, were inculcated in the employees. During their observations of the IBM employees, Hofstede and his team noticed the clear influence of national cultures, in addition to the carefully cultivated corporate one, on their behavior and attitudes. At this point, the research turned into a breakthrough work in the field of cultural anthropology, eventually forming the foundation for a whole raft of social, political, educational, and business applications.

Hofstede's team defined four key dimensions distinguishing social groups and directly influencing the choice of decision-making methods. These dimensions, named as indexes, were power distance, individualism, masculinity, and uncertainty avoidance in the original research.

Power Distance (PDI)

Power distance was defined by Hofstede's team as a given nation's acceptance that power and resources are not equally distributed.[1] Societies with a high power distance index (PDI) accept it as the norm and see nothing unnatural about the fact that some people are rich and powerful and others not. Citizens of nations with a low level of PDI take the opposite approach: they aspire to minimize the differences and to redistribute power, influence, and wealth more equitably. The five countries with the highest PDI are (in descending order) Slovakia, Malaysia, Panama, Guatemala, and Russia. The five with the lowest PDI are (in ascending order) Austria, Israel, Denmark, New Zealand, and Switzerland, followed by the Scandinavian countries.

The PDI translates into key expectations of decision-makers. In countries with a high PDI, hierarchy and the formal attributes of authority, such as the right to make decisions, are enormously significant. Organizations that exhibit a high PDI are typically run centrally, are autocratic, and concentrate decision-making within a small group of high-ranking managers. In this case, there are clear threats to an inquiry approach—even if, for cultural reasons, subordinates feel no need to get involved in the decision-making process and don't feel slighted by the decision-makers ignoring them, the authority trap and dangerously shallow analysis both lurk in the background. In black swan situations, this combination of obedience to authority and superficial analysis can be a very poor advisor. Conversely, the lower the PDI, the greater the expectations across the organization that lower-ranking employees will be involved in the decision-making process; if this doesn't happen, it can be seen as unjust and as displaying indifference to the competence and experience of the staff. Here, though, other dangers appear, because excessive discussions and consultations, typical characteristics of a democratic decision-making style, can lead to missing time-sensitive opportunities.

Individualism versus Collectivism (IDV)

The individualism index (IDV) has a very interesting influence on the decision-making process. Individualistic cultures (those with a high IDV) are seen as focusing on the individual, and a degree of selfishness and concern with your own wealth and that of your nearest and dearest is socially understood and accepted. Collectivist countries (those with a low IDV) set the interest of the group above that of the individual.[2] Among the most individualistic societies, the USA tops the rankings, in second place comes Australia, with Great Britain hot on its heels. The most collectivist countries are found in Latin America: Guatemala, Ecuador, Panama, Venezuela, and Colombia.

Professor Hofstede's team's research revealed a seemingly surprising correlation: countries with a collectivist culture typically also display a high PDI and the strong hierarchy that results from it. Explaining this, though, is not difficult. In collectivist countries, "authority" is deferred to the group to which the individual belongs, with group interests being viewed as overriding. The consequences for decision-making are similar: collectivist countries often make irrational and uneconomic decisions, because the group takes precedence. An example of this is the classic business situation where a manager decides not to release an inefficient worker because he's been there a long time and is an integral part of the company's social network.

An additional source of poor decisions in collectivist cultures can stem from people not being open to discussion, for fear of disturbing the status quo. This can be illustrated using a story in the Gospel According to Matthew: A man with two sons instructed them to go and work in the vineyard. The first son replied, "Yes, Father," but didn't go near the vineyard. The second son refused the order, but finally changed his mind and went to work on the winemaking. So, which of the sons obeyed his father's will? The Bible, obviously, indicates that the second one did. Hofstede, though, relates the tale of a Dutch missionary who told the tale in Indonesia, a very strongly collectivist nation. To the surprise of the missionary, the Indonesians all picked the first son, as in their opinion, even if he didn't ultimately carry out his father's instructions, he hadn't upset the status quo in the family, which is the most important of all social groupings.

A large part of communication in collectivist countries is what's known as high-context communication, which is composed not solely of words but also of their accompanying nonverbal language, the tone of voice, and the entire context of the conversation. In situations where decisions have to be made quickly, decoding such a message can be time-consuming and result in misinterpretation. The challenge of making quick decisions in such groups becomes worse when a decision-making team includes representatives of both individualistic and collectivist cultures: the first group will be far more extroverted, expressing their views far more boldly and assertively and making those in the other group feel uncomfortable, as they are likely to prefer to back down rather than openly oppose. A hybrid group will have little chance of engaging in open debate and conducting a thorough, multifaceted inquiry approach. RCAs will also be emotionally colored, and analyzing the causes of failure will be extremely awkward for those from a collectivist culture (after all, we're talking about mistakes made within our social group, toward which we should be loyal).

Masculinity (MAS)

Hofstede's team also divided cultures into masculine and feminine. In strongly masculine cultures, with a high masculinity (MAS) index, the emphasis is on achievement, winning, progress, and earnings, and men are expected to meet these expectations. In predominantly feminine cultures (with a low MAS index), cooperation, quality of life, and relationships, as well as care for the weak and vulnerable are more important, with both sexes being expected to display these priorities.[3] The leading masculine cultures are Slovakia, which ranked first, then Hungary, Austria, and the German-speaking part of Switzerland, followed by Japan and Venezuela. Feminine cultures were headed by Sweden, which scored the lowest MAS index, Norway, Denmark, Latvia, and the Netherlands.

As you might imagine, masculine societies are more confrontational. You can see the difference clearly in negotiations: while feminine nations aim for compromise and consensus (win-win), masculine societies prefer to win from a position of power. This had tragic consequences in two almost identical international conflicts, one of which was resolved peacefully, and the other ended in an unnecessary loss of life.

THE ÅLAND and Falkland Islands have much in common. The Åland Islands are a group of about 6,500 small islands lying in the Gulf of Bothnia in the Baltic Sea; the Falklands are composed of about 800 islands in the Atlantic Ocean, almost 300 miles off the coast of Argentina. Both island groups have been contested territories at various times. In the case of the Åland Islands, both Finland and Sweden lay claim to them, which is hardly surprising, as they are almost equidistant to the two countries. The Falklands, also known by their Spanish name the Malvinas, have been argued over by the UK and Argentina for many years.

The problem of the Åland Islands was resolved very rapidly. Although they had been settled by Swedes since the Middle Ages, and the majority of people who live on them still speak Swedish, from the beginning of the nineteenth century, they fell under the rule of various countries. In 1809, on the basis of a peace treaty signed in Friedrikshamn, the Åland Islands were given to Russia, which lost control of them half a century later as a result of the Crimean War. At the beginning of the twentieth century, there was a serious political squabble between Finland and Sweden, with both countries laying claim to the islands. The two sides decided to resolve the dispute through international law. A special commission was set up, composed of lawyers representing France, Switzerland, and the Netherlands. After much discussion, the

Council of the League of Nations awarded the Åland Islands to Finland on June 24, 1921, on the condition that they remained neutral. To this day, although about 90 percent of the inhabitants are Swedish, the Åland Islands remain a demilitarized autonomous territory belonging to Finland. A potentially dangerous international crisis was averted through negotiation.

The battle for sovereignty of the Falklands ran a totally different course, despite their backstory resembling that of the Åland Islands. The Falklands also changed hands frequently. Discovered in the sixteenth century by the British, they fell under French rule; the first colony on the islands was established by Louis de Bougainville in 1764 and was called Port Louis. The French didn't enjoy the Falklands for long. A mere three years later, they were taken over by the Spanish, who wasted no time in changing the name of Port Louis to Puerto Soledad. This wasn't the end of the drama, though. In 1771, the islands once again became the property of Great Britain, although Argentina stated its claim to the islands at the beginning of the nineteenth century, and eventually, the Falklands were declared a British colony. The Argentinians never accepted this, and in March 1982, the military junta that was currently in power under the leadership of Leopoldo Galtieri, decided to launch Operación Rosario. On April 2, Argentina sent armed forces to the islands, which were inhabited by fewer than fifteen hundred people. The United Nations Security Council condemned Argentina's actions, but the military ignored the resolution. The British obviously had no intention of standing idle, and they sent a major task force to the Falklands. Open conflict broke out, which despite the efforts of the international community (including the Secretary-General of the UN, Javier Pérez de Cuéllar), lasted for over two months and claimed the lives of almost one thousand people.

What distinguishes the two events? The MAS index of the countries involved. Finland and Sweden are strongly feminine countries,
where decisions are made via mediation and by seeking consensus,
while the UK and Argentina are masculine nations and favor direct
confrontation.

Uncertainty Avoidance (UAI)

Avoiding uncertainty is an interesting and yet decidedly counter-
intuitive factor.[4] It is difficult to establish the value of this index
simply by observing the daily behavior of a group of foreign nation-
als. Countries with a high uncertainty avoidance index are those
where the fact that the future is highly unpredictable is a source
of deep unease. This creates a need to control, which means being
less open to innovation. Nations with a low UAI accept uncertainty,
working on the assumption that some things can't be controlled,
so whatever will be, will be. At the top of the UAI rankings come
Greece, Portugal, Guatemala, and Uruguay, while the countries
with the lowest scores—where people cope with the uncertainty
of tomorrow with relatively little stress or concern—are Singapore,
Jamaica, Sweden, Denmark, and Hong Kong. It's worth remembering that a high UAI leads to unease, not to fear. Fear is an emotion
that has a clear cause (we are afraid of something); unease, however, is unjustified.

Countries with a high UAI display numerous unpleasant social
phenomena as a result of this deep level of internal stress. Research
has shown, for example, a strong correlation between UAI and
suicide rates. It should also come as no surprise that high UAI countries score a lower rating in the World Happiness Report.

In decision-making, people from a country with a high UAI will
try to make choices that shore up the status quo and don't lead to
significant change, because change leads to uncertainty, which in

turn makes the decision-maker uneasy. However, attempting to control reality fosters the adoption of the inquiry approach, as the deeper the analysis of a given situation, the more comfortable the decision-maker feels. We can see a similar mechanism in operation during purchasing decisions. Those who avoid uncertainty will prefer to buy new items, from authorized dealers and stores, and will employ specialists to perform any work that requires special competencies, as this puts them at ease. In countries with a low UAI, the secondhand goods market is far more robust, and many people try to perform small jobs around the house themselves (even if, ultimately, they hire an expert, when they eventually discover they have two left thumbs). This index, and its influence on decision-making, also affects the speed with which major innovations spread: they are adopted far more rapidly in nations that have a low uncertainty avoidance and are therefore more open to trying something new. The development and uptake of new technologies such as cell phones, the Internet, online and mobile banking, and so on illustrates this rather neatly.

AT THE company level, the situation is even more intriguing.

The mechanisms underlying the building and shaping of an organizational culture are almost identical to those of building and shaping a national culture. Individual companies create their own, unwritten approaches to the dimensions outlined by Geert Hofstede's team. In some, decisions will generally be made at the top of the management ladder, while others will favor decentralization. Some companies will culturally apply a policy of "up or out," and others will allow an employee to remain in the same position for their entire career. There are companies that approach planning and forecasting in an extremely scrupulous and restrictive fashion, and there are others that take a laid-back, almost stereotypical

Jamaican approach to things—it'll work out somehow, so don't worry about it. In some companies, teamwork is everything; others foster outstanding individuals. Every organization has its own aura, its own way of looking at the world, which translates into distinctive attitudes and behavior.

Organizational cultures are shaped, though, by slightly different factors than nations are. A tremendously significant role is played by a company's mission statement and its position in relation to the competition, because it is knowing how we want to differentiate ourselves that shapes many of our behaviors. Exceptional customer service, amazingly low prices, top-quality products or services— each of these attributes will influence the attitudes of employees to one another and to the market context. The motivational tools used to encourage employees to act in line with the organizational culture are a little different. Businesses have a vast array of carrots and sticks at their disposal. Those who operate in accordance with the company's expectations may not only receive financial rewards, but also advance up the hierarchy. Those who don't follow the written, or unwritten, rules of the culture may find their pay packet is lighter or, in extreme cases, be excluded from the social group—in other words, get sacked.

In the case of national cultures, the only reward or punishment on offer is the sense of belonging to a given group, or of being ostracized. Interestingly, the majority of companies dream of achieving the first (our employees are motivated to work simply because they are employed by us!) while retaining an entire arsenal of business sticks to beat you with (if you're not excited to work for us, then say goodbye to that bonus...). Despite these differences, organizational cultures, just like national ones, significantly affect the decision-making process.

The influence of organizational culture on the decision-making process is, in fact, one of the key topics of this entire book. I am analyzing the attitudes of leaders and key moments, looking at the behavior of teams, and discussing ways of introducing an organization to a new normal and instilling into employees novel approaches to coping with the chaos of life. Organizational culture is one of the basic forces that shapes the competence (or incompetence) of a company when it comes to making business decisions. That is where phenomena such as individualism versus teamwork in decision-making, the tendency (or reluctance) to adopt an inquiry approach, boldness (or timidity) in decision-making, a sense of personal responsibility (or not), and the desire to understand the causes of both failure and success and propensity for risk are manifested.

This last element is, in business, one of the most important, as demonstrated most dramatically in the expeditions led by Rob Hall and Scott Fischer on Mount Everest. In that extreme case, the boundaries of acceptable risk were pushed too far by the quest for greater profit and ultimately compromised safety, which should never be considered acceptable. A converse example of this was the decision taken by Eurocontrol in 2010, where risk was minimized (or more accurately, eliminated), which later turned out to have been a very poor business decision. The ability to set the parameters of acceptable risk is a crucial competence in a leader, but it can be subjected to enormous pressure from the organizational culture, which may encourage us to take unnecessary risks or to be overly cautious. The key is not only to remain objective, so we can set the applicable limits, but also to consciously shape an organization's culture in such a manner that the decision-making capacity of all employees is improved and the appropriate approach to the process adopted.

That lesson was learned in the hardest way imaginable by NASA.

THE ASTONISHING effort, described earlier, to rescue the crew of *Apollo 13* did not constitute a success, as far as the US Congress was concerned. Despite the happy outcome, the incident was viewed as an unsuccessful realization of the mission's goals, which resulted in budget cuts for NASA. As a result of this, the organization set its sights on a bold, new target: following the Moon landing, the next milestone in the conquest of space would be the construction of an orbiting space station, to facilitate further research. In 1971, a project and a budget were prepared and presented to Congress, which rejected the proposal, horrified by the sums involved. Struggling for financial survival, NASA decided to adopt the salami method and embarked on a process of getting the funding bit by bit, splitting the budget into successive stages of building the station. The first stage was the construction of a space shuttle, whose job was to carry successive parts of the space station into orbit. The tactic was successful: Congress approved the Space Transportation System (STS) program, which was officially inaugurated on January 5, 1972. The space shuttle was presented by President Richard Nixon as a means of cheap, routine space travel, and in the decade to come, NASA tried to realize this bold vision.

The prototype of the space shuttle was named *Enterprise* (in honor of the space ship in *Star Trek*), and in 1977, it completed its first test flights, the goal of which was to practice the landing maneuver. On the basis of what was learned from those tests, the first fully functional space shuttle was constructed. Designated OV-102, and known to all as *Columbia*, its maiden voyage was slated for an undisclosed date in 1978. A series of delays meant that it was actually April 12, 1981, at precisely noon, before the historic first mission, STS-1, was launched with a two-man crew, John Young and Robert Crippen. The flight lasted two days, six hours, and just under twenty-one minutes, during which time *Columbia* orbited Earth thirty-seven times. It landed at Edwards Air Force Base (EAFB) without any problems. President Ronald

Reagan, welcoming the crew back to Earth, gave a speech in which he announced that "The first priority of the STS program is to make the system fully operational and cost-effective in providing routine access to space."[5] However, in many experts' opinions, flying in the space shuttle was an enormous challenge, greater even than landing on the Moon had been twelve years earlier, and they treated the announcement of numerous commercial flights with some skepticism.

In the years to come, NASA tried its best to realize President Reagan's promise. New shuttles were put into service—in 1982, *Columbia* was joined by *Challenger*, and in later years by *Discovery* and *Atlantis*.[6] Missions were carried out increasingly frequently, and by mid-January 1986, twenty-four had already been completed. The twenty-fifth mission, STS-51L, was the *Challenger* flight, but it was repeatedly delayed for technical reasons. For NASA, this was a very awkward situation, as just prior to the scheduled date for the *Challenger* mission, an unwelcome record had been set: the liftoff of *Columbia* had been put back seven times, delaying the mission by twenty-five days. Information about problems with yet another shuttle was exploited to the full by the media, which mercilessly mocked NASA with comments such as "Once again a flawless liftoff proved to be too much of a challenge for the *Challenger*."[7] A new launch date of January 27 was finally set for *Challenger*, but yet again bad luck raised its ugly head in the form of a damaged exterior access hatch. Once more, liftoff was delayed and set for the following day. On January 28, at 11:38 local time, the *Challenger* space shuttle was finally set to leave the launch tower and begin its mission.

On January 23, at around 1:00 pm, NASA received an unpromising weather forecast. It showed an unusually low temperature for Florida, going as low as 23°F on the night before liftoff. Air temperatures before noon the following day were expected to range between 32°F and 41°F. A shuttle had never taken off in such low temperatures before—the lowest liftoff temperature to date had been 52°F, precisely a year before in January 1985. During that mission, STS-51C, an isolating O-ring connecting element of the SRB rockets used to boost the shuttle into orbit, failed. On that occasion, the backup O-ring remained sealed, which prevented a tragedy.

Larry Wear, responsible for the solid rocket boosters on the STS program, contacted the Morton-Thiokol company, which supplied the booster rockets to NASA. He asked the vital question: Could the low temperature predicted for liftoff constitute a threat to the rockets? The contractor treated the question with the appropriate seriousness. Robert Ebeling, who was the person responsible in the company for the liftoff systems for the STS project, set up two teleconferences with engineers from Morton-Thiokol and key NASA management. The second of these, which began at precisely 8:15 pm, turned out to have grave consequences. Lawrence Mulloy, a high-ranking NASA manager, requested a liftoff recommendation from the manufacturer. To his surprise, the engineers strongly advised against it. The Morton-Thiokol vice president, Joe Kilminster, therefore informed Mulloy and the other participants in the discussion that he couldn't guarantee the O-rings would remain operable at such low temperatures. He referenced the incident from the year before, when the O-ring became rigid at 52°F, and recommended delaying the start. NASA went ballistic. There followed a heated exchange during which Mulloy uttered the fateful words: "My God, Thiokol, when do you want me to launch, next April?" George Hardy, the deputy director of Science and Engineering, said he was appalled by the recommendation.[8] Then Kilminster asked to suspend the conference. During a thirty-minute break, another vice president of Morton-Thiokol, Jerry

Mason, said, "We have to make a managerial decision," thus excluding the Thiokol engineers from the process and ignoring concerns and questions from Arnie Thompson and Roger Boisjoly, engineers at NASA. Despite this, they still tried to make the others understand their concerns. Finally, it was put to a vote in which only the high-ranking managers could take part and which resulted in the earlier recommendation being changed. To the evident satisfaction of NASA's management, Morton-Thiokol gave the green light for liftoff.

During the night, yet another red flag began to wave. The team that inspected the liftoff equipment at 1:30 am noted a large buildup of ice covering the surface of the tower as well as the shuttle itself and the boosters. The inspection was repeated twice more in the early morning hours, and as a result of their findings, NASA contacted Rockwell, the company that had built *Challenger*. Here again, the contractor's engineers expressed their misgivings about the weather, suggesting the liftoff be delayed. The Mission Management Team (MMT) voted to continue the launch procedure. To the satisfaction of the MMT, at 11:25 am the countdown began, and liftoff went ahead, according to plan, at 11:38 am local time at a temperature of barely 36°F.

Fifty-eight seconds into the flight, small tongues of flame began to lick at the connector to the right solid-fuel rocket booster (SRB), indicating both seals had failed. Sixty-four seconds after liftoff, the casing of the liquid hydrogen tank caught fire, which was registered by the telemetry as a pressure drop in the tank. The crew was totally oblivious to the drama that was unfolding. At the sixty-eight-second point, the final communication between Mission Control and *Challenger*'s commander, Richard Scobee, took place. Scobee accepted and confirmed a command to increase power to the rockets—a command he ultimately could not carry out. In the seventy-third second, the connectors to the right SRB and the damaged liquid oxygen tank broke away, causing massive disruption to the flight trajectory. The resulting G-force exceeded 20, which tore the shuttle apart. The catastrophe took place at an altitude of approximately 9 miles, when *Challenger* was traveling at over 1,800 miles an hour.

Later analyses showed that the crew of seven probably survived the initial explosion. In photos that captured the moment of the explosion, the undamaged cabin is clearly visible, separated from the rest of the craft, still climbing for a few seconds, then falling in a gentle arc down toward the ocean. It emerged that after the breakup of the shuttle, three PEAPs (Personal Egress Air Packs), which supply oxygen in the event of an emergency, were activated. The PEAP activation demanded conscious action by the astronauts on board; it couldn't have occurred spontaneously. Not that it mattered. Regardless of the PEAPs, the crew would have had zero chance of surviving the impact when the cabin hit the water two minutes and forty-five seconds after the explosion. The cabin fell at a rate of about 200 miles an hour, and the impact with the ocean generated about 200 Gs—a force that neither the reinforced aluminum crew module nor the astronauts themselves could have survived.

President Reagan immediately set up an investigative committee led by former attorney general William P. Rogers, whose name lives on in the commonly used name of the committee, the Rogers Commission. The aim of the investigation, which was also their mandate, was to analyze the causes of the tragedy and present a detailed report containing recommendations to avoid similar events in future, all within 120 days. The committee was composed of numerous luminaries from the world of science and technology, including, among others, the legendary Richard Feynman, winner of the Nobel Prize in Physics in 1965; the astronaut Neil

Armstrong; and Charles Yeager, the renowned test pilot who, in 1947, broke the sound barrier.

This extraordinary set of experts met their deadline, publishing the report expected of them by the president, while the investigation itself was observed closely by the media and the public. Right from the start, there were leaks, some more outrageous than others. The turning point arrived on February 9, 1986, when the *New York Times* published an article on the front page of its Sunday edition, under the headline "NASA Had Warning of a Disaster Risk Posed by Booster,"[9] in which an anonymous but very well-informed NASA employee revealed the shocking truth to journalists: the problems with the O-rings had been well known since at least 1982—and consistently ignored. All hell let loose, and the Rogers Commission subsequently decided to hold a closed meeting on February 10, with the managers and technicians from NASA who were responsible for the SRBs and their O-rings, as well as the contractors, Morton-Thiokol. The information released following the meeting provided a deeply disturbing view of the situation. The now-infamous teleconference the day before liftoff came to light, as well as the pressure that had been applied to the engineers and Morton-Thiokol's management. It also brought to light historical details that revealed that the problems with the O-rings went as far back as 1977, four years before the first space shuttle flight and almost a decade prior to the *Challenger* disaster. Despite this knowledge, NASA took no action to avert the tragedy.

The committee's report, published on June 6, 1986, described the blatant faults and technical shortcomings that led to the catastrophe, but it also pointed to its deeper cause: the faulty decision-making process in the Agency. In particular, the committee highlighted the ineffective procedures for reporting problems to senior managers as well as general problems with the flow of information, which rendered deeper analysis of the situation impossible. The report didn't name and shame; instead, it placed the responsibility for the deaths of the seven astronauts of STS-51L on the organization as a whole.

The *Challenger* tragedy almost offers a grocery list of the classic decision-making errors described in this book, and the RCA reveals a range of additional information about its causes.

The launch conditions were the very definition of a black swan— no mission had ever been initiated at such low temperatures. The takeoff was therefore outside the zone of typical risk management, because there was no way of assessing the risk. NASA had boldly gone where no space agency had gone before and was dealing with genuine uncertainty. In this situation, an inquiry approach is essential and time needs to be bought by using salami tactics, enabling a more thorough analysis to be carried out. It would have been enough to delay liftoff to either deal with the black swan (which would essentially have simply meant waiting a few hours for the air to heat up a bit), or more thoroughly assess the degree of danger. NASA, unfortunately, decided on a typical commercial, business-oriented advocacy approach. They urgently sought out information that would show that it would be safe to lift off despite the unusual weather. They cited earlier examples of a shuttle getting back safely despite damaged O-rings (falling prey to the turkey syndrome). Another part of the advocacy approach was the pressure placed on the Morton-Thiokol engineers, who had their arms twisted to help them come around to Mission Control's view.

If we use RCA to understand the underlying reasons for the tragedy, the answers to successive "whys" are very interesting. Why did people as experienced and professional as the NASA managers make such a fundamental error? Why did the same organization that had successfully rescued the crew of *Apollo 13* several years before fail so spectacularly on this occasion? Why was liftoff allowed to proceed in such unusual conditions? Why was the wrong decision made?

Both the Rogers Commission and the other teams investigating the catastrophe have pointed to sequential pressures that may have pushed NASA's managers into making the wrong decision.

The Space Shuttle program (generally referred to as the STS) was set up at a time when NASA was desperately fighting for funding to continue its work. The shuttles were a compromise measure that the organization decided upon after Congress refused the funding to build an orbiting space station. The fundamental argument the Agency used was that an orbiting space station would make space flights routine, which meant the STS program made commercial sense. Congress was won over by the idea of space travel becoming easy and financially viable. It was therefore of the utmost importance to NASA that they kept to the schedule for the plans presented to Congress, and that they garnered the relevant media backing for the project. This led the Agency to develop a very dangerous dual nature. While it was still carrying out extremely difficult, experimental projects using untested technologies and operating with a high degree of risk, it tried to present itself to the outside world as a commercial organization. They were on time and they delivered the measurable results they promised. In this way, the risk became downplayed, and in the growing chasm between these two sides of itself, it lost sight of the fundamental priority: the safety of the astronauts.

The project that was to be one of the driving forces behind the Agency's new image was the Teacher in Space program, as part of which NASA intended to send the first civilian into space, thereby demonstrating that space travel was a routine and relatively simple undertaking. The culminating moment was to be a lesson

conducted from space by a teacher onboard the shuttle and trans-
mitted live to thousands of pupils across the United States. The
Teacher in Space program was announced by President Reagan in
1984 and generated enormous interest—as many as eleven thousand teachers submitted applications. After a long series of medical
and other tests, on July 19, 1985, a special commission selected
thirty-seven-year-old Christa McAuliffe from New Hampshire.

In line with the initial plans for liftoff on Wednesday, January
22, the space class was planned for Tuesday, January 28, the sixth
day of the mission. The delays to liftoff disrupted that schedule.
Starting the flight on January 28 meant there was still a chance to
conduct the class on Friday, January 31, though. If the liftoff had
been delayed yet again, limitations on time and organization would
mean it couldn't go ahead. Many of the experts investigating the
Challenger catastrophe pointed to this as one of the pressures that
influenced the final decision.[10]

A great many articles and commentaries also focused on the
wider political context. On January 28, 1986, Ronald Reagan was
to give his annual State of the Union address to the nation. The
presidential administration was very keen to be able to boast of
further successes in the space exploration program, including the
planned space lesson. The Rogers Commission found no evidence
of direct pressure being placed on NASA, but the decision-makers
at the Agency were well aware of the expectations and must have
been influenced by them.

There was also another significant source of pressure: the media.
In NASA's new incarnation as a commercial entity, it had to protect
its image in the public arena and in Congress, because acquiring
further funding for its projects depended on it. The repeated delays
to *Columbia*'s liftoff immediately prior to *Challenger*'s deadly mission incited widespread sarcastic commentary about NASA. So,

when new technical problems delayed STS-51L, NASA once again found itself the prime target of the media. In this situation, the pressure to launch and get the media off the organization's back was intense, and it cast a long shadow over the objectivity of the decisions taken by even the most competent and experienced members of the team.

The results of the Rogers Commission's work and its conclusions came as a big shock to many people. The situation as pieced together by the experts allowed for no ambiguity: The *Challenger* space shuttle tragedy was entirely avoidable. All that NASA had needed was somebody bold enough and high enough up the organization's hierarchy to say "No. Don't lift off, because the conditions are totally new and the experts with the greatest knowledge have the greatest fears." But nobody did.

An analysis of the events that played out in January 1986, and further "why" questions, show that the seeds of the *Challenger* disaster were sown almost sixteen years earlier, in April 1970. That's when, following the heroic efforts of Gene Kranz's team to save the three astronauts onboard *Apollo 13*, Congress essentially decided to punish the organization for the incident, refusing further funding for its program. As a result of this decision, NASA was pushed toward an unconscious and entirely uncontrolled process of moving from a research and development operating mode to one that was strictly commercial. Consequently, the priorities set out for and the expectations placed on the engineers and managers, their teams, and indeed the entire Agency began to change. People were required to alter their attitudes and behavior, which over the following dozen or more years led to a fatal decline in the organization's culture, until it was ultimately utterly inappropriate for the kind of work it was involved in. As in the case of Rob Hall's and Scott Fischer's expeditions, an extraordinarily dangerous venture

started to be treated in purely business terms, leading to an acceptance of higher and higher levels of risk. On April 28, 1986, at 11:38
am local time, this unconscious mechanism killed seven people.

Sadly, though, this isn't the end of this terrible story.

You might think that a shock of this scale would have been a
kind of catharsis for the organization, leading to profound reflection and fundamental changes in how projects were managed so
that nothing like it would ever happen again. Hard as it is to believe,
that didn't happen.

After the *Challenger* catastrophe, the STS program was halted for
over two and a half years. During this period, NASA carried out its
own investigation into the cause of the tragedy and subsequently
implemented the nine changes recommended by the Rogers Commission. Despite these actions, the culture and financial models of
the organization didn't change.

In the 1990s, NASA was struggling with two basic problems.
First, following the collapse of the Soviet Union, the importance of
many of the projects being carried out by the Agency diminished,
because they were less likely to be needed in a military capacity.
This was reflected in the dwindling generosity of Congress, which
proceeded to turn off the flow of funding. Second, budget restrictions and management failures meant the flagship program of
building an orbiting space station fell further and further behind
schedule, to the increasing irritation of the authorities, the media,
and, of course, NASA's own managers. This created a vicious cycle,
an authentic Catch-22 where, due to lack of funds, the project fell
behind schedule, which became a compelling argument for providing even less funding, which put the project even further behind
schedule, and so on. Two successive NASA administrators, Daniel Goldin and Sean O'Keefe, tried in various ways to cope with
the budget restrictions. To save money, a partnership with the

European Space Agency (ESA), Russia, and Japan was initiated, with all those partners becoming involved in NASA operations.

Both Goldin and O'Keefe put more and more pressure on the Agency's staff during their time as administrators. On assuming his post in April 1992, Goldin said that if the NASA budget was cut back and they could do only one thing, that thing must and should be figuring out how to cut the cost of going to space by a factor of a hundred and improve the reliability of going to space by a factor of ten thousand. The organization lived by the slogan "faster, better, cheaper," and indeed, Goldin turned out to be very effective at cutting costs. Over time, "faster, better, cheaper" became a mantra that impacted the decisions and actions of NASA managers. Sean O'Keefe, who replaced Goldin in December 2001, also stressed the importance of the schedule, telling his directors that at the very least they needed to a fix a date by which they would have the components sent up to the space station. Dr. James Hallock, an expert who analyzed the operations of the Agency during this period, pointed out the dangerous disparity between what was declared and what was possible. According to his calculations, to carry out the project according to the schedule set out by the incumbent administrator, NASA would need to have at least five successful space shuttle missions every year for the foreseeable future. The problem with this, though, was that five successful liftoffs per year was a massive challenge—during the STS program's lifetime, sometimes only two or three missions per year were achieved.

So, NASA entered the new millennium as an organization that had taken practically no steps to alter its culture. The Agency became an increasingly commercial outfit, demanding more and more obedience from its employees and insisting that they adhere rigidly to their designated tasks. They had to worship at the altar of financial parameters, deadlines, and public image.

The failure to learn real lessons from the *Challenger* tragedy, combined with the total lack of change in the Agency's culture and the increasing pressure from deadlines and a need for results, planted a ticking time bomb.

It finally exploded in 2003.[11] The first planned mission that year was a trip by the oldest of the space shuttles, *Columbia*, mission number STS-107, with a crew of seven, led by Rick Husband. The mission's aim was to carry out a series of experiments, including some on the Spacehab transport module. This flight, too, was delayed several times due to technical issues. It took off on January 16, five days later than scheduled. Although this time liftoff took place in good conditions, analysis of the film record of the flight's initial phases revealed an unsettling anomaly. Eighty-two seconds into the flight, a 1-pound fragment of isolating foam broke off, hitting the leading edge of the left wing. The incident occurred at an altitude of almost 12.5 miles, when *Columbia* was traveling at nearly 1,900 miles an hour. The strike was an undisputed fact, clearly recorded by the cameras. The engineers working on the Debris Assessment Team (DAT) were concerned, and after an internal discussion, they reported their worries to Mission Control, led by Linda Ham. Management's reaction was startling: the DAT report aroused little interest and the managers seemed unconcerned by the problem. They cited three arguments. First, the engineers had no hard data to prove the wing had actually been damaged. Second, such incidents had happened before without serious consequences—long-standing employees pointed, among others, to missions STS-7, STS-27, STS-32, STS-50, STS-52, and STS-62, in which isolating foam also fell off the booster rockets. The last argument used by management was nothing short of shocking. Reportedly, Ham, in conversation with engineers, said that the incident was not a factor which they were going to take into consideration, because even if the foam had damaged the wing, there was nothing they could do about it. In the face of such arguments, the engineers eventually capitulated. They tried to illustrate the risk by using a computer simulation, but they weren't able to demonstrate categorically that the foam had caused damage.

The *Columbia* mission lasted a total of sixteen days; on February 1, 2003, preparations began for the shuttle to land at Edwards Air Force Base. At 8:10 am, the shuttle's captain was given permission by the Entry Flight Control Team to begin the re-entry maneuver. Thirty-four minutes later, the shuttle re-entered Earth's atmosphere, its outer surface heating up due to friction. Within five minutes the temperature had reached over 1800°F, which is typical on re-entry. At 8:53 am, while speeding along at Mach 23, *Columbia* flew over the coast of California at an altitude of over 43 miles. The outer surfaces were glowing at a temperature of 2650°F, about two hundred degrees less than normal. The shuttle began to disintegrate around five minutes later, when tiles from the thermal protection system (TPS), damaged by the strike, began to fall off. The TPS is there to protect both the shuttle and the astronauts from the high temperatures generated on re-entry. One minute later, the Landing Control Team alerted the shuttle command that they had lost telemetry data from the sensors in the damaged wing. At precisely twenty-eight seconds before 9:00 am, Rick Husband replied to Mission Control, "Understood, but ..."

The sentence stopped midway, just like the other telemetry data.

As in the *Challenger* disaster, an investigative commission was set up—the CAIB, or Columbia Accident Investigation Board—to conduct a series of analyses to uncover the cause of the tragedy. Just as they had done seventeen years before, the experts highlighted two separate problematic areas. The direct, technical cause of the failure was obviously the damage to the TPS tiles on the wing by the insulating foam, which meant the wing had no way of surviving re-entry. The second cause had a management and organizational perspective. As one of the CAIB members, General Duane Deal, put it, "The foam did it, the institution allowed it."[12]

The report published by the board runs to several hundred pages and is one of the most shocking studies on decision-making inertia, avoidance of responsibility, poor organizational culture, and lack of leadership that I have ever encountered. The mechanism that killed the astronauts on mission STS-107 was identical to the one that ended in the tragedy of STS-51L. This means it could have been avoided in at least two ways: either by learning the lessons from 1986 and introducing specific changes to the decision-making procedures on the STS program, or, seeing as this wasn't done earlier, by learning from them during the sixteen days *Columbia* spent in orbit. The CAIB experts did not beat around the bush: they noted that, unlike the *Challenger* catastrophe, where, once the shuttle had left the launch tower there was nothing anyone could do, in this case NASA had over two weeks to try to rescue the crew. Seven people might have been saved had the Agency's management entered inquiry mode and admitted that it was dealing with a serious problem that demanded unconventional, unforeseen actions. Seven people could have survived if NASA had retained even one iota of the attitudes and behaviors that Gene Kranz's team had demonstrated in 1970.

The results from the CAIB report can be divided into several main categories that reflect the definitions of the classic decision-making errors I've described so far.

Wrong Decision-Making Mode

The first group of mistakes center on how the unexpected event of the insulation foam hitting the wing was treated. This was recognizably a black swan, because while foam had fallen off before, it had never previously struck the leading edge of the wing. The DAT engineers tried to go into inquiry mode (by asking for photos of the wing to assess the condition of and any damage done to the TPS tiles), but they were refused permission by Mission Control. The managers ignored the threat, accepting only information that confirmed it was safe to continue the mission. They even cited experiences from earlier flights in their arguments (turkey syndrome).

It is notable, though, that even the worried DAT engineers failed to fully go into inquiry mode. As they testified during the investigation, their basic problem was a lack of evidence to support the threat's existence. With the recordings available to them, and even with the computer simulations, they weren't able to demonstrate the threat to the managers, and after having their requests turned down three times, they gave up trying to look for evidence. Meanwhile, the CAIB investigation quickly revealed that the necessary data could have been obtained from at least two sources. First, it would have sufficed, as part of an inquiry approach, to conduct a detailed analysis of the shuttle's construction parameters, which is where Dr. James Hallock, a CAIB member, uncovered some surprising data. The TPS tiles were unusually fragile: they were supposed to withstand a strike equivalent to a pencil's hitting the wing from a height of 6 inches. It's easy to imagine, then, the damage that must have been caused by a 1-pound piece of insulating foam moving at a speed relative to the shuttle of over 500 miles an hour. Second, it was possible to demonstrate the threat by the simplest of tests, such as the CAIB carried out. They took a spare wing from NASA's stores and fired a similar piece of foam at it, essentially replicating what happened during liftoff. The results of the test were shocking—the foam didn't just damage the thermal isolation tiles, it actually put a hole in the wing. An even simpler test was carried out by 1996

Nobel Prize Winner Douglas D. Osheroff, who tested the foam in his own kitchen. He showed that under high temperature and pressure, the foam simply peeled off, so it could have been shown much earlier, and in a very simple way, what risk this posed during liftoff.

This all shows the power of organizational culture. It turns out that abandoning inquiry mode didn't only occur at the level of managers interested in continuing the mission. It also happened with the engineers responsible in large part for the astronauts' safety. The work of the CAIB demonstrated clearly that the DAT had simple tools and solutions to hand with which they could have demonstrated their concerns to management and so forced through a different approach.

It's no accident that people say the most effective killers of creativity and innovation in any business are the pressure to stick to existing plans and deadlines, and to keep an eye only on the bottom line.

Lack of Teamwork and Psychological Safety

During the testimony given by the DAT engineers, one other statement worthy of deeper reflection was made. Rodney Rocha, the leader of DAT, when asked why he didn't try to apply more pressure to mission control, said that he was too low on the corporate ladder to challenge any decisions made by those on the upper rungs.

It's quite startling that the head of a team crucial to the safety of a mission would feel so far down the hierarchy that he was afraid to openly express his opinions to Mission Control. In 1970, NASA had had a culture of open discussion and professionalism. How had it become a place where a competent and experienced man, vital to the safety of the astronauts, felt he could not communicate openly with his superiors?

James Bagian, a former astronaut, didn't hold back when he commented that in the 1990s, NASA did not tolerate disagreement and people knew that if they wanted to survive in the organization, they had to keep their mouths shut. Torarie Durden, who was a member of one of the teams of experts, is also on record as saying that NASA was exerting pressure on staff to meet their deadlines, no matter what it took.

There is no doubt that NASA failed to build psychological safety into its environment. Over the years, a silent process of cultural conformity took place at all levels. Senior staff expected only that deadlines were met and projects were cost-effective; any teams or individuals that challenged this were gradually moved off a project so they wouldn't upset the apple cart with their rogue opinions. From this perspective, the DAT was a trouble-maker, forcing management to revisit their preconceived positive scenarios, which in turn resulted in the sidelining of the engineers from the risk assessment process (just as the Morton-Thiokol experts were sidelined in 1986). Subsequently, changes in the organizational structure, carried out in the 1990s, saw the status of the DAT reduced to below that of flight controllers, previously seen as their equals.

Lack of Leadership

However, even in such a flawed organizational structure, you can still encourage discussion, especially if it is vital to the quality of the decision-making process, as JFK demonstrated when he created EXCOMM. An essential condition for this is excellent leadership— the presence of people who are aware of the threats and risks, and at the same time have the courage to confront the given circumstances or cultural stereotypes and to abandon routine behaviors. Kennedy was just such a person, and apparently Gene Kranz was too.

Peter Drucker once said that "management is doing things right, leadership is doing the right things." It would therefore be reasonable to conclude that while NASA had excellent *managers* in 2003, they were sadly lacking in *leaders*. The Agency's management tried to do things right, meeting deadlines and delivering the expected results. However, there was no real leadership which, as per Drucker's definition, is what you need at key moments when the right decisions are crucial.

Linda Ham, flight director of STS-107, had an impressive career history with NASA. She joined the Agency as a talented, able twenty-one-year-old, and thanks to her stamina and hard work, she climbed the rungs of the organization to the very top: in May 1991, she became the first woman in NASA history to direct space flights, and less than a year later, she was the flight director on the STS-45 mission. Ham aroused ambivalent feelings in her co-workers. No one questioned her competence or decision-making boldness, but some pointed out that she could be quite authoritarian.

During the *Columbia* mission, Ham took a range of decisions that were later heavily criticized in the CAIB report. Among the most serious errors were disregarding and later overruling the opinions of the DAT engineers, refusing the request for photos of the wing to be taken using military satellites, and fostering an attitude of powerlessness and the impossibility of carrying out repairs in the team below her. Distancing Mission Control from the engineers responsible for flight safety was nothing new, though, and neither was faulty communication between teams; they certainly weren't specific to the *Columbia* incident. The weak communications were also rooted in the lack of leadership in NASA and are illustrated quite well by a brief exchange between Linda Ham and one of the members of the investigating commission:

CAIB: As a manager, how do you seek out dissenting opinions?

Ham: Well, when I hear about them...

CAIB: But, Linda, by their very nature, you might not hear about them.

Ham: Well, when somebody comes forward and tells me about them.

CAIB: But, Linda, what techniques do you use to get them?[13]

To that question, Linda Ham gave no reply and the room fell silent.

After the final CAIB report was published, Ham was openly criticized, not only by the media but also by some politicians and members of the public, and she paid a price both professionally and personally. In 2003, she was demoted and sent to the National Renewable Energy Laboratory in Golden, Colorado; in the same year, she divorced her husband, the astronaut Kenneth Ham.

Analyzing her role in the STS-107 mission, Ham admitted in an interview with a local newspaper:

> If people say there are problems with the NASA culture, I will admit that I am part of it. I grew up there. I was there when I was 21 years old and spent 21 years there. So besides growing up in Wisconsin, the only other thing I ever knew was NASA.[14]

The fact is that flight control took a series of wrong decisions that were also reiterations of mistakes made in earlier years. Some of the decisions, attitudes, and behaviors were quite remarkable. Taking NASA's history into consideration, though, together with the system of cultural pressures constructed over the years, it's hard to place the blame on a single person. CAIB member Diane Vaughan has noted that she believed the problem was most definitely both a cultural and also a structural one, and that if the culture and structure do not change, anyone who joins that organization will inevitably adopt the same behaviors as their colleagues.

I don't think any words could express the essence of the Agency's problem quite as briefly, simply, and clearly. Those in management positions were either raised in NASA's specific culture, and so couldn't become the instigators of cultural change (Linda Ham), or were very rapidly instructed in the prevailing manner in which decisions were taken and risks managed, as well as in how to behave in the organization. So a change in personnel didn't really change anything. What's worse, the lack of leadership didn't just affect the Agency. There was nobody to be found in the whole of the USA who perceived any kind of risk emerging from the lack of a clear vision for the development of NASA (since Kennedy's time, nobody had set long-term goals for the Agency), no one in Congress or successive presidential administrations saw any danger in the deterioration of the organizational culture. The twin pressures of deadlines and constant budget cuts meant that dollars were worth more than astronaut safety. There were no true leaders.

One crucial paragraph of the CAIB final report shows how these different aspects combined to create an ideal environment for bad decision-making:

> The organizational causes of this accident are rooted in the Space Shuttle Program's history and culture, including the original compromises that were required to gain approval for the Shuttle Program, subsequent years of resource constraints, fluctuating priorities, schedule pressures, mischaracterizations of the Shuttle as operational rather than developmental, and lack of an agreed national vision. Cultural traits and organizational practices detrimental to safety and reliability were allowed to develop,

including: reliance on past success as a substitute for sound engineering practices [...] organizational barriers which prevented
effective communication of critical safety information [... and]
lack of integrated management across program elements.[15]

In one of his statements, General Duane Deal expressed his
concerns for the future of NASA. Among them were the Agency's
reluctance to implement change, which typified the organization in
earlier years and which was deeply rooted in its culture:

History shows that NASA often ignores strong recommendations;
without a culture change, it is overly optimistic to believe NASA
will tackle something relegated to an "observation" when it has
a record of ignoring recommendations.[16]

In the following years, though, NASA showed that General Deal
was wrong on this count and that his concerns were unfounded.
After the *Columbia* tragedy, the Agency opted for full transparency
in its activities, including communicating about the ongoing process of cultural change in the organization. The aim of the change
was simple: to maintain the positive aspects of functioning as
a commercial organization while restoring the cultural attitudes
and behaviors from the *Apollo 13* era and, as a result, radically
improving flight safety levels. These cultural changes were to
be accompanied by important structural changes in response to
the CAIB recommendations. An initial review of the areas requiring change was conducted by an external group led by Albert
Diaz, director of the Goddard Center. Diaz's group highlighted
seven key issues: leadership, learning, communication, processes
and rules, technical capabilities, organizational structure, and
risk management.

In order to fully understand the prevailing situation in the Agency, as well as the views of employees and contractors, NASA also turned to the consulting firm Behavioral Science Technology Solutions (BST), requesting that they conduct a detailed analysis of the organizational culture and employees' opinions, and also check how NASA's four core values—safety, integrity, teamwork, and excellence—were being interpreted. BST was also expected to propose specific organizational changes for the years 2004-09.

The results of the project, published in a final report by the consultants, were like a bucket of cold water. It turned out that the organization's longtime values had become warped, in the eyes of employees, by the pressures of its functioning as a commercial operation. Employees admitted, for example, that safety was a frequent topic within the organization, but conversations about it were more abstract, with less focus on specific solutions. In other words, there was a lot of talk, but no walk. Similarly, integrity was treated as a purely theoretical matter that didn't translate into other areas of the Agency's operations—improving management quality, shaping decision-making processes, or improving the flow of information. It's hardly surprising, then, that the level of open communication suffered—while people felt comfortable talking to colleagues of equal status, those above them in the hierarchy discouraged open communication, especially if it meant talking about inconvenient truths—like problems and risks.

The communication problem appeared to be ubiquitous, as the flow of information between the Agency's management and individual centers (including the Langley and Ames research centers, the Goddard Space Flight Center, Kennedy Center, and Johnson Center) was universally assessed as very poor. Even a value such as "teamwork" turned out to be meaningless. NASA's employees were quite unambiguous on this point: "We're not treated like experts. The organization doesn't value or respect us." Thanks to this, the BST experts revealed a dangerous schism: NASA employees felt engaged in their work, but not engaged with the Agency. This led to a dwindling sense of responsibility for the ultimate success of an undertaking via a tenet of "I have to do my job well (and be engaged in the process), but I'm not interested in the wider perspective. I'll just keep my head down and let others worry about everything else." The situation was even worse in the support functions, where there was absolutely no broader vision or understanding of those func- tions' influence on the end results.

A further problem was the lack of a precise definition of the role of contractors in decision-making. According to NASA's technical staff, subcontractors and their opinions were key from the point of view of mission safety. Unfortunately, the Agency's managers had never worked out any structures to involve representatives of outside firms in analytical processes; whenever they did become involved, it was on an ad hoc basis. The opinions of contractors were only considered when they suited the purposes of mission controllers, which is precisely what happened in the case of the now-infamous dialogue with Morton-Thiokol the day before the *Challenger* launch.

The BST experts, like the CAIB members, singled out the orga- nization's history as the direct cause of the situation, as that was what had shaped the prevailing organizational culture and decision- making methods, and criticized its leadership (or lack thereof in many areas). The fundamental accusations leveled against NASA were essentially twofold: lower-level employees were being placed under increasing time pressure, which meant they had less and less interest in situational analysis and safety, and those who did voice concerns found themselves having to prove that a problem existed rather than providing evidence it didn't; and the leaders were failing to follow internal NASA procedures.

The BST experts recommended that the Agency conduct a long-term, wide-scale cultural transformation program, including acting to resume shuttle flights, which had been suspended following the *Columbia* disaster. The overriding goal, though, was to carry out a process that seemed impossible, not only to those inside NASA, but also to even the most casual observer: to radically change the attitudes of NASA employees, especially those in management positions.

NASA implemented the majority of the BST recommendations, including providing rigorous training in risk management and decision-making in situations of uncertainty for Agency managers and 360-degree feedback for key personnel from mission management, establishing a long-term leadership development program, and introducing a system of employee assessment based on behavioral competencies. Additionally, the Agency's subcontractors, who had previously been kept at a distance, were engaged in much of the decision-making. Inside the organization a range of structural changes were introduced, which reflected the increased emphasis on mission safety.

Engineers were promoted to much higher positions in the hierarchy, which also reinforced the newly prioritized emphasis on safety. This led to deeper analysis of events within NASA and better flow of information between units. The Safety and Mission Assurance, Programs Analysis and Evaluation, Programs and Institutional Integration as well as the chief engineer all reported directly to the Office of the Administrator. These changes radically elevated the status of expert circles, which allowed them to participate in discussions to a far greater degree and exert greater influence over decision-makers.

BST also introduced five rules of operation to guide NASA's employees and contractors. They described the organizational culture that was being aimed for:

1. **Open and clear communication is encouraged and modeled**
   People at every level of the organization must be committed to the free and unobstructed flow of information up and down within the organization. This means having the courage to question assumptions, and the willingness to ask even seemingly obvious questions, to listen actively and be ready to learn. It describes a value for shared inquiry that is unimpeded by concern about "looking bad." [...] Open and clear communication means that people feel free from intimidation or retribution in raising issues. [...]

2. **Rigorously informed judgment is the sole basis for decision-making**
   Robust processes for analysis, judgment and decision-making must be flawlessly executed without cognitive bias. The only basis for confidence is properly understood data that meet safety and reliability criteria. [...] Cognitive bias is understood by decision-makers and leaders are committed to eliminating it as a source of influence on decision-making. Decisions are based on scientifically grounded assessment of risk.

3. **Personal responsibility is taken by each individual**
   Each individual is responsible for upholding a safety-supporting culture in what we do and how we do it. Each individual feels a sense of duty, responsibility, and ownership for the safety of every mission in which he or she is involved, and acts accordingly. It is unacceptable to assume that someone else will handle

your issues or questions. Each individual is fully engaged in the pursuit of long-term and short-term success, of which safety is an integral part. [...]

4. **Integrated technical and managerial competence is our shared value**
We require excellence in every aspect of our work. We hold that optimal safety follows from integrated technical and managerial competence. Mission success is accomplished by integrating all aspects of program management: safety, engineering, cost and schedule, across functional and organizational lines.

5. **Individual accountability is the basis for high reliability**
Mission safety results from actions, not just words. Our credibility is built on the consistency between our words and our actions. Procedures, values, objectives and plans are only worthwhile to the extent that they can be reliably executed. We will set new standards of flawless execution in both our management practices and our technical work. Each individual will be accountable for performing to that standard.[17]

The multifaceted nature of the actions taken by NASA can be best summarized in this short paragraph from the BST materials:

In order to achieve cultural change of this magnitude across a large, decentralized, geographically dispersed agency, perseverance and strong support from senior agency leadership will be required. Cultural effects are systemic and enterprise-wide; accordingly, cultural transformation requires a systemic, enterprise-wide approach.

Specifically, senior management alignment, focus, openness, teamwork and discipline will be required in ways that have perhaps never before been fully contemplated. Changes will be required in many deeply-embedded organizational systems and processes. Leadership attitudes, beliefs and behaviors will need to change in very significant ways, and sound management practices will be more important than ever.[18]

After various initiatives were launched, BST carried out a follow-up review, which showed a clear change in the organizational culture of NASA in the desired direction.

In the first two and a half years after the *Columbia* catastrophe, NASA also implemented almost all of the fifteen changes recommended in the CAIB's final report, which were a condition for the resumption of shuttle flights. Twelve of the changes were either fully implemented, or exceeded the expectations of the experts; as for the remaining three, NASA admitted that due to time constraints, they hadn't achieved much in that regard. On July 26, 2005, the shuttle *Discovery* was given permission to launch for the first mission since the tragedy. It successfully and safely completed a two-week flight.

Cultural changes were also perceived by the person who, during the *Columbia* mission, battled most fiercely for further analyses to be carried out to assess the degree of danger to the crew. Rodney Rocha, who led the group of DAT engineers at the time, said in a 2005 interview with the *New York Times*, "We have a voice. Engineering is more independent than ever, more assertive than ever, and more in your face."[19]

The change of leader at NASA was also not without significance. On April 13, 2005, Michael Douglas Griffin replaced Sean O'Keefe as administrator; his priority was to redefine NASA's vision, to have a long-term goal for the Agency. It was a highly significant shift in priority, because since the Moon landings there had been no such vision, and the organization's operations had become increasingly dominated by a commercial-style focus on small details, causing it to lose sight of the bigger picture. Griffin's successors, especially Charles F. Bolden Jr., who was administrator from July 17, 2009, to January 20, 2017, sustained this strategy.

RULE #11

Never stop shaping the organizational culture. It can be your greatest ally, or your worst enemy, in making the right decisions.

NASA'S HISTORY shows how vital a role context plays when it comes to the quality of the decisions taken by those in power. In earlier chapters, we looked at techniques for improving decision-making processes at the individual and team levels, but we must always remember the third level, which may, in fact, be the most important: the organizational culture within which decision-makers operate and the pressures of the environment they are subjected to. The case of NASA offers a tragic example of how not to behave after a disaster. Even though the Roger's Commission formulated a series of recommendations following the *Challenger* tragedy, the organizational culture of the Agency didn't change at all. A perfectly conducted RCA is meaningless if we don't then consistently implement and monitor its recommendations over the following years. The end result will be the same as it was for NASA—the same mechanism, ignoring black swans and failing to apply an inquiry approach, buoyed up by past successes and faulty teamwork, and a lack of leadership, will inevitably lead to another disaster.

One client I had the pleasure to work for as a consultant was struggling with a similar problem. Founded many years earlier, the company had become the market leader in its industry sector, leading to rapid but uncontrolled growth with no equivalent development of the organization. The head count went up, new units were created, new systems introduced, procedures expanded, as the board thought that only increased reporting was the key to maintaining the rapid upward trajectory. With time, though, the first cracks started to appear in this plan, although they didn't compromise the company's competitive position. However, the levels of internal conflicts grew incrementally, more and more often requiring intervention at the highest levels, swallowing up the time of the already busy management. Another issue was the gradual emergence of cliques within the organization, as every unit started to fight for its own interests and security. As one of the support function managers put it to me, "There was a hell of a mess, and we all started to lose our bearings. When things began to look dangerous, we all just covered our own backs. We started to be cautious about what information we passed on. As a team, we avoided forming unambiguous opinions. You cover yourself by leaving room for interpretation, and the interpretation is done by someone else. Then you say it was their fault." With time, this attitude affected not only teams, but individuals, too, who acted to minimize their own personal risk. It isn't difficult to anticipate the effect this had on decision-making. It became harder and harder to get a clear, concrete opinion on which to base a business decision. The company suffered a classic diffusion of responsibility. Everyone focused purely on their own job as a damage limitation measure. Simultaneously, a number of "orphans" appeared—problems nobody was looking at, because the procedures, structures, or orders didn't make clear whose wards they were. Everyone at the lower levels could see them, but no one said anything because not only were they "minding their own business," they also assumed that someone else would look after the orphans.

This is, unfortunately, a typical human phenomenon, and not one restricted to business. A tragic example of collective irresponsibility occurred on March 13, 1964, in Queens, New York.

TWENTY-EIGHT-YEAR-OLD Kitty Genovese worked as a manager in one of the district's bars; she typically finished work late at night. She rented an apartment on Austin Street in Kew Gardens, a peaceful, middle-class area. On the morning of March 13, Genovese parked her car about 30 yards from the entrance to her building. She never reached her apartment, though, as she was attacked en route by Winston Moseley, a twenty-year-old with no criminal record. Moseley stabbed Genovese twice and then fled because of her screams. It later transpired that a total of thirty-eight people in Kew Gardens had heard her screaming. None of them called the police. A semiconscious Genovese lay on the street where she had fallen. Nine minutes later, Moseley returned and attacked her again. This time, too, he fled, startled by a shout from one of the neighbors, Robert Mozer, who yelled out of his window, "Leave that woman alone!" but did nothing else. Still no one called the police. Moseley returned again, this time raping the dying Genovese, stabbing her one last time, and stealing a small amount of money. Only after this third attack did another neighbor, Karl Ross, call the police, who arrived at the scene barely two minutes later. For Kitty Genovese it was too little too late—she died in the ambulance on the way to hospital.

Two weeks later, Martin Gansberg published a shocking article in the *New York Times*, in which he described the night's events and accused the neighbors of indifference. Genovese's ordeal lasted a full thirty-five minutes and the murderer returned twice. If the police had been called after the first attack, she would have lived. The neighbors whom the journalist spoke to explained their lack of a reaction in various ways: "I thought someone else would call," "I didn't want to get involved," "I was tired"... Karl Ross had actually phoned a friend in Nassau County to ask him what he should do before he finally called the police.[20]

Although the expression "callous indifference" is hard to resist in this context, the problem was a result of the *bystander effect* (also known as bystander apathy), a term coined by social psychologists Bibb Latané and John Darley. In a situation where numerous people observe a disturbing incident, the feeling of individual responsibility becomes divided and diminished, with everyone thinking "someone else will deal with it." On March 13, 1964, in New York, for over half an hour, thirty-eight people thought precisely that, and as a result a young woman died. It's no accident that on self-defense courses today, women are instructed not to shout an impersonal "Help!" but to address a specific person in the crowd: "Please help me, sir! Sir, you, the one in the red jacket!" It's harder to resist such a direct appeal.

Let's return to our business example, though. In the case of the company I was describing earlier, the diffusion of responsibility also led to a serious incident that could have ended in tragedy. The chemicals used in the production process were stored in a warehouse. Out of laziness, one of the employees decided to store one particular fluid close to the entrance, so it would be easier to transport it to the production area. The barrels were placed below a row of shelves where some canisters containing another substance were stored. This was against the rules, because the two chemicals would react if they came into contact, creating an asphyxiating gas. Pretty much all of the warehouse employees knew about this, but in true turkey mode, they assumed that seeing nothing bad had happened so far, this was an acceptable risk. On top of that, due to the collective indifference, nobody felt any need to inform anyone about this dangerous situation.

Then, one day, while maneuvering in the warehouse, a forklift operator punctured one of the containers, and its contents started to drip onto the barrel below. As bad luck would have it, the liquid dripped directly onto a leaky barrel that no one had seen fit to report ("it's always been OK"). The two substances reacted, and the resulting compound poisoned four workers, three of whom were hospitalized. According to the doctors who treated them, they owed their lives to the rapid responses of their colleagues, as breathing the gas in for only a few minutes more would have irreversibly damaged their central nervous systems.

When an internal health and safety team spoke to warehouse workers during their investigation of the accident, they encountered identical attitudes to those exhibited by the thirty-eight people who stood back and let Kitty Genovese die. All the employees questioned denied responsibility:

> "It's not part of my job description to report such things."
>
> "Everybody knew about it. I was sure that the management knew, too, after all, the logistics director was here not long ago."
>
> "Someone must have reported it to management, seeing as they did nothing about it, it meant it was okay to store it like that."
>
> "No one else did anything about it, so why should I? That's above my pay grade."
>
> "There were more important matters."

The board took a lot of convincing that the statements were genuine.

DECISION-MAKING IN organizations is a complicated game between often conflicting forces and interests that can pull the decision-maker in different directions. The process is rooted in the evolution of the work environment, replete with conscious and unconscious habits, practices, and behaviors, many of which can seriously compromise the objectivity of the final decision. More and more often, then, the key to making the right choice requires an acute awareness of these covert games and an ability to resist emotional pressures with the hard logic and concrete facts that only an inquiry approach will provide. This combination is what distinguishes authentic leaders—those who, regardless of the circumstances and pressures, have the courage to make Drucker-like correct choices. They not only introduce perfect decision-making processes, or create systems for analyzing data, but also shape an organization's culture to promote an inquiry approach throughout the company, engage disaffected groups of workers who have unique knowledge bases, and prohibit personal emotions from interfering with a rational, cool-headed assessment of a situation.

The NASA example shows that even the most professional and competent organization can undergo an invisible and dangerous cultural metamorphosis when it submits to the influence of external and internal pressures, exchanging former behaviors and attitudes for new ones with which everyone feels comfortable, even if that comes at the cost of safety, quality, or profits. This is actually characteristic of two very different types of business: large corporations and relatively small private companies. In the case of corporations, there comes a point at which purely rational arguments are overtaken by a desire for stability and maintenance of the status quo, and procedures and regulations are introduced, which gradually shape a culture of blind obedience. The same thing can happen in privately owned businesses, except that instead of procedures, it is the opinions and views of the owner that prevail. Here, too, cultural change evolves to ensure employees enjoy a quiet life, rather than being blinded by the harsh light of reality. The true purpose of leadership—to keep everyone focused and on task—becomes lost.

Thus, in both large and small businesses, the cultural re-education process eliminates people bold enough to express their opinions openly, people who by nature are constructive devil's advocates and whose presence is invaluable in a proper inquiry approach. The phenomenon is lethal, not only for the quality of communication and the depth of discussions, but also for leadership and the future of those with the potential to lead the company through important changes. Cultural inertia and pressure to conform can kill the engagement of even the most competent person…

UNLESS, OF course, they're an authentic leader.

IN SEARCH OF

AUTHENTIC

LEADERS

7

L EADERSHIP. THERE'S PROBABLY no other topic in business that exerts such fundamental influence over the quality of the decisions taken within a company and creates such a strong feeling of unease in me. Everyone talks about it. Google will find you over half a billion pages if you search for the word *leadership*. The number of self-proclaimed experts running training sessions on it seems to grow with every passing hour, at every turn we can apparently learn "how to become an outstanding leader in a weekend," and more and more people, whom you might not immediately associate with the topic, are crawling out of the woodwork to offer their two cents on the topic. The debate about whether leadership is innate or learned, or whether being a leader is a question of personality or of experience resounds at ever more conferences and seminars, leaps at us from the pages of magazines, rampages through the blogosphere and social media.

However, while we can gorge ourselves on theories, in one form or another, we are positively starving when it comes to people who can take those theories and turn them into practices. Thus, we find ourselves constantly repeating the mantra about a lack of leaders. We say there are no authorities, no clear vision, no strong characters to inspire us to challenge our own limitations and improve ourselves. According to many, this problem, this lack of real, authentic leaders, has even intensified in recent years. They're right. Authentic leaders have always been a rare thing in the business ecosystem, and the pace of change in the environment means we need more of them than ever before, especially as a lack of leadership can have only two consequences: if we're lucky, stagnation and a lack of development; if we're unlucky, catastrophic errors like those that hit NASA in 1986 and 2003.

Today, sound management isn't enough. It's not enough now to just "do things in the right way"—in the new normal, even the error-free implementation of decisions and following procedures will get you nowhere when you're faced with a black swan. The second part of Peter Drucker's definition of leadership has become key: success or failure is decided by the ability to "do the right things," making the right decisions and the right choices, which we expect our leaders to do. The psychology of change has also begun to play a role, as the vast majority of people are afraid of change and are not keen to leave their comfort zone, which in the face of today's macroeconomic, political, technological, and social turbulence is a pipe dream. People need a clear vision for sure, especially in times of uncertainty; therefore, they are looking for visionary leaders they can trust.

Leadership ability has been admired and debated over millennia. In the beginning were the men, and the occasional woman, who changed the world, generally military, political, or religious leaders, or great scientific minds. Their common denominator was the ease with which they attracted a following, even if what they were offering wasn't immediately attractive (take religions, for example, which involve respecting a set of rules and consciously limiting pleasure today in return for a very remote promise of reward in the afterlife). The power to inspire and motivate others to behave in specific ways is both fascinating and terrifying—just look at the ease with which Adolf Hitler persuaded the German nation in the 1930s of the need to increase their *Lebensraum*, their living space, which led to the bloodiest conflict in human history. There are numerous examples of authentic leaders who attracted masses of people to follow them: Benito Mussolini, Chairman Mao, and even Osama bin Laden, to name but three.

The definition of a leader is only simple at first glance. If we consider the multiplicity of roles a leader has to play, it's actually extremely difficult to capture the essence of leadership in one or two sentences.

For many years, the key words were *vision* and *inspiration*, and leaders were those who had a clear idea and were able to convincingly present it to others. Over time, those ideas were supplemented by *authority*, built on a range of factors: competence, personality, experience, and success. The next stage was the aspect of initiating change and leading others through crises, as well as making decisions in situations of uncertainty, which have all taken on a great deal of significance in recent years.

In a business context, there is a clear distinction between managers and leaders. If we adhere to Drucker's definition, we could say that managers are an organization's "stabilizers"—they ensure that processes run as intended, making sure that previously agreed-upon goals are achieved and that tightly defined procedures are followed. Managers ensure that an organization behaves predictably. Leaders, on the other hand, make strategic choices, set out a vision, and inspire others to follow them, often challenging the organizational status quo. Note, though, that leaders often have no formal position of power in an organization's structure; sometimes they are employees in specialized positions who have earned their place as authorities in the eyes of others. This clearly delineates the different sources of power and influence in the two roles: a manager uses the power invested in them by virtue of position, while a leader influences others by inspiring them to follow. Leadership is becoming more and more diffuse within an organization and is embodied by people at all levels of the hierarchy and in different areas of operation—even if at first sight we perceive the person at the head of the firm to be the leader.

Of course, for an organization to grow healthily, there must be a balance between these two forces, as we require both inspiring visionaries and thorough practitioners. The first drive development, shaking the company out of its equilibrium, an ever-more dangerous state of being nowadays; the second ensure that plans are precisely executed, goals are achieved, and actions remain transparent.

From the point of view of decision-making, then, leaders must keep a lot of balls in the air. They are strategists, responsible for formulating a convincing vision and making decisions that affect the long-term direction of development. Leaders mold the organizational culture, thus affecting the attitudes and behavior of others. In many cases, they also become the foundation for innovation as initiators of and the driving force behind organizational change, encouraging the company to develop; they are also responsible for creating tools and nonstandard procedures that improve decision-making processes.

The Leader as a Visionary and Strategist

The most obvious role of a leader in the decision-making process is to make the most important, breakthrough decisions. We look to leaders to make the final call on vital matters and expect them to shape the strategic perspective. It is the leaders who are responsible for the long-term consequences that result from decisions.

From the strategic perspective, the prevailing understanding of the definition of a leader is also the most obvious one: a person from whom we expect a clear vision and direction. Human history is awash with visionary leaders. Think about President John F. Kennedy. In May 1961, he articulated an inspiring vision, which we've already discussed, that essentially set in motion the long-term, extraordinarily bold project to put humans on the Moon.

Life isn't a bed of roses, of course, and history also offers a plethora of examples of leaders making a strategic decision that was far from successful. Take, for instance, 1964, when President Lyndon Johnson decided to send US troops into Vietnam.

The 1960s were characterized by an increasingly ruthless arms race accompanied by a political struggle between two superpowers for global domination. One of the regions that underwent powerful changes but remained something of a no-man's-land in terms of spheres of influence was Southeast Asia. This area had a stormy history: since the second half of the nineteenth century, it had been part of the French colony of Indochina, composed of today's Cambodia, Laos, and Vietnam, as well as a dozen or so other protectorates, which were gradually incorporated into the expanded colony. The second-most powerful colonial power in the region was the UK, which exerted its influence in Burma (Myanmar) and Siam (Thailand). The golden age of Indochina in the 1920s and '30s didn't last long. The German invasion of France in 1940 rocked French authority in the region, and the British had far more important things to worry about by then than some remote Asian colonies. The Japanese took advantage of French weakness and attacked the northern part of Indochina at the end of 1940, moving forward in the following months to eventually take control of the entire area. In a bit of a twist, the French managed to negotiate with the Japanese, who, busy battling the USA, ultimately left the entire French administration in Indochina in place. This lasted until 1945. At that point, the situation turned around—defeated by the Americans, the Japanese, who had just had atom bombs detonated over their cities, were helpless, and the French decided once again to take full control over their colonies. It turned out, though, that the locals had their own ideas about that, and in 1945, Hồ Chi Minh declared Vietnam's independence, while Norodom Sihanouk did likewise in Cambodia. Because the French weren't inclined to lose the opportunity to regain control over the recently lost territories, an eight-year war broke out (the First Indochina War), which ended in France's spectacular defeat in the Điện Biên Phủ valley in 1954.[1] The loss led not only to the withdrawal of Europeans from the contested territories, but also to significant political decisions at the Geneva Conference that same year. During the conference, it was decided to split the former territory of Indochina into four independent nations: Laos, Cambodia, and North and South Vietnam.

In this way, Southeast Asia became a mosaic of highly politically discrete countries. Thailand favored the USA, which ended up launching the majority of its flights over Vietnam from there. Burma was shaken by internal conflict (in 1947, the ruling General Aung San was murdered), fighting off the Chinese Kuomintang, who were advancing more and more boldly into the north of the country, and trying to remain independent of any of the world superpowers. So, while the Burmese were fighting communist movements, they also bluntly refused to join the Southeast Asia

Treaty Organization (SEATO), an American initiative set up in 1954. In Laos, which gained independence in 1953, the Pathet Lao communist movement was powerful—so powerful, in fact, that it seized full power in the 1970s. The story was similar, albeit far bloodier, in Cambodia, where at the end of the 1970s, about 25 percent of its 8 million inhabitants were killed in a grisly civil war started by the Khmer Rouge. In the years prior to the war in Vietnam, Cambodia, ruled by Prince Norodom Sihanouk, tried, like Burma, to remain independent and neutral; it had some success in this respect until a certain Saloth Sar, a.k.a. Pol Pot, took power.

Looking at the culturally diverse and vivid political patchwork of postcolonial Southeast Asia, the schism in the worldview of Vietnam should come as no surprise. The pro-American south, with its capital in Saigon, soon came into conflict with the North Vietnamese Viet Minh movement. The Geneva Accord had assumed there would be only a temporary division of the country along the 17th parallel and had required both sides to conduct elections in preparation for reunification by the end of 1956, but things didn't quite turn out that way. The ruler of South Vietnam, Ngô Đình Diệm, called off the elections in his part of the country, under the pretext that the communist regime in the North would interfere with the process. The country remained divided and the conflict between Saigon and Hanoi became more apparent, occasionally leading to partisan fighting incited by units from the communist North, which at the same time was trying to foster the communist movement spreading through South Vietnam. The communist partisans grew stronger, which disconcerted the Americans, who were unconcerned about the communists coming to power in little Laos but balked at the prospect of a 40-million-strong Vietnam supported by the Soviets, considering it a serious threat to its global interests. So, when a frightened Ngô Đình Diệm turned to them for help, a significant military force was added to the group of military and political advisors who had already been supporting him: at the end of 1961, the USS *Core* sailed into the port of Saigon, with over thirty assault helicopters and several hundred crew onboard. The American contingent in South Vietnam thereby crept above a thousand. It didn't help Ngô Đình Diệm, though. The government in Saigon was growing weaker, and attacks by the communist partisans from the North became more and more audacious. Communist movements in the South grew stronger, and Ngô Đình Diệm paid the ultimate price—he was murdered in November 1963 during a military coup d'état.

This prompted President Lyndon Johnson, who had taken office after the assassination of President Kennedy, to deploy additional forces to South Vietnam to stabilize the situation. Command of these increased personnel was assumed by General William Westmoreland. Simultaneously, President Johnson authorized Operational Plan 34 Alpha, sending American destroyers to patrol the waters off the coast of Vietnam and carry out intensive surveillance operations to gather precious military intelligence.

The events that led directly to the decision to begin the US military operation in North Vietnam are a rather farcical series of mistakes and misunderstandings, though some claim it was a setup from the start. The prelude to the American attacks was an alleged August 4, 1964, Vietnamese attack on the USS *Maddox* and USS *Turner Joy* while they were patrolling the waters of the Gulf of Tonkin. It's important to note that this wasn't the first attack—a couple of days earlier, the USS *Maddox* had come under machine gun fire. That attack, described in detail and reported back to Washington, didn't provoke an immediate reaction, though many in the military pressured Johnson to respond with significant force. Among the politicians and generals unfavorably disposed toward

Johnson, the oft-repeated opinion that Johnson was "too soft" and allowed the Vietnamese to get away with too much prevailed, thereby harming the United States' image and threatening American interests. In such an atmosphere, it was impossible to ignore information about a torpedo attack on August 4, and so the Secretary of Defense, Robert McNamara, who would become one of the central figures in the events to come, was duly informed.

McNamara lived an extremely interesting, and in the opinion of many, controversial life. Born in 1916 to a family of Irish immigrants, he was a graduate of Harvard Business School and later became its youngest-ever assistant professor at the time. In August 1940, he worked for Price Waterhouse. He spent World War II in the air force, and in 1946 went to the Ford Motor Corporation, where he helped to rebuild the company, which was suffering enormous losses at the time. In 1960, McNamara became the first president of the company to come from outside the Ford family. He didn't manage to do too much in this role, though, as barely a year later, the president-elect, John F. Kennedy, offered him the position of Secretary of Defense. McNamara accepted, and he quickly became one of the most trusted and influential people in the Kennedy entourage—he actively participated in the resolution of the Cuban Missile Crisis in 1962. He stayed in the post until 1968, making him the longest-serving Secretary of Defense in history at the time. After stepping down, he became President of the World Bank and occupied that post until his retirement in 1981.

On August 4, 1964, it was Robert McNamara who received the first report of the torpedo attack in the Gulf of Tonkin. The Secretary of Defense fully grasped the seriousness of the event and that in the coming hours he, the Chiefs of Staff, and the entire presidential administration would be required to prepare the essential information to enable Lyndon Johnson to make the correct decision to resolve the problem. It's worth remembering that the president was in a difficult position: he had taken office as a result of the Kennedy assassination, and not by winning an election, which his opponents frequently, and more or less openly, reminded him of. At the same time, he was preparing to go head to head with an extremely tough rival—the prospective Republican candidate in the November 1964 presidential campaign, Barry Goldwater, a descendant of Polish immigrants who was a fervent anti-communist. In comparison to him, Johnson came across as calm, hesitant, and defensively-minded. The events of February 1964, when Fidel Castro cut off water supplies to the US base in Guantánamo and provoked no reaction from the president, were still fresh in Johnson's mind. He knew that if he were to have any chance in the upcoming elections, he would have to change his image and convince Americans that he could also play hardball when necessary. He was convinced of this by a meeting with Kenneth O'Donnell, one of the White House secretaries and previously an advisor to Kennedy. O'Donnell himself later recalled that during the meeting, he and Johnson had agreed that "his leadership was being tested and that he must respond decisively."[2] This opinion resonated with the words spoken earlier by Senator Richard Russell, Johnson's friend and mentor, who noted after the Guantánamo episode that there was "a slowly increasing feeling in the country that we are not being as harsh and firm in our foreign relations as we should be."[3] The Gulf of Tonkin incident thus gave Johnson an excellent opportunity to present a different face to the world.

McNamara, of course, knew about the president's dilemma and directed a very clear question to Admiral Sharp: How long did he need to prepare air attacks on targets in North Vietnam? General David A. Burchinal was able to include the aircraft carrier USS *Ticonderoga* in the plans, so an attack could be launched by 6:00 am local time (6:00 pm in Washington). That gave Johnson a chance to make the relevant announcement to the media at 7:00 pm, right in time for the main evening news. McNamara and his advisors therefore rushed around and called a sitting of the National Security Council (NSC). The majority of the two-hour discussion, though, was focused not on an analysis of the military situation but of the political consequences of the decision to attack. Johnson was interested not only in the potential reaction of his rival Barry Goldwater, public opinion, and the media, but also the reactions of politicians from other countries. Ultimately, Johnson took the decision to attack, but in a more limited manner—he didn't agree to the bombing of Hanoi or Haiphong; the only targets were to be Vietnamese patrol boats located in five ports, together with gas installations and storage in Vinh.

When McNamara met the Joint Chiefs of Staff (JCS) and passed on the president's decision, work began on drawing up the attack orders. Meanwhile, though, something happened that McNamara hadn't foreseen, and that brought the entire operation into question. Captain John Herrick, who was commanding the patrol on August 4, contacted the Pentagon to inform them that, following a subsequent assessment of the situation, he had doubts about the veracity of the attack. The report read as follows:

> Review of action makes many recorded contacts and torpedoes fired appear doubtful. Freak weather effects and overeager sonarmen may have accounted for many reports. No actual visual sightings by *Maddox*. Suggest complete evaluation before any further actions.[4]

A startled McNamara sought confirmation of this report from Admiral Sharp, who admitted that he wasn't 100 percent sure that the attack had actually taken place, although, in his initial report, which had started the whole thing, he had given very precise details about it, including the number of torpedoes used by the Vietnamese. Sharp requested more time to check the facts and recommended postponing the armed response until the matter was resolved. McNamara organized an urgent meeting of the Chiefs of Staff, during which he tried to establish whether or not the American destroyers had been attacked as reported. Under pressure from the Secretary of Defense, Admiral Sharp ultimately concluded that the attack had occurred—although he did so using words which were ambiguous to say the least. To McNamara's final question about whether the attack had taken place or not, Sharp hesitated as he replied, "Oh, no doubt about that ... I think."[5]

Meanwhile, President Johnson anxiously awaited confirmation of the order to attack, and regularly contacted McNamara, expressing his increasing impatience and placing him under ever-greater pressure. The hours passed. It was late in the evening, and he still couldn't make his announcement on the situation in Vietnam and the US's response.[6] Finally, shortly after 11:00 pm, McNamara confirmed the plans for the military operation; half an hour later, sitting in the Oval Office, the President announced that he had authorized "limited and fitting" retaliatory strikes on targets in North Vietnam. As a result of the subterfuge by McNamara and the other advisors, Congress unanimously voted for the Gulf of Tonkin Resolution, which gave Johnson the power to increase the American presence in Vietnam. War had begun.

From the perspective of the decision-making process, a clear error is immediately evident: operating in a totally new context, dealing with a country and a culture with which they had had little contact previously, responding to a startling and not entirely confirmed incident, the Americans adopted the advocacy approach, despite the evidence positively screaming out for a deeper analysis. They didn't try to gain extra time; in fact, they did quite the reverse, setting a deadline by which time the decision had to be made (in time for Lyndon Johnson's television appearance), thus placing everyone under extra pressure. An inquiry approach was immediately rejected as too time-consuming, and those trying to cast doubt on the official interpretation of events and wanting to thoroughly analyze the incident—Captain Herrick, for example—were pressured by those in authority to ease off. This trap was repeated on all levels: Captain Herrick was pressured by Admiral Sharp, who was being pressured by Robert McNamara, who in turn was being pressured by President Johnson. The combination of the time pressures and the authority trap meant that the decision was made on the basis of false indications—the documents released in 2005 confirmed that on August 4, 1964, no attack took place in the Gulf of Tonkin.

The former Secretary of Defense later featured as the main character in the 2003 documentary film *The Fog of War*, directed by Errol Morris. In it, an aging McNamara recalls the key events that led to the outbreak of the war in Vietnam and describes the role of the central figures involved. It's telling that he admits at the end that the decision to attack was made based on false assumptions and was the result of a host of poor decisions made by President Johnson and his advisors. McNamara clearly stresses three issues. First, the root of the errors made on August 4, 1964, was, in his opinion, the pressure that led all those involved—both in the Gulf of Tonkin and in Washington—to "[see] what they wanted to see." Second, in this instance, there was no equivalent of Tommy Thompson in the vicinity of the president, no reliable source of information about ambitions and motives in Hanoi. The effect, as McNamara says in the film, was that the Americans got things terribly wrong. Third, he points to the words used by President Johnson in one of his speeches:

> If this little nation goes down the drain and can't maintain her independence, ask yourselves, what is going to happen to all the other little nations? [...] America wins the wars that she undertakes. Make no mistake about it. And we have declared war on ignorance and illiteracy, we have declared war on poverty, we have declared war on disease, and we have declared war on tyranny and aggression. We not only stand for these things but we are willing to stand up and die for these things.[7]

In tribute to turkey syndrome, the assumption that this war would be won (just like the previous ones had been won) made it easy to ignore the potential threat from the Vietcong and take for granted that it would be a pretty simple conflict, with little required in the way of preparation. That attitude would come back to haunt the US.

The following years saw a massive escalation of military action. The United States didn't stop at air attacks—in 1965, it sent in the army, whose numbers rose in a matter of months to 200,000. There was still a complete lack of an inquiry approach, and many army units had no idea at all about the kind of enemy they would be facing, or on what terrain and in what weather conditions they would be fighting. The conviction remained that this would be a potentially boring conflict, and one that should be relatively easy to win. There was no comprehension of what the war meant to the Vietnamese, for whom it was not a conflict between two opposing political blocs as part of the Cold War, but a struggle for independence and reunification of a country divided by the Geneva Agreement. In *The Fog of War*, McNamara recounts that precisely these words were used during a meeting in Hanoi in 1995 between him and Vo Nguyen Giap, Commander in Chief of the North Vietnamese forces during the 1960s. Vo Nguyen Giap bluntly told McNamara he was ignorant of Vietnam's history and laughed at his assumption that North Vietnam had been part of an alliance with communist China and the USSR. And in fact, given the hundreds of years of conflict between the Vietnamese and the Chinese, such an assumption was, at the very least, dangerous, and it demonstrated that the Americans had not analyzed even fundamental questions about the region.

The effects of this were significantly more serious than the president's circle could ever have imagined. In July 1965, President Lyndon Johnson uttered the following words, immortalized in Morris's film, about the decision to send thousands more soldiers to North Vietnam: "Nobody believes that sending another fifty or hundred thousand will change anything. We're doing a bad job. We're losing... losing the terrain we've got."[8] Despite this, military involvement increased in the following years, as the Americans' situation grew more and more difficult. In other words, they also failed to take the correct, courageous decision to bring a rapid end to the action (seeing as they'd lost the war anyway) and minimize their losses. This is an early example of the sunk cost effect—it swayed Johnson and his successors, and none of them was prepared to make a Drucker-style right choice. In this light, some other words of McNamara, which I came across in his book about these events, offer an interesting commentary on the subject of leadership and taking strategic decisions:

> Having reviewed the record in detail, and with the advantage of hindsight, I think it is highly probable that, had President Kennedy lived, he would have probably pulled us out of Vietnam [...] I conclude that John Kennedy would have eventually gotten out of Vietnam rather than move more deeply in ...[9]

The leader's error lay, in this case, in accepting a view that turned out to have no solid basis in fact (building a position in Southeast Asia through military force, assuming the USA was vastly superior in both a technological and a military sense), which led to the making of poor strategic decisions (attacking North Vietnam) as well as operational ones (e.g., increasing the involvement of land forces). Additionally, the attitudes of the key personnel, including President Johnson, made it impossible to begin an open discussion about the possible options and, as with the Bay of Pigs, only one scenario was taken into consideration.

Lyndon B. Johnson won the elections in November 1964, defeating Barry Goldwater by a landslide, and held office till January 1969. The war in Vietnam dragged on for nearly four more years, until it was ended by the signing of the Paris Peace Accords on January 27, 1973.

MARK TWAIN once said that good decisions come from experience, and experience comes from bad decisions. The wisdom of life, therefore, should come from drawing conclusions from past mistakes—preferably ones made not by us but by others. I get the impression that among Lyndon Johnson's advisors at the time there was no one who possessed such wisdom. No one looked at the historical context, which led to the acceptance of false assumptions, and no one looked at similar military failures—decision-making errors that had been behind the failure of the Nazi's Operation Barbarossa of 1941, an event that fell well within the boundaries of living memory.

Although it might be controversial to say so, Adolf Hitler became an authentic leader during the 1930s, presenting a defeated Germany with a tempting vision of restoring the country's power. The failed painter proposed an alluring image of a strong economy and of increasing *Lebensraum*, which later became the underlying motive for military action. Rejected by the Academy of Fine Arts in Vienna, Hitler took up politics and joined the NSDAP (the Nazi party), eventually becoming its leader. As head of the NSDAP, in 1923, he led the Munich Putsch, which also became known as the Beer Hall Putsch due to the place where it was started (in the Bürgerbräukeller beer hall). This led to his being arrested and sentenced to five years' imprisonment. Hitler made best use of his time while incarcerated in Landsberg prison, writing the infamous *Mein Kampf* ("my struggle"), in which he outlined the ideological framework for the national-socialist movement. Meanwhile, his party grew stronger, and its radical messages became more and more popular toward the end of the 1920s, as the country struggled with economic crisis and poverty; the NSDAP entered the Reichstag, in time becoming the main political force in the country. Adolf Hitler himself came to power in 1933, when he was chosen to be Chancellor of the Reich; one year later, he combined the roles of president and chancellor, declaring himself the *Führer* (leader).

The first actions that essentially started the war, though at the time they appeared relatively benign, were the remilitarization of the Rhineland (breaking the Locarno Treaties) and the annexing of Austria into Germany in 1938. Several months later, on the basis of the Munich Accord, and taking advantage of the political expediency of the UK and France, Hitler first annexed the Sudetenland and then partitioned Czechoslovakia, thus creating the Nazi-administered Protectorate of Bohemia and Moravia. Encouraged by the passivity of the signatory countries of the Treaty of Versailles which had demilitarized Germany, Hitler escalated his territorial demands and, in 1939, set his sights on another neighbor: Poland. During a meeting with the Polish Foreign Minister, Józef Beck, Hitler demanded extraterritorial highways to the Free City of Danzig across what was referred to as the Polish Corridor to the Sea. Despite ongoing diplomatic discussions, the Third Reich drew up at the same time the *Fall Weiss*—the plan for an attack on Poland, which became further solidified by the signing of the Molotov-Ribbentropp Pact with the Soviet Union on August 23, 1939.

On September 1, 1939, the Wehrmacht invaded Polish territory and the Luftwaffe began airstrikes on Polish cities. Because of the overwhelming superiority of the German forces, the campaign ended within a month. The Third Reich then established a General Government on Polish land and turned its attention to the west. In 1940, Hitler decided to attack another neighbor—France, and included the Benelux countries in the assault, setting things in motion with the German army's new doctrine of *Blitzkrieg*, or lightning war. The operation was launched on May 10, 1940, with a Luftwaffe strike on targets in Belgium and the Netherlands, followed by paratroop landings and land forces entering French territory. Although both sides were numerically similar (the Allies' total armed forces in terms of men was even greater than that of the Germans), the battle was a short one, due to the highly effective operating method applied by the Nazis, together with its superb execution on the ground. The main Belgian fort, Eban Emael, was soon taken, a defeat that inflicted an enormous psychological impact—the Netherlands capitulated on May 14, and Belgium continued fighting for barely two weeks more, surrendering on May 28. Meanwhile, the French, supported by the British army, tried to put up resistance but were pushed further and further back by the Wehrmacht and decimated by precise bombing attacks. In addition, on May 24, the leader of the British Expeditionary Force took the decision to withdraw his troops, which outraged the French. Despite protests from Paris, in the following week, Operation Dynamo was put into action—over 330,000 British soldiers were evacuated from Dunkirk back to the UK. An isolated France could not defend itself any further and abandoned Paris, declaring it an open city on June 13. As a result, on the following day, Parisian streets and squares were swarming with German troops, while the French government evacuated to Bordeaux. Further decisive inroads made by Hitler's armored formations led to the capitulation of France, announced on June 22, 1940. From the ruins of the country arose the puppet government of Vichy which, led by Marshal Philippe Pétain, supported the occupiers. In this way, in little more than a month, one of the largest European military and political powers fell, and the Germans reveled in their new approach to waging war, the *Blitzkrieg*.

The approaching war with Russia was perceived by Adolf Hitler in a somewhat surprising manner. He considered the assault on Moscow not as an attempt at conquering another country, but as an important step in the ongoing air battle with the UK, which he viewed as his major rival in Europe. Franz Halder, Head of the German General Staff, cited Hitler's opinion in his memoirs:

With Russia smashed, Britain's last hope would be shattered... Decision: Russia's destruction must therefore be made part of this struggle. [...] The sooner Russia is crushed the better.[10]

The Führer thought that the UK, like France, was a defeated country and that it was clinging to the hope that the Soviet Union would enter the war. In this, he completely underestimated the military potential of Russia. General Erich Marcks, whom Hitler entrusted with preparing the analysis preceding the attack, estimated Russian forces at 151 divisions of infantry, of which barely 100, in his opinion, could be sent into battle. On top of this, Marcks thought that the Red Army, with its KV-1 and T-34 tanks, would be defenseless in the face of the *Panzerwaffe* brought from France—that assumption turned out later to be painfully wrong. The German leaders' dominant conviction of their total superiority over the Soviets was rooted in a stereotype—dignitaries of the Third Reich viewed the Russians as backward simpletons, incapable of fighting. Influenced by this, Marcks estimated the campaign would last for about five to seven weeks, in which time the Wehrmacht was supposed to get to Moscow without encountering any difficulties. Any opinions that this was rather optimistic were rejected for not being in accordance with the Führer's view (advocacy approach!). Even Halder, who in earlier years had occasionally had the nerve to contradict the dictator, changed his point of view. Hitler meanwhile, drunk on his success in France, went so far as to state that, in comparison with what had already been achieved, defeating the Soviets would be child's play—*Sandkastenspiel*, or literally "playing in a sandpit." It was also to be another lightning war. As it turned out though, in this case, the *Blitzkrieg* had very little *Blitz* and a whole lot of *Krieg*—the operation dragged on interminably, the literal size of the battlefield became a serious obstacle to supplying the German armies, and the Red Army turned out to be far better trained and organized than the Germans had thought.

Operation Barbarossa was launched on June 22, 1941, although Hitler had actually signed the order authorizing it in December 1940. Many of his advisors were concerned about waging a war on two fronts at the same time, but nobody was bold enough to stand up to the Führer (it would be absurd to make any kind of comment here about the lack of psychological security), and so the decision to strike the Soviet Union along three corridors was made. At 3:15 am, the *Heeresgruppe Südukraine* (Army Group South) set off in the direction of Donbass, *Heeresgruppe Mitte* (Army Group

Center) started on the march toward Moscow, and *Heeresgruppe Nord* (Army Group North) began operations on the territory of the Baltic states, headed toward Leningrad. Simultaneously, more than six hundred Luftwaffe planes bombarded key targets in western parts of the USSR. It was an unprecedented operation: around 3.5 million German soldiers were involved, with over 7,000 cannons, and almost 4,000 tanks at their disposal. The strike came as a total surprise to the Soviets, even though the possibility of a German attack had been discussed repeatedly. In addition, on June 25, Finland declared war on the Soviet Union, actively fighting alongside the German forces.

The first weeks of Operation Barbarossa went according to the German plan, though the Soviets put up far fiercer resistance here and there than had been expected. The first serious challenge for the Wehrmacht arose at the battle for Smolensk, which took place in July 1941 and delayed the march of the Army Group Center on Moscow. Despite this, the German forces pushed on, and in September scored a spectacular success, which Hitler dubbed the greatest in history, by encircling and destroying considerable Red Army forces at Kiev. The road to Moscow was open, and at the beginning of October, Operation Typhoon, whose aim was to capture the Soviet capital, began.

In the same period, though, numerous previously unexpected (albeit entirely predictable) developments began to unfold. The most significant of these was the rebuilding of the Red Army in terms of manpower, which the USSR achieved by the straightforward method of drawing on its enormous population, with endless more divisions being formed throughout the country and hurled into battle. The Germans, who suffered serious losses in the first few months of Operation Barbarossa, had no such resources at their disposal. A second unexpected development concerned supplies.

The operation had been planned as a lightning strike, and supplies had been issued with a short duration in mind. As the operation dragged on, major problems arose with the supplies (fuel to begin with, as they had only three months' worth). These problems were exacerbated by the sheer expanse of the Soviet territory, which was taking longer to traverse than the Germans had imagined. The third wrench in the works was thrown by Nature. The Germans were not prepared for the Baltic winter—again, they'd expected to be done and dusted by that point—and the winter of 1941–42 was a particularly bitter one.

On December 5, 1941, something happened that even Hitler hadn't contemplated. The Red Army he had treated with such contempt launched a counterattack. Later referred to as the winter counteroffensive, it turned the German forces back from Moscow, causing heavy losses (it's estimated that Army Group Central lost tens of thousands of troops during Operation Typhoon). While this didn't give the Soviets the upper hand, it was the first snag in a hitherto unbroken string of German successes. Operation Barbarossa was at a standstill, sinking in the spring thaw that had paralyzed military movement on both sides. Moscow had been saved, and an irritated Führer ordered the start of an operation named *Fall Blau* in the south, even though the German army chiefs favored regrouping and maintaining the current position. The plan for Fall Blau involved cutting the Red Army off from the Caucasus and capturing Stalingrad by way of a grand finale. The main burden of the task rested with the 6th Army, led by Field Marshal Friedrich Wilhelm Paulus. He initially handled the job brilliantly, and by fall 1942, the Wehrmacht had managed to take most of the city, massacring its inhabitants in the process. But then the German army found itself facing an old adversary—Nature swept in a second monumental winter, for which Hitler's soldiers were not prepared, because a supply chain to the remote units at the front still hadn't been established. The effects were appalling: Paulus's soldiers starved, suffered dreadfully from frostbite, and indisputably lost their fighting spirit as attempts to provide them with food and ammunition by air proved insufficient. Faced with this situation, Paulus asked Hitler for permission to withdraw and regroup, but the Führer refused and demanded they go back on the attack. This was mission impossible—they were instantly caught in a pincer movement by divisions led by Generals Konstantin Rokossovsky and Andrey Yeryomenko that encircled Paulus's exhausted 6th Army. The Field Marshal himself was called on to surrender, but initially refused. So, on January 26, 1943, the Red Army began an operation that sealed the fate of the German soldiers, and the Field Marshal, against Hitler's wishes, threw in the towel five days later. At Stalingrad, not only did hundreds of thousands of people die, so too did any German hopes of turning around the war.

The end of 1942 brought the Führer yet more problems on other fronts: the defeat of the legendary Afrika Korps of Erwin Rommel at El-Alamein[11] meant the situation in Africa had reversed, and Japan, one of the Axis countries, was defeated at the Battle of Guadalcanal. Despite this, Hitler didn't give up on his offensive strategy, and in spring 1943, he gave the order to launch Operation Citadel, aimed at cutting off divisions of the Red Army grouped near Kursk. The attack, whose launch date was repeatedly delayed due to ongoing supply problems, was slated to begin on the night of July 4 with a strike by German armored units with air support. Unlike the beginning of Operation Barbarossa, this time the Soviets knew all about the German plans, as military intelligence had supplied detailed information on the planned attack several days earlier; hours before the Germans launched their operation, the Soviets bombarded the positions held by the Wehrmacht. This delayed the onset of Operation Citadel, giving the Red Army extra time to prepare their defense.

The Battle of Kursk lasted for almost two months and became a breakthrough event not only in terms of fighting in Soviet territory, but also in terms of the entire war on the Eastern Front—it was a battle that changed the course of World War II. It was also one of the biggest clashes in the history of humankind, as both sides mobilized forces exceeding 1 million soldiers. During weeks of fierce fighting, dozens of clashes and battles took place, of which the most important was one of the first. On July 12, in the vicinity of Prokhorovka, a massive tank battle, totaling more than a thousand vehicles, raged for several hours. Germany lost the battle, suffering heavy losses in equipment that they could not replenish given the existing strain on resources, forces spread far and wide, and supply chains stretched to breaking point. Smelling blood after the destruction of the German armored forces at Prokhorovka, the Soviets went on the counteroffensive with Operation Kutuzov, pushing the Wehrmacht onto the defensive as its situation became progressively more desperate. In August, it became clear that all was lost and that the Germans' only option was to retreat. The Red Army followed in relentless pursuit, bludgeoning their way west through Poland and eventually arriving in Berlin less than two years later, in April 1945. The disastrous strategic decisions made by the Führer led the Germans to defeat and brought the bloodiest war in human history to a close.

The causes of the catastrophe that befell Hitler and the German army were identical to those that raised their heads in the Gulf of Tonkin and Washington almost twenty-five years later: The lack of an inquiry approach and thorough assessment of the strength of an opponent, resulting from delusions of one's own greatness fueled by a recent history of success. Pressure from a leader who totally ruled out any discussion about the vision they imposed (any analyses that were presented, just as in the Gulf of Tonkin situation, distorted the facts and presented the picture the leader wanted to see). And the sunk costs effect, which made it impossible to withdraw or change course once it became clear that the original strategy wasn't providing the desired results.

We could go a step further and say that Adolf Hitler failed to learn the lessons of history when he decided to start a war against the USSR in that way and under those circumstances. General Carl Gottlieb von Clausewitz, a Prussian military strategist and author of *On War*, published in 1832, commented on Napoleon Bonaparte's Russian defeat, suffered twenty years earlier, thus:

> [The Russian campaign of 1812 showed that] Russia is not a country that can be formally conquered [...] certainly not with the present strength of the European States and not even with the half-a-million men Bonaparte mobilized for the purpose. [...]
>
> The 1812 campaign failed because the Russian Government kept its nerve and the people remained loyal and steadfast. The campaign could not succeed. [...]
>
> [Bonaparte's fault] lay in his being late in starting the campaign, in the lives he squandered by his tactics, his neglect of matters of supply and of retreat.[12]

Many historians believe that if Hitler had chosen another, more considered strategy after conquering France—as some advisors suggested to him—the war would have turned out very differently, as the Germans, utilizing their resources more sensibly, would have been much more difficult to defeat.[13]

Leaders assume an enormous responsibility when they make decisions regarding the strategic direction of developments. The slightest error at the preparation stage can have dire consequences later on, when it's impossible to turn things around. Hence the absolute necessity of conducting a thorough analysis and instigating an inquiry approach, and of surrounding yourself with the right people and giving them the requisite psychological security to enable open, honest dialogue.

RULE #12

Great leaders are distinguished by their awareness that greatness is no guarantee of infallibility.

MAKING STRATEGIC decisions and setting out the path for others to follow seems to be the magnum opus of most leaders, and it is perceived by many as their greatest challenge. I think, though, that leaders have more difficult issues to cope with. One of these involves the introduction of radical changes in an organization, especially if they are supposed to reshape the organizational culture.

The Leader as an Agent of Change

Strategic decisions usually mean that certain changes will have to be implemented. And while it's probably reasonable to assume that most of us would see the sense in making changes if things are going badly, it is possibly more beneficial to look at cases where an organization was successful but a leader opted to defy the conventional wisdom of "if it ain't broke, don't fix it" and decided to introduce major changes.

This was the backdrop to what became a classic case of change management. In 1981, John (Jack) Welch took over at General Electric, the company founded by Thomas Alva Edison. The company was in excellent shape at the time, and the position of chairman had opened up following the retirement of the legendary Reginald H. Jones, who had led the business since 1972 and—in addition to doubling its earnings—had transformed it into a radical, forward-thinking company, based on a strategy of business units, rather than more traditional structures. Most analysts thought the very young, by GE standards, CEO would simply continue along the lines of his illustrious predecessor. The first couple of years soon disabused them of such ideas.

Despite his relative youth, Welch, who had been with GE for over twenty years, knew the strengths and weaknesses of the company inside out. He realized that the transformations carried out by Jones were just the beginning, and that continuing growth was dependent on further change. Welch's vision was simple: GE, despite its size (at the beginning of the 1980s, the corporation employed over 400,000 people and operated in dozens of sectors), was to become as dynamic as a small company, and its employees were therefore expected to think like entrepreneurs, showing genuine customer orientation. Welch, nicknamed "Neutron Jack" by his colleagues, touched down like an atomic bomb: by 1985 he had slimmed down the organization to 299,000 employees, eliminating numerous levels of management and flattening the structure. This was accompanied by a rule—a controversial one in the eyes of many—whereby, regardless of the results of a unit, every year, in accordance with his "rank and yank" policy, the 10 percent least effective employees were given the push. Welch's obsession with leadership extended into the market dimension. During the 1980s, he implemented the unprecedented strategy of selling off business units that were not and had no chance of becoming leaders in their sectors. This gradually turned the unwieldy giant into a super-dynamic organization in which the overriding goal was to be number one in every field of operation. GE, meanwhile, didn't forget about quality, which is often a victim in such transformations. From 1995 onward, the company consistently implemented the Six Sigma system, developed by Motorola, to reduce the number of errors generated by processes and people. Its implementation not only required an enormous effort in terms of training and reorienting the organization toward the customer and their satisfaction, but also was a test of the quality of the leadership and engagement of the employees.

The solutions resulted in changes, not only financially and in terms of customer satisfaction, but also in the attitudes of employees. As one of the managers of Morgan Stanley Dean Witter observed, GE achieved not only extraordinary levels of quality but also sustainable solutions. In the initial phase, while many initiatives identified and eliminated problems in the organization, after the new system had worked efficiently for a while, the old problems resurfaced. The Six Sigma approach, however, created a feeling of responsibility among the Black Belts[14] for continuing the new way of working. A characteristic feature of the GE management culture at the same time was that managers and specialists were more and more involved in the decision-making process. Welch knew that nothing generated more engagement in people than an awareness of being a co-author of a solution.

GE sped forward, and Welch's approach won greater and greater acceptance, even among his earlier critics. The 1990s did not see Neutron Jack resting on his laurels—instead, he constantly forged ahead, actively seeking out new business opportunities. The company bought up players that fit with its competitive model, and continued to rid itself of those units that were unable to achieve or maintain their position as leader.

GE shares at the beginning of the 1980s cost a little over $1.00. When, after more than twenty years at the helm of the corporation, sixty-five-year-old Jack Welch retired, the share price stood at over $50.00. The company's market cap was at $12 billion when Welch took over and peaked at $596 billion in August 2000—a record for GE. When he left, it had dropped to $400 billion.

A SIMILARLY interesting story was played out in another American corporation, which for many years had been a symbol of the country's business success, only to find itself in serious trouble and then become a fascinating story of rebirth driven by an exceptional leader.

At the beginning of December 2016, I flew to Phoenix for some workshops as part of the Marshall Goldsmith 100 Coaches program. I didn't know that it would be a weekend that would alter my views on managing change. I knew I was embarking on an intensive couple of days in the company of fascinating people, but I was in no shape or form prepared for what happened on Saturday, December 3. That day, I met Alan Mulally, and the story he told me turned my perception of the role of a change leader in transforming an organization upside down.

Mulally was born shortly after World War II in Oakland, California. He studied at Kansas University and MIT. Though he spent almost his entire career with Boeing, where he was highly successful, particular attention should be paid to the years 2006-14, when he accomplished a seemingly impossible task: despite being an industry outsider, he not only led the Ford Motor Company back onto the straight and narrow after the 2008 financial crisis, but also repaid the government funds the company had received, making Ford unique among the country's Big Three in this respect. His introduction to Ford had been less than auspicious, though. When William Clay Ford Jr., a descendant of Henry Ford, announced that his successor in the role of President and CEO would be someone who had spent his entire career with Boeing, few believed that the legendary company would survive. The internal organizational and financial problems were bad enough (in 2006, Ford lost $17 billion on its core business!), but the global crisis two years later almost tapped the final nail in the coffin, as it wreaked havoc throughout the auto industry. So how did an outsider achieve the impossible? He turned to radical change, of course[15]—restructuring the brand portfolio, changing the management personnel, implementing major cost-cutting accompanied by tough negotiations with trade unions, and mortgaging almost the entire assets of the company for a sum exceeding $23 billion... and yet, it was Alan Mulally's personality that proved to be the key to his extraordinary success. I summarized the lessons on leadership I took away from the December meeting in five points:

1. **If you don't believe in your people, you'll get nowhere.** People come first. If you can't build a team characterized by open, honest communication, trust, respect, and genuine engagement, you will get nowhere, no matter how great your strategy is. Leadership is about building the capability of the team and its members. If you are better and know more than your direct reports, you are in trouble.

2. **Truly including everyone is crucial.** Compelling vision, comprehensive strategy, and a relentless implementation plan are key, and you should make sure that everyone understands and trusts them. If people know where the company is going and are up to date with its status, they feel safe. Uncertainty, gossiping, and lack of engagement are rooted in insufficient communication.

3. **Emotional resilience comes from having a process you trust, whether you are a manager or an employee.** If you have both a process and a plan, these are your support network when the going gets tough. Trusting in the process and the plan helps you sleep well at night. However, there are two important points to note about this approach:

   a. When organizations face a problem, their instinctive reaction is to say, "We have to change our plan." Mulally's lesson: don't do this; instead, be more creative in your search for a solution.

   b. Rely on facts and data. You cannot manage secrets, so honesty and transparency are fundamental. Data sets people free.

4. **Have zero tolerance for those who violate norms and expected behaviors.** This one might seem surprising: although individual performance is important, values and norms are what really matter. Mulally is okay with someone who has no idea how to solve a problem they encounter (see Lesson 5), but does not tolerate those who violate values and expected behaviors.

5. **Having no solution to a problem is OK.** In my opinion, this is the most powerful lesson to be learned from. We work in ego-driven organizations and environments in which admitting you have no idea what to do is tantamount to professional suicide. This is embedded in the managerial and decision-making culture: How many times have you heard, "Don't bring me problems, bring me solutions"? Empowering people and making them accountable makes sense, but what if someone faces an issue they can't find an answer to, despite their best efforts to do so? In such a situation, the "bring me a solution" approach encourages people to sweep

problems under the carpet. Mulally's lesson: it is OK to have no answer. The team is there to help—this is what teamwork is all about. This is common sense, but uncommon practice.

Alan Mulally's achievement deserves special recognition, because the transformation of organizational culture is an extremely difficult type of change management.

The Leader as Architect of Organizational Culture

Organizational culture, as we saw in the previous chapter, is of fundamental significance for decision-making processes, and it is leaders who are responsible for shaping it. This responsibility is more important today than ever before, and if that weren't enough, it is one of the most difficult processes of change to oversee in business, not only because people resist it, but also because the actual transformation concerns things that are difficult to measure. Changing the tools used in the sales process, changing the program for managing warehouse levels, changing purchasing procedures, and so on, all share one pleasant feature: they're measurable. It's not difficult for a project manager to define the criteria and parameters of such things, so it's not difficult to find out fairly rapidly whether or not the change is having the desired effect, or whether the approach needs to be modified. In the case of modeling organizational culture, setting hard, measurable indicators is far more difficult, and frequently impossible.

Leaders are not helpless, though, as long as they apply a technique that until recently was treated as superfluous and typically pushed to one side: managing organizational values.

Values are basically beliefs and guidelines that an organization identifies as standards that they want to adhere to and be associated with. They set the tone of an organization and are part of its brand.

The foundation of an organization's values is usually specific to its corporate priorities. For some, this will mean that innovation and constant change are key; for others, it will be stability and predictability. Every sector has a place for companies that back experimentation (like fusion restaurants), as well as those for whom uniformity and standardized service and product are key (such as McDonald's). The important thing is that employees act in accordance with the values promoted by the company and that their leaders encourage such behaviors. Values should be a kind of lighthouse, helping to steer employees toward the right decision when conditions are uncertain—they answer the question "how," unlike a strategy, which answers the question "what."

Values are frequently at the root of vital decisions that will directly affect the success or failure of a company. An excellent example of this was the decision taken in 2009 by Hyundai in the United States. Like their rivals, the Koreans were struggling at the time with the catastrophic collapse of sales in the US market, caused by the financial crisis and the massive uncertainty accompanying it. Americans, fearing for their futures and job security, and reluctant to take on more debt, decided en masse that their current vehicles weren't so bad after all and put off buying a new car until more predictable times returned. This led to the collapse of the market in 2008. The year-on-year drop in new car sales was 18 percent, the worst slump in the sector's history. Almost every brand was affected, the few exceptions being manufacturers of luxury and sports vehicles, where demand remained relatively stable. The slump hit the automakers hard—Chrysler, for example, declared bankruptcy, and many had to apply for support from public funds. That wasn't the end of the crisis, though—in 2009, sales dropped even more, falling 22 percent year-on-year. Meanwhile, Hyundai (which manufactures neither luxury nor sports vehicles), like its competitors, lost sales in 2008 (-14 percent), but achieved the seemingly impossible in 2009. It didn't just maintain sales levels from the previous year, it increased them by 8 percent! Industry experts couldn't believe their eyes—this lowly Korean manufacturer was coping better than top-drawer car makers. The secret was simple: for years, Hyundai employees had been trained to put themselves in their customers' shoes and to think like them. They had no difficulty, then, in understanding the decision to put off buying a car. This awareness was a common denominator in the decision-making process whereby they rapidly launched a campaign transferring the risk from the customer to the producer—all the dealers of the Korean brand declared that, in the event of a customer losing their job within the next twelve months, Hyundai would let them return the car and would reimburse them, taking into account the depreciation of the vehicle's value so the amount customers received was fair to both parties. For purchasers, it was excellent news—you didn't have to give up your dream of purchasing a new car because the seller was shouldering the risk for you. It shouldn't come as any surprise to learn, then, that anyone who had previously intended to buy a Hyundai went ahead with their purchase as planned, and, on top of that, that the brand attracted a lot of customers for whom the Korean manufacturer hadn't been their first choice but whose outstanding offer had encouraged them to transfer their brand loyalties. In this way, applying the company's value of understanding the customer was a key factor in making and implementing a business decision, which in turn led directly to a significant success—Hyundai's market share in the USA almost doubled in 2008-12.

So, values not only matter, they can also generate a real, bottom-line return on investment. But what should we do if other people don't respect our values? The most striking evidence for the importance of values, together with the key role played by leaders in modeling organizational culture, comes from a somewhat surprising sector.

THOUGH THE birth of the Italian Mafia is lost in the mists of time and shrouded in mystery, one thing is certain: however strange it may sound, the Mafia (and in particular, the Sicilian Mafia, or Cosa Nostra), was and remains an organization built around a very precise set of values. In its history, of all the amazing stories it has to tell, three stand out: the building of a powerful market position based on a system of organizational values, followed by a deep crisis provoked by the transgression of those values by its leader, and, after losing its position, the implementation of an organizational culture change project.

Ladies and gentlemen, sit back and prepare to absorb some business wisdom from the underworld.

The Cosa Nostra is one of the four main Italian Mafias and is beyond question the best-known grouping. It was the subject of a series of novels by Mario Puzo that later formed the basis of *The Godfather* film trilogy. Although the films' action is set mainly in the United States and the events presented in them aren't a completely faithful or accurate depiction of the realities of the operations of the Cosa Nostra, the trilogy was a hit, reaping as many as nine awards from the Academy of Motion Picture Arts and Sciences. In this manner, a true classic among gangster films was created, and the Sicilian Mafia became global headline news. The success of the films led to the (obviously unintentional) popularizing of the Sicilians' modus operandi all across the world.

The true story of the Cosa Nostra actually began over a hundred years earlier, although there are many traces of its activities dating back even further. Some enthusiasts maintain that the roots of the Sicilian Mafia lie in the resistance movement against Charles I of Anjou, a ruler of Sicily who lost power due to the actions of the

Sicilian Vespers, when the local population rebelled against the French regime. According to one of the popular, but untrue, stories, *mafia* was an acronym of the chant shouted during the rebellion, *"morte alla Francia, Italia anela"* (death to France is Italy's cry). Despite this story's having very little connection with the actual facts, the Sicilian Mafia was in its own way a resistance movement— an attempt by locals to protect their interests when political games too frequently deprived them of the benefits of their hard work. Sicily passed from ruler to ruler. After the overthrow of Charles I of Anjou, the island fell under the rule of the kings of Aragon, who attacked the exiled Angevins. In the middle of the fifteenth century, it seemed that, thanks to Sicily having reunited with the kingdom of Naples, peace would finally prevail—but then the Habsburgs took power. They were replaced by the Bourbons, who remained in power until 1860.

Meanwhile, the legendary Italian hero Giuseppe Garibaldi was attempting to reunite a fragmented Italy, starting his march from Sicily. In May 1860, his modest, thousand-man division launched a desperate attack on Palermo—and to everyone's surprise, emerged victorious. After three days of fierce fighting, the exponentially stronger Bourbon forces withdrew from the city, and soon after from the entire island. Garibaldi led his Redshirts toward Naples, which they finally took on September 6. The process of reuniting Italy had begun.

This didn't signal the end of Sicily's problems, though, as integrating the island's 2.4 million inhabitants into Italy didn't go smoothly. Further battles and minor revolts were the order of the day, leading at a certain point to the imposition of martial law. It's hardly surprising that the population, tired of the repression, gradually began to organize in defense of themselves, and the more important local families became the fundamental unit of resistance and protection. However, no one had yet named these increasingly powerful families a "mafia." The word entered the vernacular partly via Giuseppe Rizzotto and Gaspare Mosca, authors of a very popular opera titled *I mafiusi de la Vicaria* (in which "*mafiusi*" denoted a group of prisoners), and partly via the authorities themselves, who, in the wake of the opera's popularity, started to refer to the Palermo families in this way. The word *mafia* probably comes from the Italian-Arabic slang that the inhabitants of Sicily used at the time and that contained such words as *mu'afa* (protection) or *marfud* (rejected, outside the law). The actual members of the Mafia didn't use the term at the time, naming their organization at the end of the nineteenth century simply Cosa Nostra—"our thing."

For centuries, the Cosa Nostra was treated by many locals as a power for good, or at worst a neutral entity. This resulted from Mafia members' consistent observance of certain unwritten rules, constituting the basis of the code of shared values of the organization: the principle of not hurting local people without good reason, not engaging in unnecessary fighting with other Mafia families, not attacking the state authorities and their representatives (unless it was absolutely necessary), not earning money from prostitution, and the rule of *omertà*—absolute silence on matters related to the Mafia. The members' adherence to these rules made fighting the Cosa Nostra incredibly difficult, and none of the inhabitants of Sicily had either the desire or the intention of cooperating with the authorities.

Observation of the rules was policed over the decades by the heads of the most important Mafia families, though the details of the structures of the organization and the decision-making mechanisms remained a secret up until the 1980s. Only then were investigators able to use the testimony of former members to establish a clearer picture of the organization. It emerged that the Cosa

Nostra was made up of *cosche* (families or clans) from all over Sicily, with those from Palermo being consistently the most powerful. The most important *capi* (bosses) formed a kind of consultative group called *la Cupola*, which basically functioned in the same way as a management board of a regular business organization—it served as a forum for discussion, a platform for the exchange of information, and a place for making the biggest decisions. One of the most important of these decisions was the choice of the *capo di tutti capi* (boss of all bosses), the person who could be regarded as top dog and who essentially ran the Cosa Nostra as the president of the board and enforced observance of the rules of the game by the individual families. The *capo di tutti capi* was invariably a member of one of the Palermo *cosche*.

Simultaneously, though, a curious tale was unfolding, one that went unnoticed, or ignored, by Palermo for a long time. During Mussolini's dictatorship and later the war years, the significance of the Mafia family from the small town of Corleone, in the northwest part of the island, began to grow. At the head of the *Corleonesi* (the Corleones), as the family was called locally, at that time was Dottore Michele Navarra, a highly respected doctor in the community, whom the locals called *U Patri Nostru* (Our Father), the same words used in the Sicilian dialect to address God. Navarra demonstrated a fair degree of political flexibility—as one of the few important people in town, he decided in favor of discreet cooperation with the prefect Cesare Mori, Benito Mussolini's emissary, who took decisive action aimed at eliminating criminal activity from the island and breaking up the most important old Mafia clans. Navarra's involvement allowed him to kill two birds with one stone: it ensured the authorities left him alone and at the same time eliminated his most serious rivals. The arrival on Sicily of nearly half a million of George Patton's soldiers was a mere blip for Navarra, who made masterly use of his family ties (his cousin, Angelo di Carlo, who had emigrated to the United States more than ten years earlier, was not only a Mafia hitman but also … a captain in the Marines) and began collaborating with the new powers.

In Michele Navarra's times there were a great deal of scores to settle, and in the short period between 1944 and 1948, the modestly sized Corleone was the site of 150 murders. The good doctor was not a man who attracted suspicion. He surrounded himself with a small group of trusted people who carried out the operations he planned. One of his closest and most trusted collaborators was Luciano Leggio, a modest, albeit highly impulsive man from a poor farming family. Over the years, it was Leggio who eliminated witnesses and rivals on his boss's orders, all the while implementing his own ever-more intricate and refined plan. Leggio's ambition was to build his own clan, but he had to do this without threatening, or seeming to threaten, Navarra's interests.

At a certain point, though, their areas of interest began to collide dangerously. A particularly significant clash occurred over the matter of a contract to build a dam, which Leggio was heavily involved in. The families allied with Navarra had a vested interest in the dam's not being built, as they were shareholders in the existing water supply system, which enabled them to dictate pretty much whatever prices they liked to the local residents and businesses. The building of the dam would put an end to this bounty. Navarra let his position on the matter be known in a relatively direct manner—his people ambushed Luciano Leggio and shot him in the shoulder.

The doctor assumed that the lesson would suffice for his loyal henchman to remember who was head of the Corleone clan. Don Michele Navarra believed totally in the sanctity of his position and reputation—and that he was utterly unassailable. He often traveled alone, without bodyguards, and one of his solo driving trips proved to be his undoing. On August 2, 1958, his car was blocked by two other vehicles, and then machine gun fire broke out; struck by ninety-two bullets, Navarra didn't have a chance. He died where he fell. The killer turned out to be none other than Luciano Leggio, who, as you can see, drew an entirely different lesson from that which Dottore Navarra intended.

Leggio took over from where Navarra left off, which meant that the careers of two of his closest allies, Salvatore "Totò" Riina and Bernardo Provenzano, blossomed. The whole trio would play a key role in the Cosa Nostra in the future.

Over the next few years, Luciano Leggio solidified his position with a perfect balance of carefully chosen alliances and ruthlessness toward opponents. He was renowned for the scale on which he planned and carried out his operations—for example, in June 1973, he collaborated with *'ndràngheta*, the powerful Calabrian Mafia, to kidnap John Paul Getty III, the grandson of one of the richest people in the world at the time, from Palazzo Farnese in Rome. After long negotiations, the seventeen-year-old's family, who had been sent, among other things, the boy's chopped-off ear, paid close to $3 million for his release. The teenager was released in southern Italy shortly after the ransom was paid, over half a year after his kidnapping. As it turned out, kidnapping the grandchild of such a wealthy person had its consequences, because capturing Leggio became a priority for the local police and Carabinieri. The authorities achieved their goal at dawn on May 14, 1974, when they arrested the unsuspecting gangster at his lover's house. He was given a custodial sentence but, like his predecessors, he tried to maintain control over the operations of the Corleonesi from behind bars. It turned out, though, that history likes to repeat itself, and standing in his way was his closest collaborator,

Salvatore Riina, who, in turn, gradually took over where his boss had left off. Information about this reached Leggio, who ordered his people to start taking orders from Provenzano, and not Riina. In response, Riina torpedoed the plan to release his boss from prison—as a police informer said many years later, all it took was a word from Riina and Leggio "could escape a hundred and fifty times"; instead, though, a shadowy game of intrigue and power plays dragged on.

In 1975, it became necessary for the Cupola to meet in order to address a number of matters, including the question of the families' approach to kidnappings (which, as Leggio had learned the hard way, caused more harm than good in the long run) and the choice of a new *capo di tutti capi*. Giving Riina one more chance, Leggio decided that Provenzano and Riina should represent him at the meeting.

The families from Palermo were resolute in their desire to stop the kidnappings, pointing to the unnecessary risks they entailed. The only dissenting voice was that of Riina. The meeting ended in a bitter conflict that soon after escalated into open warfare. Riina decided to show who was really in charge of the Cosa Nostra, and despite the prohibition imposed by the Cupola, organized the abduction of Luigi Corleo, who was not only one of the richest Sicilians, but also a relative of two influential bosses from Palermo and so considered himself untouchable. His outraged family refused to pay the exorbitant ransom demanded—reputedly over $25 million—counting on settling the affair through their regular contacts.

It ended tragically for the kidnapped man, who was murdered, as Riina made a bid to take control of the Cosa Nostra by force. The Palermo families had a chance to stop him, as the united *cosche* of Gaetano Badalamenti and Stefano Bontade had significantly more firepower at their disposal; however, falling prey to turkey syndrome, they remained doggedly faithful to the methods that had served them well over many decades, ignoring Salvatore Riina and the Corleonesi, whom they dismissively labeled *i viddani* (peasants), forgetting that the big bosses of the 1940s, like Genco Russo and Calogero Vizzini, had also come from the countryside. Badalamenti and Bontade did not consider Riina a threat, as no one had ever undermined the authority of the families from Palermo. They soon realized just how big a mistake that was.

The basic goal of the Corleonesi was to control the narcotics market, on which the older bosses looked with distaste, just as they did prostitution. The values nurtured over the centuries were not highly rated by Riina, they limited his opportunities to entrench his power and domination, so it's hardly surprising that he pretty rapidly departed from the majority of them. He demanded total subservience from the local population, and any kind of criticism was severely punished. For example, the Corleonesi murdered Mario Francese, a journalist from the popular paper *Giornale di Sicilia*, which over the years had reported on the activities of the family headed by Riina. Francese's only error was to publish a short interview with Ninette, the boss's fiancée at the time, whose comments, Riina believed, showed him in a poor light. The journalist was shot dead a few years later, in line with the Corleonesi's principle that *il miglior perdono è la vendetta* (the best forgiveness is revenge). At the beginning of the 1980s, another taboo was broken when the clan turned against the authorities and police in a clear breach of the rules of the Cosa Nostra. Anyone whose activities could in any way damage the Corleonesi family would be killed: they murdered, for example, Boris Giuliano, deputy chief of police in Palermo and Emanuele Basile, captain of the Carabinieri, as well as Cesare Terranova, head of the court of appeal, Piersanti Mattarella, president of the Christian Democrat party on the island,

and Michele Reina, secretary of the Christian Democrat party. None of these killings were sanctioned by the Cupola, whose members were outraged. Immediate action against the Corleonesi was ordered by Stefano Bontade, one of the most influential members of the Cupola, the *capo* of the powerful Santa Maria di Gesù family from Palermo.

Riina responded in his characteristic style, breaking the rules of the game again. On his forty-second birthday, in April 1981, Stefano Bontade died in his Alfa Romeo when he met a Kalashnikov-wielding Giuseppe Greco, the Corleonesi's leading hitman. Riina didn't stop at removing Bontade. With his perfect understanding of the rules and logic of Sicilian vendettas, he decided to eliminate anyone and everyone who could possibly threaten him in the future. He had Bontade's right-hand man, Salvatore Inzerillo, shot along with his sixteen-year-old son, who, following tradition, had announced that he would avenge his father when he grew up; meanwhile, in New York, Salvatore Inzerillo's brother Pietro died. This series of killings could not go unchecked, which led to a *mattanza*—a bloody Mafia war—in which more than a thousand people reportedly died over the next few years.

The state couldn't ignore what was happening, and so Carlo Alberto Dalla Chiesa, a legend in his own lifetime, was sent to the island. Dalla Chiesa was a Carabinieri general who commanded the region of the Aosta Valley in Piedmont, and from 1974 had led an antiterrorist unit in Turin, battling against the radical left-wing *Brigate Rosse* (Red Brigades), who were responsible for the kidnap and murder in 1978 of former Italian Christian Democrat prime minister Aldo Moro, among other things. Thanks to Dalla Chiesa, the local founder of the Brigate Rosse, Renato Curcio, was arrested along with his close colleague, Alberto Franceschini, which led to the collapse of the organization at the beginning of the 1980s.

Dalla Chiesa was therefore an ideal candidate to fight organized crime on Sicily and was nominated prefect of Palermo, with a clear order from the authorities: get rid of the Cosa Nostra, and in particular the Corleonesi. The general arrived on April 30, 1982, the same day that the Communist MP Pio La Torre was assassinated.

Dalla Chiesa threw down the gauntlet to Riina and his people, and soon after his arrival organized a meeting of the mayors of the most important Sicilian towns... in Corleone. During the meeting, he demanded total loyalty from the mayors, and insisted that they pass on any information that might concern the Cosa Nostra. He also contacted the American consul in Palermo, Ralph Jones, from whom he expected support. These steps, together with the general's well-earned reputation, unsettled the Corleonesi, who solved their new problem in the old-school way: precisely one hundred days after arriving on the island, Carlo Alberto Dalla Chiesa and his wife, Emanuela Setti Carraro, died in a hail of bullets fired by eight hitmen, at the head of whom stood Giuseppe Greco.

All of the above events were watched closely by one of the Palermo bosses, Tommaso Buscetta, nicknamed, on account of his contacts in the United States, *boss dei due mondi* (the "Godfather of Two Worlds"). Buscetta understood that the code that had underpinned the power of the Cosa Nostra no longer existed, and that the activities of the Corleonesi had destroyed the old rules of the game. On top of that, Riina's people had also attacked his family, murdering two of his sons and a brother, and he would be their next target. So, in July 1984, Buscetta decided to take the unprecedented step of breaking *omertà* by cooperating with Judge Giovanni Falcone. As he said in his testimony, it wasn't he who had betrayed the Cosa Nostra, but the Cosa Nostra that had betrayed him.

Judge Giovanni Falcone was an extraordinary figure. Born in 1939 in the port district of Palermo, he was faced with a relatively natural career path within the structure of one of the Mafia clans, much like his friend from the same district, Tommaso Spadaro. Falcone, however, made a different choice and decided to study law at the University of Palermo, after which he became a judge. In the 1980s, he and Paolo Borsellino, a childhood friend, became the cornerstones of the struggle against the Cosa Nostra.

Buscetta's testimony was a double blow: not only did it reveal the operation methods of the Cosa Nostra and enable the arrests in later years of many of its members, but it also encouraged other gangsters—270 in total—to collaborate with the authorities. They formed a group named the *pentiti* (or "penitents"[16]), and the information provided by them led to the first *Maxiprocesso* (Maxi Trial), the biggest body blow dealt to the Sicilian Mafia in its history. The main architect of the trial was the judge, Giovanni Falcone, and a total of 474 people were tried.

Ultimately, the court sentenced nineteen members of the Cosa Nostra to the maximum punishment allowed under Italian law: life imprisonment. Among those sentenced was Salvatore "Totò" Riina, found guilty in absentia. A further 338 people received sentences totaling 2,665 years in prison.

The police and Carabinieri began hunting down the missing gangsters.

Riina did not intend to go down without a fight, and his enemy number one became, of course, Judge Falcone. After several failed attempts, the Corleonesi got their man: on May 23, 1992, a several hundred pound explosive, placed in a pipe under the Palermo-Trapani freeway, killed Giovanni Falcone, his wife, and three bodyguards. Less than two months later, the Mafia dealt another blow to justice—in Palermo, Paolo Borsellino was killed after he took over the investigation of the Cosa Nostra following the death of his friend.

The assassinations, though, had an effect that the Mafia did not foresee. The local population, which had lived for decades in a better or worse symbiosis with the Cosa Nostra, turned their backs on the gangsters. The killings aroused enormous social outrage and put powerful pressure on the authorities to deal once and for all with the problem of violence on the island. Members of the Sicilian Mafia, many of whom were deeply religious and wore their religion like a badge, were condemned in May 1993 by Pope John Paul II during the culminating event of a three-day visit to Sicily. In a mass delivered before 100,000 faithful, in the vicinity of Agrigento, an evidently angry pope abandoned his earlier prepared sermon and, in a highly emotional manner, demanded that Mafia members repent. These words were burned into the memories of those present. The authorities set about dealing with the Cosa Nostra, now decimated by arrests, with renewed vigor, and the locals more and more openly supported these operations. One of those who decided to turn against the Mafia was Baldassare Di Maggio, who for a time had been a close collaborator of Riina and knew where the boss was hiding. His testimony provided the breakthrough the authorities needed, and on January 14, 1993, at 8:52 am, a division of the Carabinieri surrounded the building he was in and Captain Sergio De Caprio personally arrested the gangster. During his arrest, the surprised *capo di tutti capi* did not put up any resistance.

The weakened Corleonesi collected their strength one last time, and in the next few months carried out another series of killings, now aimed clearly at the Italian state itself. Bombs exploded in various towns and cities, including Rome and Florence, where a part of the famous Uffizi Gallery and some of its priceless collection was destroyed. However, two crimes in particular shocked the nation to its core, crimes in which the Cosa Nostra crossed two more boundaries. Revenge for the words of John Paul II came in the form of a bomb explosion in the Archbasilica of St. John Lateran on July 27, 1993, and the murder of a priest named Pino Puglisi, who openly condemned the Mafia, less than two months later. With these actions, the Corleonesi turned against the Church, which was something the deeply religious Sicilians could not forgive. The citizens' outrage reached a peak, though, when the Corleonesi kidnapped eleven-year-old Giuseppe Di Matteo, the son of a *pentito*. After being held in captivity for two years, the boy was strangled and his body dissolved in acid. This act of violence led even some of the gangsters to say "enough," and the number of Mafiosi who broke the code of silence grew to almost 500. The police and Carabinieri caught more of them, destroying the Cupola. Among those arrested was the mastermind behind the assassination of Giovanni Falcone and the kidnapping of Giuseppe di Matteo, Giovanni Brusca; in 1995, Leoluca Bagarella, a relative of Riina's who had tried to take control over the entire Cosa Nostra and become the new *capo di tutti capi*, was also captured.

After years of pretending that the Mafia problem didn't exist, the Italian state carried out its first effective, large-scale operation since the time of Mussolini, which ultimately led to the breaking up of the Cosa Nostra. Their success was possible only because of a fundamental mistake made by the leader Salvatore Riina, who abandoned the sacred organizational values that formed the basis for *omertà*. If not for the family war in 1981, the direct attacks on the Italian state and Church, and the unprecedented brutality toward the local populace, there would have been no *pentiti*, and the anti-Mafia activities would still be nothing more than a demonstration of the impotence of the authorities. In the second half of the 1990s, the Italian police declared victory in their war on the Cosa Nostra and turned their attention to the increasingly powerful Camorra—the Neapolitan Mafia.

But what was Provenzano up to while this was all going on? Well, it turns out he employed the wisest tactic of them all, as he managed to avoid arrest in the 1990s. One of the biggest problems facing the investigators, who had been on his trail since 1963, was that the only photo they had of the gangster was from 1959. Unlike the other bosses, Provenzano was an unusually modest man who always tried to remain in the background. There's an old Russian saying that translates into English as "ride quietly and you'll ride farther," and this perfectly sums up the story of Provenzano, who, after the arrest of Leoluca Bagarella, took over the reins of the entire Cosa Nostra in the absence of any competition. His first decision was to introduce a strategy he called "submersion," which effectively meant totally disappearing off the radar and silencing media reports. This was intended to help restore the organization's strength and regain the support of the local populace. The facts testify to Provenzano's influence on the Corleonesi and other Mafia families: after 1995, the number of killings committed on Sicily fell dramatically, as did petty crime. The *capo di tutti capi* knew that this was the only way to rebuild the Cosa Nostra and openly backed the return to the old values of the organization (e.g., he set up financial support for the families of arrested gangsters, something Salvatore Riina had abolished, and prohibited reprisals against the families of the *pentiti*). The other Mafia families grew increasingly appreciative of his conciliatory style, thanks to which more and more decisions were of a win-win nature and mutually beneficial to all those involved; Provenzano himself repeatedly used the phrase *"mangia e fai mangiare"* (eat and let eat). This approach earned him the respect of others and cemented his position as the leader of the entire organization, which in turn gave him even greater influence over the behavior of others, and, consequently, the organizational culture of the Cosa Nostra. Provenzano also displayed an ability to think strategically and, at the end of the 1990s, chose a new direction for the Mafia. Seeing the annually increasing support for the

Italian economy from various European Union structural funds, he decided to increase the presence of the Cosa Nostra in the public service sector and construction, which were the main beneficiaries of this aid. Companies controlled by the Sicilian Mafia won contract after contract, and frequently expressed their appreciation with shows of generosity toward the decision-makers. In line with Provenzano's logic, the Mafia ate and allowed others to eat. Everyone was happy, and the Cosa Nostra once again re-entered the game, this time as a stealthy spider controlling a strategically located and managed web, entangling thousands of businesses in Italy and abroad.

In this extraordinary way, Bernardo Provenzano, an authentic leader managing the organization's values, succeeded in rebuilding the power of the Mafia, which the authorities had classified as a mission impossible, and restored its old culture and values.

In the letters that the *capo di tutti capi* sent from his hideout near Corleone, seven rules were apparent, which the leader called on his people and other families to observe:

1. **Be invisible:** Don't raise a fuss. It's better you are not spoken about at all than that others speak ill of you. In the worst case, suspend your activities.

2. **Negotiate:** Be calm and determined; express yourself clearly. Teach your people the art of negotiation—it's better than imposing your will by force.

3. **Work for the community:** You must be seen as working for the good of your society. So always listen to people who come to you with personal or business problems, and as far as you can, give them aid and assistance.

4. **Have God on your side:** Show that you are a man of deep faith and morality, and that you respect the rules, including the need for punishments and justice.

5. **Be politically flexible:** Do not get attached to a single ideology. Seek allies everywhere.

6. **Be creative:** In case of scandal or bankruptcy, you must reinvent yourself, show how much you've changed.

7. **Be modest:** Show you are a normal man, just like anyone else. Do not be arrogant or snobbish. Be close to the people.[17]

Seventy-three-year-old Bernardo Provenzano was finally arrested on April 11, 2006, not far from Corleone, and subsequently incarcerated, having been sentenced to life imprisonment in absentia in 1992. He died on July 13, 2016, from complications following bladder cancer surgery. The Cosa Nostra that he rebuilt is currently viewed as one of the most dangerous Italian Mafias, and the annual income from its illegal activities is estimated at over $100 billion.

The Leader as Architect of the Decision-Making Infrastructure

The charismatic leadership model has been seriously devalued, not only because people look for other features in a leader these days, but above all because it is so fallible, as demonstrated by the innumerable people who once basked in glory from earlier successes and later tumbled headlong into failure in the context of the new normal. The once popular saying that it's lonely at the top sounds today more like a warning than an observation. If you're truly alone in making decisions, the risk of making an error becomes gargantuan. As a result, many far-sighted, intelligent leaders try to surround themselves with teams that can provide the support required for making better decisions. An excellent example of this is EXCOMM, which was set up by President Kennedy and played a vital role during the Cuban missile crisis in 1962 (see Chapter 4). A similar thing happens in business organizations, where the measure of a leader is the caliber of people they can attract to the company and surround themselves with.

So, creating a good decision-making infrastructure isn't just about establishing procedures, principles, and norms; it's also about ensuring that the process involves the right people, people who understand their role and have a sense of responsibility toward their employees. This might make it look like a recruitment issue, but it's not—although finding suitable candidates is a real challenge. The greatest issue lies in motivating those you already employ and focusing their energies in the right direction. In other words, you have to get them truly engaged.

Highly interesting, but none too comforting, results emerged from research carried out by Professor Heike Bruch from the University of St. Gallen in Switzerland. Bruch, who specializes in engagement, motivation, and organizational energy, decided to investigate a simple question: What percentage of managers in a typical company combine the two aspects in their daily practice— focusing on the organization's priorities and investing energy in their job. As a result of her experiment, Bruch identified four groups of managers:

1. **The procrastinators (lack both energy and focus).** They work because they have to and they are frequently diligent. However, they lack initiative and don't go the extra mile that would set them

apart; and, of course, they put off today what really can't wait until tomorrow. They may look busy, but they achieve very little, if anything. As Professor Bruch's research showed, on average, 30 percent of the managers in a company are of this variety.

2. **The disengaged (display focus but lack energy).** As the name suggests, managers in this category tend to distance themselves from their jobs. They lack motivation and a sense of responsibility and many exhibit what Bruch refers to as "defensive avoidance"— they hide from problems, convincing themselves the problems don't exist rather than facing them and looking for solutions. Other disengaged managers opt not to act, even when they understand a problem and its magnitude. This category accounts for 20 percent.

3. **The distracted (well-intentioned with high energy level but correspondingly low levels of focus).** These people are often perceived as the driving forces within an organization because of their propensity to confuse motion with action—you'll see them buzzing about everywhere, in an apparent frenzy of activity. They tend to respond to crises by acting rather than reflecting, which can make them all the more dangerous. They typically find it difficult not only to develop strategies, but also to adapt to change. To top it all off, this enthusiastic, albeit misguided, bunch frequently overcommit themselves, thus putting even more pressure on their already fragile ability to focus and prioritize. According to the research carried out by Professor Bruch's team, these people can make up to as many as 40 percent of the management cadre.

4. **The purposeful (focused and energetic).** This is the group that everyone we employ ought to belong to—this category of managers are engaged and clearly understand the organization's vision,

strategy, and priorities. They work hard and are the most likely to achieve critical, long-term goals.[18] Some simple math tells us that effective managers constitute barely 10 percent of the managers in organizations.

In other words, 90 percent of the managers we employ or who work alongside us, despite apparently working hard, are ineffectively engaged, something that Professor Heike Bruch named "active nonaction"—they work intensively but produce nothing. They're the corporate equivalent of hamsters running on a wheel.

In terms of decision-making, each of the three ineffective types create serious consequences in their wake. The procrastinators typically generate a crisis of inaction, ignoring what really matters. A similar problem appears in the case of distracted managers—even though they are far more engaged in their work than the procrastinators, their efforts resemble firing a single large cannon at lots of random targets, none of which is the right one. Decisions taken by distracted managers are also typically botched, causing amazement among their peers: How could such a hard-working and energetic person miss something so important? Disengaged managers, though, are another matter—the key factor in the decision-making process in their case is the quality of their team, because while these managers set out the right path, they cannot drive the machine in the right direction. If their team and colleagues were able to take over this task, the decision would be implemented properly.

Frustrating tales of such people are everywhere, arousing incredulity and irritation in equal measure. I recall a highly talented and experienced marketing person who worked for one of my clients and who enthusiastically launched himself into repositioning the company's products. He was fully engaged, sacrificing his personal life and spending long evenings and entire weekends at his desk. At first, his team was delighted, because their new director was competent, professional, engaged, and hard-working. Sadly, though, after a few months he was fired because, while he was changing the image of the company's products, he was doing it in a manner that was totally at odds with the accepted strategy and vision for the development of the product portfolio. He displayed a classic mix of high energy, poor concentration, and inadequate understanding of strategic priorities.

Even more striking is the example of someone I worked with for over a year. Observing this individual was reminiscent of watching a lizard basking in the sun, gathering its strength for its next move. Mr. Lizard (let's call him so, seeing as we've already met Mr. Turkey on these pages) behaved just like this, punctuating spells of relative activity with long periods of idleness. What was worse, though, is that Mr. Lizard possessed a truly extraordinary mind—he was a highly rational and logical person, with an excellent business instinct; thought strategically; and was also unusually creative. In short, he would have been an ideal leader, were it not for his lizard-like habit of basking in the sun. Unfortunately, his was an independent, specialist position where it wasn't possible to assign him a team to implement his ideas. Mr. Lizard had to do that himself. He fell out of favor in the company because of the irritation created by his coming up with great ideas and decisions but not following through on them. Mr. Lizard could think, but he didn't act. The irritation grew exponentially when it was noticed that some of Mr. Lizard's brilliant, unimplemented ideas were being adopted by the competition.

Promoting a culture that fosters good decision-making means creating an environment in which employees are fully cognizant that they must take responsibility for any consequences of their decisions. This demands setting precise, unambiguous boundaries within which any given person can make decisions. Research by J. Richard Hackman, a psychology professor at Harvard University, showed that the best combination was to set out the direction and limits, and then leave the employee to choose their own path to meet the agreed parameters and norms.

The recipe for success in constructing an effective decision-making infrastructure therefore means combining two elements: setting up sensible decision-making processes and procedures, which are constantly revised (RCA is a great help here), and constantly communicating the vision and goals that a given individual or team is responsible for. People who know where they're going and who are given the freedom to make their own choices within their own area feel a much greater sense of responsibility toward achieving their goals than when methods are imposed on them. Micromanagement, whereby the way to carry out every step is minutely detailed and there's an almost obsessive need to show employees what to do at every single step, is a perfect way to kill engagement—especially in the case of talented individuals with the potential for significant professional development.[19] The way to motivate a builder isn't to tell him to put one brick on top of another, but to show him the glorious cathedral he's involved in building. Antoine de Saint-Exupéry once said, "If you want to build a ship, don't drum up people to collect wood and don't assign them tasks and work, but rather teach them to long for the endless immensity of the sea." Authentic leaders always remember this.

AS DEFINED by Peter Drucker, leadership is inextricably connected with decision-making, and vice versa. Leaders bear a heavy burden—they're expected to make the right strategic choices about issues that have powerful potential consequences and to improve the world around them so that the decisions they make are as good as they can possibly be. The quality of leadership affects the quality of decision-making, something that can be observed in every organization, not only in the world of business, although it is much more measurable there. Following Drucker's line of thinking, good management, or "doing things in the right way," isn't enough nowadays, because an unpleasant feature of the new normal is the paradox we looked at earlier: you can behave in an entirely rational manner that is profitable and logical yet still make a fatal error if a decision contradicts your declared values and the promises made by your organization's brand.

However, courageous decision-making often turns people into leaders. Those who aren't afraid to step forward in a difficult situation and make the right decision are perceived by others as extraordinary individuals worth following. When people are seeking reassurance, they look to brave individuals who have a clear vision and who are self-assured and, above all, successful. Leadership emerges when there is authority composed, on the one hand, of knowledge, experience, and outstanding personality, and on the other, of achievements resulting from making the right decisions (few wish to follow those who consistently fail).

Anyone who has ambitions to become a leader should bear in mind that knowledge and experience are gained over many years, but our characters are shaped throughout our lives. This aspect of the leadership puzzle, then, is developed long-term, with experience gradually filling in the gaps. The good news is that you can't suddenly go backwards in this respect, because it's impossible for us to lose our experience, or for our character to change overnight. Far more dangerous are the paradoxical challenges of good decision-making and the successes that result from it. In a world of black swans and the new normal, it's easy to slip up and to lose your authority and position as leader through a single decision. And if that weren't bad enough, the most common cause of spectacular errors lies not in external factors, but in ourselves. Even worse, we have little control over many of these internal processes, as we shall discover in the following chapter.

In our crusade to become better leaders, we are our own worst enemy.

The Four Roles of a Leader in Decision-Making

1. **Visionary and strategist.** As a leader, you decide in what direction the entire organization will go, and you ultimately choose the strategy. Be led by solid data and logic, and don't allow yourself to be seduced by past successes and a sense of invincibility. Don't forget about the soft aspects of an organization's functioning, as they play an ever-more important role these days. Be bold and prudent at the same time. Engage as many competent and intelligent people as you can in the process, ensuring that there's room at the table for those who most often disagree with you. Don't make the same mistakes as Napoleon, Hitler, or Johnson. Be aware of the pressure you place (consciously or not) on those under you. The stronger your force of personality and the greater your successes, the more likely you are to become an authority to them, someone whose opinions and decisions they accept uncritically. It is an extremely dangerous state of affairs, and one that is difficult to escape—after all, we all like it when people agree with us. Authentic leaders constantly question the status quo, even if they created it.

2. **Agent of change.** You are responsible for shaping reality. If you are able to carry out the first task of a leader, and you set out a bold vision, taking strategic decisions for the organization, make sure the system is going in the same direction. Force the organization to accept that change is necessary to realize that vision. Decisions made but not implemented are among the saddest and most infuriating reasons for failure, and the world is full of great ideas that were never realized (don't fall into the same trap as Mr. Lizard). Change not only people's attitudes,

but also the systems and tools the organization uses. Changes for the better are often hindered by an outdated system, gripping people in the talons of old solutions.

3. **Architect of organizational culture.** Shaping the mode of operation and people's attitudes and behavior is an especially difficult aspect of change management to implement. As a leader, you are the driving force behind the organizational culture, and your actions have an enormous influence on the attitudes and behavior of others. People observe you more closely than you think. Encourage others to make decisions that support your vision. Reward model students, who contribute the most to achieving those goals and create measurable values. Remove those whose attitudes and behavior are not consistent with what you have chosen for the company. Be like a wise *capo di tutti capi:* be led by values that make the organization strong, and be merciless with those who abandon them.

4. **Creator of the decision-making infrastructure.** Remember that in the new normal, "loneliness at the top" is both outdated and ineffective. You need allies, as you won't be able to analyze the gigantic amount of information and impulses flowing from the exponentially unraveling world of the new normal without help. Build courageous, competent teams whose members understand and support the vision and values you want to promote. Create wise procedures, build mental security, engage lots of co-workers in the discussion. Trust your people, but be ruthless with those who betray that trust. Build your own EXCOMM.

8

MY

FAVORITE

ENEMY

N CHAPTER 3 we met three very poor advisors in the decision-making process: authority, sunk costs, and conformism. Each of these demons uses the same bait, our faulty cognitive mechanism, which tricks us into making apparently rational decisions that may not actually be quite so rational. Under real or imagined pressure, we make choices that aren't the best, and stunned, we only realize the folly of our decisions when it's too late.

If you thought these three seemed threatening and difficult to avoid, then brace yourself for what you're about to read, because they are only the tip of the iceberg. In this chapter, we'll meet the greatest foe of leaders and decision-makers.

NOT MANY people can boast such a spectacular professional career as the Frenchman Dominique Strauss-Kahn. Born to a wealthy family (his father was a successful lawyer), he received an excellent education and, most importantly, graduated from one of the best business schools in the world, the absolute number one in France, the École des hautes études commerciales de Paris, commonly known as the HEC. HEC graduates are said to be doomed to succeed, and so it was in the case of Strauss-Kahn, who went on to defend his PhD at the Sorbonne. Strauss-Kahn first became a university lecturer in Nanterre; later, as a member of the Socialist Party, he was delegated to the National Assembly Committee on Finances, becoming its chairman. This position, despite later political vicissitudes, led to the key moment in his career: in 1997, when Lionel Jospin announced his cabinet, Strauss-Kahn received one of the most important posts, Minister for the Economy, Finance, and Industry. Strauss-Kahn served Lionel Jospin well, radically reducing the budget deficit and preparing France to enter the Eurozone.

Basking in his success, Strauss-Kahn became one of the leading figures in the Socialist Party, and as a result was among the potential candidates for the presidential elections of 2007. The right-wing L'Union pour un Mouvement Populaire (UMP), up against the socialists, backed Nicolas Sarkozy; the Socialist Party couldn't make up its mind between the leader of the Poitou-Charentes region, Ségolène Royal, ex-PM Laurent Fabius, and Strauss-Kahn. Ultimately, Royal was selected to stand, and Dominique Strauss-Kahn had to be satisfied with second place.

On the evening of May 6, 2007, it became clear that the right was going to win the second round of the elections, taking over 53 percent of the vote. Dominique Strauss-Kahn was bitter, as he felt that he'd had a far better chance of beating Nicolas Sarkozy than Ségolène Royal, whom—he believed—François Hollande, the head of the Socialist Party, had nominated in error. The defeat didn't trouble him for long, though, as only a few weeks later he became the number one candidate to become managing director of the International Monetary Fund (IMF), one of the most important and powerful posts in the world economy. You might be interested to learn that Strauss-Kahn's candidacy was supported particularly strongly by his erstwhile political rival, Nicolas Sarkozy. After Marek Belka, a former Polish prime minister, withdrew from the battle for the post, Strauss-Kahn was practically guaranteed victory, and so it turned out—on September 28, 2007, with the support of EU member states, the USA, and China, the French candidate was formally nominated as head of the IMF. In France, it was open knowledge that this success was just a staging post on the road to an easier presidential battle planned for 2012.

Dominique Strauss-Kahn, then, had it all. He had a fantastic career behind him, even better prospects for the future, a lot of money (the basic remuneration from the IMF was over $500,000, tax-free per annum) and shares, and last but not least, a devoted and supportive wife, the journalist Anne Sinclair, whom he married in 1991. A small blip came in the form of the investigation conducted in 2008 by an internal IMF commission into Strauss-Kahn's alleged affair with a subordinate, the Hungarian economist Piroska Nagy. The IMF board ultimately decided that Strauss-Kahn's behavior was "regrettable" and "reflected a serious error of judgment," but cleared him of abusing his position, not finding any evidence of sexual harassment in the affair. Strauss-Kahn publicly expressed his regret over the affair, but Nagy was forced to leave the organization.

It turned out, though, that the events of 2008 were just a prelude, an opening act. The real performance began with a bang three years later, on May 14, 2011. That day, the media reported that the

IMF's managing director had been arrested by New York police at JFK airport minutes before boarding a plane bound for Paris. The cause of his arrest was even more shocking. Apparently, thirty-two-year-old Nafissatou Diallo, from Guinea, who worked as a maid at the Sofitel hotel, had accused the head of the IMF of attempted rape, which she alleged had taken place the day before in the apartment Strauss-Kahn had been staying in.

In the following days, the events were reported by media worldwide, and Strauss-Kahn was forced to resign in the face of public outrage. The trial in a New York courtroom was also followed in forensic detail. The case ultimately ended with an out-of-court settlement (neither side revealed how much the maid received), and prosecutors dropped the case. On August 23, 2011, the court ruled that oral sex had taken place, as confirmed by DNA testing, and that it had been consensual, and Strauss-Kahn was cleared of the charges. Although, as in 2008, the politician publicly apologized, he wasn't reinstated, and he lost his wife, too: Anne Sinclair divorced him following the events.

What led a man with the world at his feet to behave so irrationally as to risk his marriage and career? If Dominique Strauss-Kahn could turn back time and find himself once more in the hotel apartment, would he do the same? Would he make the same decision? Is it even possible, in such situations, to talk about MAKING a decision?

Of course, it was neither the first, nor the last such case. A similar scandal had played out in 1996 in the rooms of the White House and involved someone holding higher office even than Strauss-Kahn—the President of the United States, Bill Clinton. His affair with the twenty-two-year-old intern Monica Lewinsky almost led to his impeachment. Was it really the president who was calling the shots in this case?

Perhaps the legendary Eldrick "Tiger" Woods, whose romance with Rachel Uchitel in 2009 ended not only Woods's marriage to Elin Nordegren but also several of his marketing contracts (sponsorship deals with, among others, AT&T, General Motors, TAG Heuer, and Accenture were terminated), would be able to enlighten us on the topic. Was sex with Uchitel a conscious decision made by the sportsman, preceded by rational analysis and risk assessment?

A similar hurricane of sexual misdemeanor swept away the career of the renowned Hollywood producer Harvey Weinstein at the end of 2017. While rumors had abounded within the profession for years regarding the magnate's practices (remember Seth MacFarlane's apparent joke at the Oscars in 2013?), it wasn't until a series of articles were published by the *New York Times* and the *New Yorker* that Pandora's box flew open. Over eighty women accused Weinstein of sexual harassment. The producer tried to defend himself, claiming all the incidents were consensual, but to no avail: the Academy of Motion Picture Arts and Sciences removed him from its list of members, he was forced to leave The Weinstein Company, and the relentless wave of outrage initiated the #MeToo movement in social media, which fought back against not only sexual harassment, but also its being swept under the carpet.

What happened to Weinstein, Strauss-Kahn, Clinton, and Woods (and millions of other men who were fortunate enough that the mass media weren't interested in their cases) is a phenomenon as old as time—after all, folk wisdom tells us that the brain is not the only organ that men think with. However, so as not to rely exclusively on the vagaries of folk wisdom, we shall turn to a more serious source. The influence of sexual desire on decision-making has been researched thoroughly, including by a professor of behavioral economy at Duke University, Dan Ariely. Ariely asked himself three simple questions: Would a sexually aroused man make different decisions to those he would make while not aroused? How does libido influence our opinions and preferences? Can our sex drive to some degree eliminate rational thinking?

Ariely conducted an experiment (which, by the way, generated a deal of controversy) with male students from the University of California, Berkeley. The young men were informed that the research would take place in two phases, and they would be asked to answer a series of questions about their preferences and sexual behaviors. In both phases, they were to answer the questions individually, while alone at home. Prior to starting the first round of questions, Ariely asked the subjects—before they began to answer—to imagine that they were in a state of sexual excitement. Note that it was about *imagining* that condition as realistically as possible, only imagining it.

Sometime after the answers were submitted, the second stage of the research was conducted. The students gave answers to the exact same set of questions as in the first round, but this time Ariely asked them, before they started to fill out the questionnaire, not to imagine anything, but to actually *become* sexually aroused. Pornographic magazines (hmm, I wonder if they were purchased out of the research grant, as it would make it one of the more interesting expenses financed by the university!) were on hand to help them with this.

As you might have guessed, the research confirmed what folk wisdom has long told us—the answers given in each phase were significantly different from each other. Influenced by their libido, the vast majority of the subjects were more open to taking greater risks (e.g., having unprotected sex) or engaging in unusual sexual behavior. In some cases, the percentage differences in their answers varied by several dozen, to even several hundred percent! For instance, in the first round (unstimulated), to the question, "Can you imagine having sex with a fifty-year-old woman?" 28 percent of the students responded positively. In the second round, while sexually stimulated, the number of students prepared to take such a step doubled (55 percent). Even more striking was the difference in the case of another version of the same question, concerning a sixty-year-old woman. While "cold," barely 7 percent of those tested said they would do so, whereas while masturbating, that number rose to 23 percent, and so by 229 percent. In the second round, there were also more subjects willing to agree to a threesome involving another man (the question: "If an attractive woman proposed a threesome involving another man, would you agree?" got 19 percent and 34 percent positive responses respectively), and things looked the same in the case of anal sex (the question: "Would anal sex arouse you?" got 46 percent and 77 percent positive responses respectively). Ariely observed similar differences in the case of each of the dozens of questions the students were asked.

The situation began to look far more sinister when it came to the analysis of another group of questions concerning hypothetical behavior on a date. Ariely wanted to test whether, when aroused, the proportion of subjects ready to engage in unethical, even illegal actions would increase. Here, too, the number of people expressing their readiness to behave in such a manner went way up.

For example, in the first round, only 30 percent of the students answered the question, "Would you tell a woman that you loved her if you thought it would increase your chances of going to bed with her?" positively. Under the influence of sexual stimulation, over 50 percent of those tested were prepared to do so. Even more unpleasant is the conclusion that can be drawn from the following question: "Would you try to try to initiate sexual intercourse even after a woman has said 'no'?" In the first stage, 20 percent of the students said "yes"; in the second, it rose to 45 percent. However, things actually get disturbing with the question, "Would you slip a woman a narcotic if it increased your chances of going to bed with her?" In round one, only 5 percent of the students would consider such an act. It was enough to simply masturbate, and so turn on the sexual drive, for that figure to rise to 26 percent.[1]

The worst thing about all this is that at the moment of our making the decision, we're convinced we're making the right choice, and that we're doing the right thing. This, by the by, is the mechanism behind "moral hangovers," which are nothing more than the consequence of returning from stage two to stage one and looking anew at the decisions that we made and, alas, implemented.

Sexual drive is a terrible advisor. Unfortunately, though, it's incredibly difficult to counteract, as it resides in the most primitive recesses of our brains, the parts responsible for encouraging us to reproduce and ensure the survival of the species.[2] For the last couple of decades, scientists have had access to functional magnetic resonance imaging (fMRI) using MRI scanners, a fascinating tool that enables us to understand a little better how our brains work. While almost 3 pounds is less than 2 percent of the total body mass of an adult human, the brain is one of our most vital organs; it is both the foundation of and the driving force behind civilizational, social, and technological advance. Despite this, we know surprisingly little about how it works, mainly because it is the most complex object we have yet encountered in the entire universe. The average brain consists of several hundred billion glial cells and—more importantly—about a hundred billion neurons, each of which creates about ten thousand synaptic connections, building an unimaginably intricate pathway for the flow of electrical impulses. Thanks to MRI scans, we're able to capture this activity in specific regions of the brain under the influence of specific stimuli received by the senses. So, in recent years, there has been a lot of research conducted in which people are placed in MRI scanners and perform various tasks; thanks to this research, scientists can identify the areas of the brain responsible for dealing with specific stimuli, and as a result, better understand, for example, how specific emotions are triggered.

It should come as no surprise then to learn that sexual drive has also been tested in this way. Serge Stoléru of the French Institute of Health and Medical Research and Jérôme Redouté of CERMEP conducted research with young men who watched three six-minute-long films while in an MRI scanner.[3] The first was essentially neutral, the second was a comedy, intended to arouse positive emotions, and the third included a heavy dose of erotica. The research enabled the identification of five regions of the brain that "light up" in response to sexual impulses: the lower temporal gyrus (dealing with visual stimuli), the right side of the orbitofrontal cortex (emotions and motivation), the cingulate cortex (the allocortex, responsible for basic physiological reactions), the right insula (initiating specific responses such as increasing heart rate or stimulating an erection), and the right caudate nucleus (influences emotions and possibly whether sexual activity follows sexual arousal). The activity in each of these regions increased under the influence of the images depicted in the third film, and of course, the subject had no way of controlling the activity. It's no accident that sexual drive is governed by the most ancient areas of our brains, which makes us incapable of eliminating them from our decision-making processes. I don't know if this is any consolation to Weinstein, Strauss-Kahn, Clinton, or Woods (it certainly makes no difference to their wives), but they fell victim to one of the most powerful forces Nature can throw at us, one that destroys the ability to consider and assess a situation rationally—sexual drive.

Just how much our actions are dominated by the activity of these five regions can be shown by another simple experiment: a group of male subjects was shown a series of photos of models and asked to pick the most attractive ones. The trick was that some of the photos had been Photoshopped to give the models... slightly dilated pupils. Those were precisely the photos the subjects identified as the most attractive, though they had no idea why; none of them consciously recognized that the pupils were larger. Yet, the oldest parts of their brains reacted instantly—there, evolution had encoded that dilated pupils connote female sexual arousal, and immediately prompted the subjects on what decision to make.

It's worth raising one further question about the inconvenient influence the libido exerts over behavior and decision-making: Why am I writing only about men? The answer is simple: It affects men to a massively greater degree than it does women. This has also been shown scientifically, by, for example, Dr. Stephan Hamann, of Emory University in Atlanta. As in the earlier experiments, Hamann used MRI technology. Twenty-eight young men and women looked at two types of photos. The first group of photos showed people of the opposite sex, selected so that they contained no erotic element; these were the most neutral photos the scientists were able to find. The second group of photos were unambiguously erotic and showed lone men, lone women, and heterosexual couples. The subjects were asked to assess their levels of sexual arousal while at the same time the researchers observed the activity in the key regions of their brains. As you may imagine, the men reacted neurologically far stronger than the women. Interestingly, this even happened when the women's self-assessments of their levels of sexual arousal exceeded those of the men. In other words, even if the women thought they were more influenced by libido than the men, in terms of the observed levels of brain activity, the men were more affected. Sadly, the results of these tests in laboratory conditions were disturbingly similar to actual police observations: men commit sexual assault around fifty times more than women.

That's not all, though. Just like libido, both positive and negative emotions created in the brain influence our ability to rationally assess a situation and make the right choice.

I think we've come far enough now in this book for me to tell you openly and honestly: you're a bunch of ignoramuses who haven't got a clue how to make decisions.

Whoa there, cowboy! I hope you haven't hurled this book against the wall, even if you had a momentary desire to do so. Stop. Think about your emotions when you read that—what did you feel? Disbelief, surprise, irritation, anger? If I managed to rile you, what did you want to do in that split second? Burn the book? Demand your money back? Find the author and strangle him?

If any of those emotions made a guest appearance, it means that your amygdala leaped into action and you were affected by something that Daniel Goleman (who popularized the concept of emotional intelligence) called an "amygdala hijack." Amygdala hijack occurs when we react in a way we later assess as having been excessive. This phenomenon has been described in purely neurological terms by US scientist Joseph LeDoux. He demonstrated that in certain circumstances, a brain signal travels directly from the thalamus to the amygdala, bypassing the part of the brain responsible for rational thinking. The amygdala then activates something called the HPA axis (the hypothalamic-pituitary-adrenal axis), which together with the sympathetic nervous system puts us into fight-or-flight mode. So, if the impulse gets from the thalamus to the amygdala faster than to the neocortex, we experience a primitive reaction bereft of analysis or rational thought. The neocortex is only activated later, leading to... another moral hangover and embarrassment that we got carried away by our emotions.[4]

Think about the times someone has angered you with their behavior on the road. Sometimes, you maybe felt like killing them, right? Or at least getting out of the car and reminding them of a few of the rules of the road with your fists... Several hours later, the incident seems trivial, you let it go, frequently surprised that such a banal situation made you so angry. With time, conflicts, arguments, and misunderstandings pale in significance, though at the time we were ready to fight to the death. This is the same mechanism as the one revealed in Dan Ariely's experiment: uncontrolled anger is like the second stage (sexual excitement), and rational reflection only comes once we stop masturbating, or our anger subsides.

Just how dangerous anger can be at the wrong time and in the wrong place was perfectly illustrated by an incident that outraged Americans in April 2014. The nation was rocked by recordings published on TMZ.com that featured Donald Sterling, a US real estate magnate and longtime owner of the Los Angeles Clippers. A few months earlier, in fall 2013, while speaking with V. Stiviano, a friend of his some fifty-one years his junior, the irritated millionaire had voiced some, to say the least, inappropriate opinions on the subject of African Americans. Stiviano recorded the conversation and, at the end of April 2014, pretty much on the day of the eighty-year-old's birthday, handed it over to the media. During the minutes-long chat, you hear the owner of the Clippers, clearly upset by a photo of Stiviano with the legendary Earvin "Magic" Johnson, which she had posted on Instagram, saying, among other things:

> It bothers me a lot you want to broadcast that you're associating with black people. Do you have to? [...]
>
> You can sleep with [black people]. You can bring them in, you can do whatever you want. The little I ask you is not to promote it on that... and not to bring them to my games. [...]
>
> I'm just saying, in your lousy [expletive] Instagrams, you don't have to have yourself with, walking with black people.[5]

I've listened to the whole recording, and I honestly have to say it doesn't sound to me like authentic hate speech, so I have no idea if Sterling really is racist or if he's just another jealous man who said things he shouldn't have said in a fit of anger. The question is, to what degree did the emotions involved affect his ability to assess the consequences of his words? Did he consider that, as a wealthy public figure, he might be recorded? Was he aware that his words might be presented to the American public, for whom racism is a particularly emotive topic? Did he consider how the NBA might react, and all the teams that are dominated by players of color? In other words, in deciding to talk to Stiviano about the photos in such a way, did Sterling make a conscious, rational decision?[6]

It's hard to comprehend the events, similarly drenched in powerful emotions, that occurred in the home of Oscar Pistorius, the South African athlete who for so long was the golden boy of the media and public opinion. Pistorius, also known as Blade Runner, lost both his legs before the age of one as a result of serious illness and for the rest of his life used artificial limbs. However, he didn't see this as a barrier to practicing sport, and alongside athletics, he played tennis and boxed. Eventually, though, he settled on the 400 m, in which he achieved better and better times. This was thanks not only to a natural talent bolstered by intensive training but also to the ever-improving prosthetics he ran in. In 2007, the sportsman achieved something that had previously been considered impossible: he participated in an official IAAF race meeting, competing against able-bodied athletes. In the years that followed, Pistorius set himself higher and higher goals, and while he wasn't able to compete at the 2008 Summer Olympic Games in Beijing, four years later he again made his mark in the annals of track and field by becoming the first disabled athlete to compete in the Olympic Games, held in London that year.

Simultaneously, Pistorius became a more public figure. TV stations and magazines of all types followed his life and achievements, creating a high-profile image of him as a sporting celebrity. The vast majority of people spoke positively about him, admiring his determination in achieving his dreams and citing him as an example of how to conquer personal challenges. A few criticized the admission of the runner to IAAF competitions, commenting that the ultra-modern carbon fiber prosthetics actually gave Pistorius an advantage over his able-bodied rivals.

This beautiful fairy-tale picture was shattered by the tragedy that took place in Pistorius's Pretoria home on February 14, 2013. That day, early in the morning, the runner shot his girlfriend, model Reeva Steenkamp, through the bathroom door, later claiming that he'd thought she was an intruder. The trial revealed at least several anomalies in his version of events: Pistorius fired two shots, but some sources claimed that, before her death, Steenkamp was also hit by a cricket bat, and neighbors testified that there had been previous arguments in the sportsman's home. Friends of the athlete admitted that he was quick to anger and had previously fired shots into the air.

Regardless of the truth of the matter, and whether or not Oscar Pistorius murdered his girlfriend, or if the whole sad story truly was a tragic accident, the same question arises: Did Pistorius, in either of the two scenarios, make a conscious decision, or was he guided by emotion, which prevented him from properly assessing the situation and the possible consequences?[7]

Bypassing the neocortex, responsible for rational thinking, happens not only under the influence of emotion or stimuli, but also in response to chemical stimulation. For example, the effects of C_2H_5OH on decision-making can be seen every weekend—just swing past a club or bar at night and observe the behavior of both sexes.

Just like unfaithful husbands, drunk clubbers mostly have the great good fortune that their unsavory behavior remains only in the memories of their partners in crime and probably results only in a hangover (this time both physical and moral) the following day. The actor Mel Gibson wasn't quite so lucky—his drunken antics provoked outrage in the media and were later analyzed in detail by US neurologist David Eagleman in his excellent book titled *Incognito: The Secret Lives of the Brain* (Gibson might not feel the same way about the book as I do, of course). On the night of July 28, 2006, the actor was stopped by California police on the Pacific Coast Highway for speeding and also asked to take a breath test—a reasonable request, seeing as his passenger was a half-empty bottle of tequila. The results of all this were not good for the actor, as not only did the test show a breath alcohol concentration (BrAC) of 0.12 percent, but the actor also lost his temper and his abusive comments were all placed in the report drawn up by James Mee, the police officer who had stopped Gibson's vehicle. A few days later, the report was leaked to the media and was published on— yes—TMZ.com. Internauts from across the globe learned that a drunk Mel Gibson said to the officer: "Fucking Jews ... the Jews are responsible for all the wars in the world," and went on to ask James Mee: "Are you a Jew?"[8]

When he sobered up and realized the scale of the problem, Gibson reacted immediately. The next day he read out a statement and apologized for the incident, explaining it was down to his alcoholism and declaring his will to continue battling it. Gibson added a further statement that was directly addressed to Jewish communities, which had been particularly offended by the actor's words:

> There is no excuse, nor should there be any tolerance, for anyone who thinks or expresses any kind of anti-Semitic remark. I want

to apologize specifically to everyone in the Jewish community for the vitriolic and harmful words that I said to a law enforcement officer the night I was arrested on a DUI charge. [...] The tenets of what I profess to believe necessitate that I exercise charity and tolerance as a way of life. [...] But please know from my heart that I am not an anti-Semite. I am not a bigot. Hatred of any kind goes against my faith.[9]

These words provoked a heated debate. Some took the actor's side, stating that Gibson wasn't the first person to say something under the influence of alcohol (or other substances) that didn't reflect their actual beliefs. It's worth noting that this attitude was strongly supported by film producer Dean Devlin, who is Jewish and one of the actor's closest friends, who stressed Gibson's devotion and loyalty to his family. Opponents put forth equally strong arguments that alcohol should not be shouldering the blame: TV host Mike Yarvitz actually got drunk on air to the same degree as Gibson had been and ironically ensured viewers that, despite being decidedly fuzzy-headed, he felt no urge to insult the Jews.

David Eagleman, then, asks an extremely interesting question: Will the real Mel Gibson please stand up? Are his authentic convictions and attitudes revealed in his sober statements to the media, or was his true face shown via the alcohol? *In vino veritas*? Or are there, in fact, two different Mel Gibsons, and both of them are ... true?

In the case of the film star, a similar mechanism to amygdala hijack seems to have occurred. Certain circuits appear to have been activated and, for a period, stomped all over the rational brain, switching off the processes of conscious analysis of the situation and drawing conclusions.

IN EACH of us, there appears to be an ongoing battle between logic and emotion, conscious and unconscious. Two mechanisms conflict, one trying to make choices based on cold, factual analysis (even if it's struggling with deficits in the cognitive mechanisms), the other, not so keen on this type of approach, unleashing the powerful forces lurking within us, such as sex drive or anger. Libido, powerful emotions, and alcohol are only a few examples of our frenemies—the range of foes inside our heads is much wider. Our unfettered emotions constantly battle our desire to make rational and considered decisions. Every single one of us has at some point said something we wish we hadn't, and the only thing that saves us from ourselves is that we're not famous—unlike the people above—and thankfully the mass media isn't remotely interested in our stupid utterances.

The two conflicting forces were named by Daniel Kahneman, the renowned psychologist, economist, and Nobel Prize winner, as System 1 (emotional, automatic) and System 2 (rational, logical). System 1 is also about thinking fast; System 2 about thinking slowly.[10] System 1 is responsible for creating automated decision schema, accelerating our actions. System 2 is a kind of supervisory board, making sure that important matters aren't treated in a routine manner (just like the approach to decision-making described in Chapter 4—routine versus the advocacy and inquiry modes). The problem is that System 2 doesn't always manage to get its voice heard, as the protagonists in this chapter found out to their cost when their rational thinking was overtaken by stimulants or libido. Worse still, when our "supervisory boards" lose control over our decision-making, we ourselves carry on thinking everything is fine and that we're still making considered rational decisions.

A classic experiment illustrating this trap, which our automated rapid thinking system sets for us, is the baseball bat and ball puzzle. It goes something like this:

A baseball bat and ball together
cost 1 dollar and 10 cents.
The bat costs a dollar more than the ball.
How much does the ball cost?

The puzzle looks ridiculously easy, and the majority of students tested answer right away without thinking that the ball costs 10 cents. Admit it—that's what you first thought too. If so, you made exactly the same mistake as the students, as the automatic, rapid response is given by System 1. However, if we set System 2 in motion and look closer at the problem, we see that the ball must cost 5 cents, and the bat $1.05. If the ball were to cost 10 cents, we'd have to pay $1.10 for the bat, giving us a total cost of $1.20, and so 10 cents too much. If you were taken in, don't get upset—you're in good company. More than half the students at Harvard, Princeton, and MIT whom researchers tested made the same mistake, and in some schools, the proportion of wrong answers was as high as 80 percent. Of course, the less focused we are, the more likely it is that our System 2 will miss the traps set for us by System 1. On the other hand, if even the form of the question demands that we concentrate, our analytical thinking is far more easily engaged. If the problem is presented in a typeface that's difficult to read, the number of right answers goes up significantly.

In another of Kahneman's uncomplicated experiments, he showed that it's enough to simply rephrase a question to get radically different answers. In 1982, at an international conference, he divided participants into two groups whom he asked to assess the prognoses for oil consumption for 1983. The first group was given a statement formulated in the simplest possible way: Demand for oil will fall in 1983 by 30 percent. The information given to the other group had slightly different information: Demand for oil in

1983 will fall by 30 percent due to increased prices for crude. As you may imagine, those in the second group presented a prognosis that they received as being far more credible and likely, thus falling headfirst into the trap of the narrative paradox. When we see information accompanied by a narrative that justifies what is being said, we see that information as more valuable, without bothering to test the cause and effect relation in the content.

In social psychology, this phenomenon is called *priming*, which involves triggering unconscious associations in the test subject that influence their decision-making. This effect is achieved by making subtle suggestions without the subject's noticing.

An example of how powerful priming can be is the famous experiment conducted by the psychologist John Bargh, in which New York University students participated. He divided them into two groups and asked them to solve simple questions involving four-word sentences from a mix of five words. The words were different for each group: the first set was chosen to be suggestive of tiredness and old age, the second set was not emotionally marked. Bargh and his associates observed the behavior of the students on finishing the experiment and measured how long it took them to walk down the corridor leading to the exit. The people from the first group walked significantly slower. This research was continued in further experiments demonstrating priming. For example, two English-speaking groups were primed with different sets of images and words. The first was bombarded with things connected to food (spaghetti, restaurants, cutlery, etc.), the second had things associated with the bathroom (shampoo, showers, towels, etc.). The two groups were later asked to perform a very simple task, supplying the missing letter in the word SO_P. It turned out that the vast majority of people in the first group chose the word SOUP, while almost all those in the second group wrote SOAP.

John Bargh carried out one further experiment, whose results have far more serious implications for our daily functioning. As in the test above, the students were divided into two groups, primed with different words. The first group solved tasks using words like *aggression, strength, hooligan, attack*, and so on; the second used words connected with gentleness (e.g., *compromise, respect, harmony*). On completing the experiment, Bargh asked the students to go one by one to the office of one of his associates to receive further instructions. When they arrived, the associate whom the students had gone to see was busy talking to someone else in his office. This pair carried on talking for ten minutes, paying no attention to the waiting student. Bargh wanted to measure the time it took for the waiting student to decide to interrupt the conversation. The difference between the two differently primed groups was massive. The "aggressively" primed students interrupted after about five minutes; those who were primed to be gentle ... didn't interrupt at all, patiently waiting their turn! I wonder what would have happened if the conversation time hadn't been limited to ten minutes ...

While tests like these have no influence on how we make decisions, they reveal the underlying decision-making mechanisms. Think about the last time you felt undermined and irritated the whole day, without any clear reason. Or the other way round—you got out of bed on the right side and spent the whole day feeling positive about things. If you can't recall a specific incident from the morning that could have evoked such feelings, it's entirely possible that you were unconsciously caught in the priming trap. It's a trap that businesses are using more and more frequently on their customers. Have you ever walked into a pricy, organic grocery store and bumped into a vase of fresh flowers by the entrance? Was the produce displayed on a tray of ice? Were the prices written in chalk on a blackboard? As if they changed every day ... Don't be fooled, all those accessories are deliberately placed to evoke associations of newness and freshness.

Another interesting phenomenon frequently encountered in business is the anchoring trap, a derivative of the priming trap. During the workshops on decision-making that I have the pleasure of running for managers of leading companies, I invite the participants to try a simple experiment. Each person gets a small piece of paper on which are written two questions, and each person is asked to answer them as quickly as possible. The exercise is individual, and participants are not allowed to use the Internet; if they don't know the answer, they have to guess, to answer according to their intuition. After a minute or so, I ask everyone in turn to read their answers to the second question, "What is the population of Burma?"[11] out loud. I write the answers on the flipchart. I start from one side of the room and initially nothing surprising happens. The values given are relatively close to one another and range from several to a dozen or so million. The surprise comes when I reach the second half of the participants on the other side of the room. They display more boldness, claiming the population of Burma is tens or even hundreds of millions. The effect is startling, and the difference is as plain as day. I have conducted this experiment several hundred times in the last few years, and it's always the same—there's always a massive difference between the answers of the two groups. The trick, though impressive, is extremely simple: although the second question for each group is the same, the first one is slightly different. Half the participants get a card with the question "Do more than 6 million people live in Burma?" with the option of answering YES or NO, followed by a question asking for a specific figure. The other half get a card with the first question "Do more than 50 million people live in Burma?" The number in the first question constitutes the anchor in this mini-experiment, which the participants' thoughts circle around. The phenomenon of anchoring is a popular tool for negotiators—if they have to purchase, for example, a certain product or service, they immediately propose a dramatically low figure, knowing full well that it's unrealistic but that, as the initial value, it becomes the anchor for further negotiation. In the sales situation, the technique is reversed, with the first figure stated being massively inflated.

What's worse, sometimes even what our senses perceive and pass on to our rational thinking brains (and so to Kahneman's system 2) can also be a delusion, leading to poor decisions. It's bad enough when this concerns a simple experiment where subjects are asked to switch on a light signal that the researchers have delayed by a few milliseconds (which our senses cannot perceive), and then, after several repetitions, remove the delay, completely surprising the test subjects, because to them, the signal started appearing before they pressed the switch.[12] But it's far worse when these types of delusion affect such a fundamental topic for some as... wine.

One of the biggest scandals in the world of enology unfolded on May 24, 1976, in Paris. This was a period of unquestioned domination by French wines, which were considered the best—period. However, someone decided to question the unquestionable—a British man called Steven Spurrier. Spurrier devoted his whole life to wine and was a top connoisseur. In 1970, he began working at a renowned London wine bar, later moving to Paris, where he opened his own wine store and set up the Académie du Vin, which became the first serious sommelier training school. Spurrier decided to test the quality of the wines from the New World that were ever more boldly marching onto the market in a blind-tasting comparison to which he invited leading French wine tasters. The test took place in Paris, and the jury consisted of nine leading French restaurateurs and sommeliers. Spurrier told the experts that they were going to taste ten well-known red and white wines, but that the bottles would be covered up, so as to conceal which wine was in their glasses. This was to enable them to focus exclusively on the wine and preclude the eventuality of favoritism or dislike in relation to specific producers. In both of the two tastings, four bottles contained French wine, the remaining six were Californian. Among the producers of red wines in the test were renowned French names from Burgundy and Bordeaux: Château Mouton-Rothschild, Château Montrose, Château Haut-Brion, and Château Leoville Las Cases. California was represented by Stag's Leap Wine Cellars, Ridge Vineyards Monte Bello, Heitz Wine Cellars Martha's Vineyard, Clos Du Val Winery, Mayacamas Vineyards, and Freemark Abbey Winery.

The results of the tests were shocking (especially for the French), as the expert ranking looked like this:

1. Stag's Leap Wine Cellars (California)
2. Château Mouton-Rothschild (France)
3. Château Montrose (France)
4. Château Haut-Brion (France)
5. Ridge Vineyards Monte Bello (California)
6. Château Léoville-Las Cases (France)
7. Heitz Wine Cellars Martha's Vineyard (California)
8. Clos Du Val Winery (California)
9. Mayacamas Vineyards (California)
10. Freemark Abbey Winery (California)

For white wine, the battle involved Domaine Roulot Charmes, Meursault, Beaune Clos des Mouches, Joseph Drouhin, Bâtard-Montrachet, Ramonet-Prudhon, and Puligny-Montrachet, Domaine Leflaive les Pucelles, representing France; while Chateau Montelena, Chalone Vineyard, Spring Mountain Vineyard, Freemark

Abbey Winery, Veedercrest Vineyards, and David Bruce Winery represented California. In this case, the puzzlement of the experts and observers was even greater, when the post-test ranking shaped up as follows:

1. Chateau Montelena (California)
2. Roulot, Meursault Charmes (France)
3. Chalone Vineyard (California)
4. Spring Mountain Vineyard (California)
5. Beaune Clos des Mouches Joseph Drouhin (France)
6. Freemark Abbey Winery (California)
7. Batard-Montrachet Ramonet-Prudhon (France)
8. Puligny-Montrachet Les Pucelles Domaine Leflaive (France)
9. Veedercrest Vineyards (California)
10. David Bruce Winery (California)

This famous Paris experiment ended less than positively both for the jurors and Spurrier. While only one journalist, from *Time*, had been present at the tasting—because wine enthusiasts throughout France claimed it wasn't worth bothering with anything so exotic as wine from the USA—the article he published provoked a storm. The French, who were totally unable to come to terms with the defeat (it would have been bad enough if their competitors had been from Tuscany or Ribera del Duero—but the USA!), treated the entire incident as a conspiracy, the Briton was declared *persona non grata*, and they questioned everything connected with the testing. The jurors were subjected to a barrage of criticism—one of the restaurateurs, for example, found some of his regular customers were boycotting his restaurant. And FYI, similar tests have been repeated many times since then. Spurrier himself, in collaboration with the wine magazine *Decanter*, carried out an identical duel in

2006, on the thirtieth anniversary of the Judgment of Paris, as the test came to be known.

When it comes to wine, it's a case of *de gustibus non est disputandum* (in matters of taste, there can be no disputes), but the experiment demonstrated a very interesting phenomenon from the point of view of decision-making. Our brains create a representativeness heuristic in order to help us negotiate a highly complex world, simplifying it somewhat by suggesting, for example:

French wine = better wine

Such a simplification can often lead us astray, and when we try to bypass the heuristic (by covering up the bottle), the effect can be surprising.[13]

Another classic heuristic, affecting not only wine, is the unconscious assumption that a more expensive product is a better one. It's been tested repeatedly, and the results are the same every time. One test subject was wine: in one classic version of the experiment, the subjects were told that they were to taste two wines, one costing a dozen dollars or so, the other several times that amount. Of course, the majority proclaimed that the second one tasted better, even though it was precisely the same drink as the first one. More shocking, though, were the results of the experiment when the subjects were placed in an MRI scanner and their brain activity measured while they tasted the wine. It turned out that while they were drinking the purportedly more expensive wine, there was more activity in the orbitofrontal cortex region (OFC). That's the region responsible for, among other things, experiencing pleasure. What does this mean? Well, it means the subjects were being truthful. It wasn't their wine snobbery telling them to praise the more expensive wine. No, that wine *really did* taste better, because their

brain responded more positively to the taste of the "more expensive" wine.

Each of these things means that even if we think we're behav-
ing rationally and logically, thoroughly analyzing the pros and cons
when we're trying to come to a decision, oftentimes we remain
under the influence of things that effectively render our choices
less than optimal. The world around us is certainly to some degree
an illusion, something we discover quite painfully only after we've
made up our minds.

Even if we operate entirely on a rational level and don't succumb
to any of these misapprehensions, we still remain under the influence of yet another powerful force—our social motives. Though
the subject is not a new one and has been thoroughly researched,
it is rarely considered in the context of decision-making, which is
surprising, bearing in mind the enormous influence motives have
on our choices. Research into social motives was conducted in the
second half of the twentieth century by an American psychologist and lecturer at Harvard and Boston University named David
McClelland. McClelland carried out a series of studies on personality and behavioral competencies, together with their application
in business, but his key accomplishment was the book *Human Motivation*. While the history of research into social motives dates back
to the work of Henry Murray, who worked out, among other things,
the Thematic Apperception Test (TAT), which examines projected
motives, McClelland was the first to go a step further and apply the
results of the research to leadership and decision-making.

There are three kinds of social motives. The first, called the need
for achievement—more commonly referred to as the *achievement
motive*—appears in the unconscious search for challenges, individual tasks presenting difficulties, which, when overcome, give
someone a strong feeling of internal power and satisfaction. People

with a high need for achievement will therefore try to take up new activities and aim to break records to do things better than anyone has done them before, to compete with those regarded as the best. McClelland's research showed that the achievement motive relates to success, especially in specialist and expert roles (I want to be the best in a given field, to overcome barriers, to constantly improve). One project also demonstrated a correlation between the popularity of this motive in society and overall levels of wealth.

The need for affiliation, or *affiliation motive*, is expressed through participating in social activities and joining groups characterized by harmony and good relations. Affiliative types are highly empathetic; they also unconsciously choose situations and tasks where they will have occasion to feel needed, liked, and accepted. In business, which as a rule isn't a very friendly environment for affiliative types, they can be found in roles connected with addressing customer needs and satisfaction, or as business partners improving cooperation with outside companies.

The need for power, or *power motive*, is displayed by those who feel a strong need to influence and control the world around them. People with a strong power motive will try to dominate, to deal the cards, all while creating an image of themselves as an important, influential, and high-ranking individual. While many people may regard the power motive as somewhat aggressive or unattractive, in business it is of enormous significance. People with a power motive usually develop excellent managerial skills, especially in difficult circumstances involving change. McClelland himself repeatedly stressed the importance of the power motive, in, for example, an article with the unambiguous title "Power Is a Great Motivator," published in the *Harvard Business Review*.

Every mentally healthy person harbors all these motives, but we vary in the degree to which we are driven by them. For some of us, affiliation will come first, power a little lower, and achievement last. Others will put achievement first, affiliation second, and power third. Yet others may have a strong need for power combined with relatively low levels of achievement and affiliation. What matters are the consequences that arise from which of the motives dominates in our personality, as this will quite strongly condition our actions toward those that will bring us the best motivational returns for our efforts.

The dominant social motive relates not only to our effectiveness in particular business roles, but also to our attitudes when decision-making. Each of the three motives exerts positive and negative influences on our choices.

People with a high achievement motive will look favorably at difficult but realistic scenarios and will make bold decisions that give them an opportunity to test themselves. A negative of the need for achievement is having a relatively low ability to engage others in the decision-making process, as the achievement motive also relates to a high degree of individualism. In business, managers with a high achievement motive don't cope well with delegating responsibilities and empowering others to make decisions, as they assume (often correctly) that they themselves would make a better choice.

People with a high need for affiliation face a different problem: they tend to avoid making decisions that in their opinion will upset or hurt others. Such difficult, but often essential decisions, like firing an ineffective employee, are a nightmare for an affiliative manager, which they will—more or less consciously—avoid by deciding to give the employee one more (last) chance. On the other hand, affiliative types are natural supporters of an inquiry approach, as they promote teamwork and always try to involve others in discussions. Even if they do so unconsciously, acting not so much to improve the analysis of a situation but to keep others happy by asking for their opinions, the positive influence on the decision-making process is unarguable.

The power motive, in turn, is useful when making tough decisions in a crisis or period of change management. Decision-makers with a high need for power will, and most often quite autocratically, promote radical solutions that they directly control. There are two huge minuses here: The first is the same as for those with a high achievement need, in that they will bypass other people's opinions, which occasionally makes it difficult to view a problem objectively. The second is their tendency to use their position to force through certain decisions, even if they are not the best ones. It's no accident that many charismatic leaders have a high power motive. Just how dangerous that can be was discussed in Chapter 3.

THE EMERGING picture is not reassuring. In everyday life, we assume that the reasons for bad decisions are scattered in the world around us. We blame others, who gave us crappy information; we curse our competitors, who got their new product right when we didn't; we criticize those who persuaded us to change our minds. Alas, we seem oblivious to the fact that we are our own greatest enemy—or more precisely, we are hostages to the highly volatile combination of our senses filtered through a fantastic and intricate thought-processing machine that controls our behavior: our brain.

We understand better and better how our brains work, how our emotions are not only created but also affect our decision-making. Conscious of our fallibility, we try to create systems and tools that will eliminate cognitive errors and improve the decisions we make. Hundreds of tests are in progress using MRI scanners, but in the case of some decisions, even they are helpless.

Maybe in the future, a solution will appear to protect us even against these errors.

9

PEERING THROUGH THE LOOKING GLASS

B EARING IN MIND how dangerous the world of black swans is, and how easy it is to succumb to turkey syndrome, anyone trying to predict how things might develop should go about it with a large dose of humility. There have already been innumerable predictions devised by professional analysts that turned out to be totally wide of the mark. For example, in 1964, the RAND Corporation, a think tank specializing in creating scientifically supported short-, medium-, and long-term scenarios, set up a group containing a dozen or so renowned experts from a variety of fields whom they asked to estimate when certain technologies might appear and when specific breakthrough events for humankind might occur. As far as landing on the Moon went, the experts got it pretty much on the nose, because, just like President

Kennedy said, they assessed that it would happen by 1970 at the latest. However, they also reckoned that there would be a permanent lunar base there a mere five years later. Also, by 1975, we were supposed to have 100 percent accurate weather forecasts, and by 1985, at the latest, there was supposed to be a manned mission to Mars. Humans as a species were also supposed to become entirely resistant to disease by 1997.[1]

The fact is that foreseeing the direction in which things will go in response to the appearance of new technologies and how people will utilize them is a minefield. Remembering how easy it is to under- or overestimate an event or trend, it's certainly worth looking at forces that not only have an enormous impact on the way we currently make decisions but will increasingly influence us in our decision-making.

THE POLISH science fiction author Stanisław Lem, when asked by a journalist in 2004 about how he envisioned the future of the world, replied in his inimitable style, "It will be the same, only more so." For me, this encapsulates what the main driving force behind decision-making in business will be in the years to come.

Although we have at our disposal the fantastic instrument that is our brain (despite its weaknesses), we are functioning in a world that is accelerating exponentially. We have less and less time to analyze data and apply a thorough inquiry approach, and the number of decisions demanding our attention is constantly increasing. The good news is that we have gained a natural ally in this crazy world, which—if we use it wisely—may provide decision-makers with very valuable support. Because, while the amount of information around us is increasing dramatically, so too are the technological capabilities to analyze that data.

Today, we are able to gather practically limitless amounts of data, which provides the foundation for business intelligence and tools supporting human decision-making. This is thanks to the technological revolution, which has drastically cut the price of digital memory. The cost of a 1 GB hard drive has dropped equally exponentially: in 1980, it cost an average of $440,000, though it could be even more expensive (e.g., Apple charged $3,500 for its 5 MB hard drive, so the cost of a gigabyte would amount to $700,000). Ten years later, the average cost of a gigabyte had dropped to just $11,000, and by 1995 that figure was 10 percent of that. In 2000, 1 GB of hard drive space cost a touch over $11.00, in 2005 that fell to $1.00, and five years after that it was calculated in cents (9 cents per GB on average). For example, the Seagate Barra-Cuda disk, with a capacity of 1.5 TB was priced in June 2010 at $89.00, or less than 7 cents per gigabyte. In 2017, the price of the latest version of the same disk was half that price, but by then cloud computing and the attendant cloud storage had arrived, so it really didn't matter anymore. Storing almost limitless data had become both absurdly simple and ridiculously cheap.

All this combined to lay the foundations for the developing phenomenon of what's currently termed Big Data, which has essentially revolutionized business analysis. Companies that find a way to use the bounty of data harvested wisely get a priceless support instrument, not only at an operational level but also in terms of strategic planning. Of course, support in making operational decisions is important, but using Big Data only to this end, despite its current domination, means failing to fully utilize its potential to improve strategic decision-making (this is excellently illustrated by the words often attributed to Mark Twain: "Most people use statistics like a drunk man uses a lamppost—more for support than illumination"). Making full use of Big Data, however, enables us to spot new market trends, new consumer behaviors, and the market potential for new products or services and breakthrough inventions.

Big Data is a great ally for the inquiry approach. It's now possible to access highly detailed information that might give us the answers to the questions that are troubling us.

RULE #13

Don't be a "decision drunk"—use data for illumination, not only for support. Data can be a great ally, when properly analyzed.

REGARDLESS OF the industry, technology is the hottest topic in business today. IBM's Global C-suite Study, conducted every two years with company presidents and CEOs, has been showing a clear trend in recent years. While in 2004 "technological factors" were rated sixth by the respondents in a list of factors identified as influencing the participating companies' futures, by 2012 they were in first place, and have remained there ever since.

Technological factors include more than just processing data. The Internet of Things (IoT) is important here, as it enables devices connected to the Internet to communicate with one another in real time to optimize their operation (in other words, making instantaneous decisions based on data without human involvement). All devices labeled "smart" use some application of the IoT: from smart cities through smart grids to smart homes. The number of appliances operating within the IoT today is in the tens of billions,[2] and the renowned advisory company McKinsey estimates that by 2025, the potential economic impact of the IoT will be worth $11.1 trillion.[3] With the development of deep learning (postulated in

1957 by Marvin Minsky) and deep neural networks, creating truly "intelligent" AI is just a question of time—AI in driverless cars is already becoming more reliable than a human decision-maker behind the steering wheel.

There is also enormous potential in blockchain technology, which some consider the most important innovation in the financial world in many years. The uses of blockchain go far beyond banking—in September 2017, the French insurance giant AXA introduced blockchain technology and the use of smart contracts to automatically compensate passengers for flight delays, for example.

Regardless of the accuracy of the predictions, we can be sure of one thing: in the years to come, rapidly changing technology will have ever-greater influence, as will rapidly changing methods of gathering, analyzing, and using data. This, in turn, will lead to increased automation of decision-making processes. If we don't fully understand these changes, we should seek out people who can navigate seamlessly through this new reality because they were born into it.

The passing of time means the arrival in the world of new generations who, every now and then, radically alter the view of reality through the values and attitudes they express. An example of such a change was the appearance between 1945 and 1965[4] of the Baby Boomers, who saw themselves as a generation of change. Among other things, the sexual revolution of the 1960s and '70s occurred during the period in which Baby Boomers were young adults. That period also heralded the arrival of the first wave of businesses availing themselves of new technologies and creating businesses based on new values—not using traditional "hard resources" and making things that lasted, but drawing on innovation and human capital. Members of that generation include Bill Gates, Paul Allen, Larry

Ellison, and Richard Branson. Steve Jobs was a Baby Boomer, too. With time, the Baby Boomers began being replaced by Generation X, people born between 1965 and 1983.[5] A characteristic feature of this generation was the further liberalization of attitudes and habits (affecting religion, race, sexuality), but this was accompanied by a less revolutionary approach to reality. Where the Baby Boomers genuinely aspired to overthrow earlier ideals and behaviors, replacing them with their own, the majority of Generation X was keener to fit into the existing scheme of things (hence, for example, the blossoming trend in recent years for classic corporate careers and unfettered consumerism).

In the middle of the 1980s, there appeared a new generation, named Generation Y, or, from the turn of the century, Millennials. We can easily see that Generation Y consists of people who have spent almost their entire, conscious lives enjoying the benefits of virtual lifestyles and technologies which were innovations for earlier generations who had to learn to use them.[6] Research carried out by Boston Consulting Group in 2012 showed that the basic difference between Generations X and Y lies (not surprisingly) in how they use the Internet. While both generations spend a similar amount of time online, Millennials spend that time predominantly on social media platforms, building and expanding their virtual world. Not surprisingly, social media and mobile devices have become fundamental means of communication for Generation Y.

This natural ability that new generations have for assimilating and using technologies that constituted a sea change for older generations is brilliantly captured by Don Tapscott (himself a classic representative of the Baby Boomers) in his book *Grown Up Digital*, where he describes a scene that played out one day in 1997 in his own home, with his twelve-year-old son Alex as the unwitting lead role. That day, Alex discovered that Don, a noted figure in the world of new technology, was taking part in a TV program, during which he was to demonstrate to viewers a newfangled piece of technology called the Internet. When Alex's mom told him about the program he reacted like this:

> That's the dumbest TV show I've heard of. Why would anyone want to watch Dad use the Internet? [...] Mom, this is so embarrassing. All my friends are going to see it. You don't need to show people how to use the Internet.[7]

When Don heard about Alex's reaction, he asked his son why he thought that way, and got the following reply:

> Dad, no offense, but I think you adults are obsessed with technology. You call this a technology revolution and you are so fascinated by how technology works. Imagine some other technology, Dad. [...] The television—is that a technology to you, Dad? Imagine a TV show where people watch you surf television! Wow! Let's see if my dad can find a football game on television! Now my dad is going to try and find a sitcom.[8]

If that wasn't enough, Don's daughter, one year older than Alex, chipped in with her two cents:

> Yeah Dad, how about a refrigerator? Remember, it's a technology, too. Why don't we have a TV show where we can all watch you surf the fridge? Check this out, my dad has found some meatloaf...[9]

That just about sums it up. Something that seemed a breakthrough to Generation X and the Baby Boomers, and that they had to make a conscious effort to adapt to, is to Millennials, who were born into a digital world, as natural as breathing.

RULE #14

Never ignore the values and convictions of other generations, especially those only just entering the market. Even if their influence on decision-making today is minimal, the new normal means this may change sooner than you expect.

ONE OF the most interesting mechanisms enabled by technology and social media is *crowdsourcing*, a term coined by Jeffrey Howe in *Wired* magazine in June 2006. Put simply, crowdsourcing involves using modern technologies to engage large groups of people—often millions—in a specific task. It is used both in business and in projects of a social and academic nature.

One of the oldest examples of crowdsourcing is the SETI program, which has been running since the 1960s. SETI—the Search for Extraterrestrial Intelligence—was initiated in 1960 by American astronomer Frank Drake of Cornell University, and its aim was to analyze signals from outer space registered by radio telescopes that were looking for specific patterns that might indicate that the signals had an intelligent origin. The first targets were the stars Tau Ceti and Epsilon Eridani (chosen because they're at the relatively close distance of 12 and 10.5 light-years, respectively), which the Green Bank Observatory's radio telescope listened into at a frequency of 1,420 MHz. While the project didn't provide the hoped-for results, the researchers weren't deterred, and the next phase of observations extended to monitoring as many as 650 stars over four years. One of the listening instruments used in this stage was Ohio State University's Big Ear radio telescope. With the help of this device, on August 15, 1977, an unusually strong signal was registered. It was named the WOW! signal, after a note made by Dr. Jerry Ehman, who observed it. The signal came from the constellation of Sagittarius and was never repeated, but it gave scientists new hope of using their method to find intelligent life elsewhere in the universe. Other institutes (including Berkeley University) joined the SETI program, and even NASA showed an interest. More and more listening installations were used, including the largest single radio telescope in the world, near Arecibo in Puerto Rico.

Initially, only the scientific personnel of a dozen or so institutions were involved. It soon emerged, though, that there was a prodigious amount of data to be analyzed, far exceeding the capabilities of the computers the scientists had at their disposal, and so a bottleneck developed. In 1999, someone had a bright idea. Seeing the limitations on their computing power and the impossibility of adding further supercomputers to their inventory, the scientists decided to turn to scaling. They asked hundreds of thousands of Internauts from around the world to participate in the project, asking them to download onto their home computers a special screensaver that analyzed packs of data taken from the Internet while the computer wasn't being otherwise used. When the owner wanted to use their computer, the screensaver and the analysis were switched off.

The SETI@home project was officially launched on May 17, 1999. The scientists hoped to acquire 100,000–150,000 users, but such hopes turned out to be modest, to say the least. Over 5 million people from 233 countries signed up, and their combined computer power in the following years provided a calculating time of over 2 million years (yup!). By mid-2013, the total calculating power of SETI@home was 670 teraflops (that's 670 trillion floating-point operations per second).

While the SETI@home project hasn't resulted in any contact with extraterrestrial intelligence, it does offer an amazing example of exploiting the possibilities of new technologies in developing crowdsourcing campaigns. Another milestone in this area was Wikipedia, where the combined intellectual effort of millions of Internet users led to the creation of the largest compendium of knowledge in human history. These were just two of many events that encouraged other firms to attempt something similar. Two interesting examples of business applications of crowdsourcing against a backdrop of open innovation were My Starbucks Idea, set up by the coffee chain, and IdeaStorm, set up by Dell. Another was InnoCentive, an open innovation platform that helped to connect the world of large corporations seeking a solution to a specific problem with that of millions of experts (be it individuals or small organizations) who might be able to help.

When it comes to decision-making, crowdsourcing can be an interesting ally on several levels. First, in the case of decisions affecting the customer, engaging a large number of them gives an organization a unique perspective, so we can very precisely assess which choice will win the greatest approval among those whose opinions are of the greatest importance to us. This approach is also used in some places by local communities and authorities trying to decide how to allocate what are often referred to as citizens' budgets: a pool of public finances that local residents, not the authorities, can decide how to use by voting for—in their opinion—the most beneficial initiative. The point of this is to ensure that funds are allocated in a way that reflects locals' priorities. Some businesses have behaved similarly, allowing customers and partners to decide to whom a company distributes its corporate social responsibility (CSR) funds.

Second, crowdsourcing can be used to provoke or deepen the inquiry approach. If we can engage people from different circles and with different points of view in the discussion, we have a better chance of examining a problem from every possible angle.

Third, we can use crowdsourcing in decision-making to multiply the potential for compiling a complete picture of a situation and questioning the status quo, which in the world of the new normal is enormously beneficial. Many companies that take this path use the dispersed leadership approach, in which every employee is expected to display leadership, speaking out about any threats and opportunities they perceive, and actively promoting new approaches and solutions to the company. There will be more on this topic in the Epilogue.

Crowdsourcing and its related tools are also revolutionizing areas that at first glance might not seem threatened by the growth of online social networking mechanisms. An obvious example is the *Encyclopædia Britannica*, whose activities and product seemed far removed from the dynamically developing new technologies, but which eventually was seriously impacted by new trends and forced to radically reorganize its business model. Other traditional businesses have been similarly affected (Uber, Airbnb), and have also been forced to admit that crowdsourcing and its related tools have turned their worlds upside down.

Internet communities and the solutions emerging from them, such as crowdsourcing, are the natural environments of and an obvious mode of operating for Generation Y. Due to their nature (virtually free to use, increasingly credible and valuable), they are attracting more and more people of a slightly older vintage, for whom they have also become a priceless tool in making the best possible decisions with the help of Big Data.

RULE #15

The world of data overload is also a world of new possibilities.
Actively seek out opportunities to engage a cost-free force
that can radically improve the quality of your decision-making.

FAR MURKIER possibilities lurk in the current and future development of nanotechnology and digital biology. As you probably know, one of the commonest reasons for bad decisions being made is the fallibility of human memory. Scientists disagree wildly in their assessments of the capacity of the human brain: according to Paul Reber, a professor of psychology at Northwestern University, we have at our disposal a gigantic memory capable of storing around 2.5 petabytes (!) of data; Ralph Merkle, a nanotechnology and cryptography expert, is far more cautious, estimating its capacity at a "mere" several hundred megabytes. This enormous disparity isn't actually very significant to our current context, because the problem lies elsewhere. As humans, our bottleneck isn't the quantity of data we can store, but the permanence of its recording. Unlike the hard drive of a computer, where data can only be erased through the deliberate action of the user (deleting data), in the case of the human brain, data can be retained only fleetingly—think of the times you've forgotten the five things you went to the store for, within minutes of making a mental list of them. We simply forget, whether it's important data, stakeholders we need to take into account, or our previous experiences in similar situations, and so on.

Our susceptibility to illusion (see Chapter 8) and imperfections in our memory combine to form one of two fundamental barriers to our making full use of the capabilities Big Data provides; the second is the fallibility of intelligence ... artificial intelligence, which, in comparison to our amazing brains, is still limited in pattern recognition. We still can't get computers to emulate the workings of our brains.

It's only a question of time, though. Ray Kurzweil, the American visionary and futurologist, believes we are hurtling toward an epoch in which these weaknesses will be eliminated, or—if you prefer—there will be a fusion of the strengths of both computers and the human brain. In practice, this phenomenon will take the form of better and better machines enabling faster and better decision-making in situations where a human wouldn't normally have even a hypothetical chance of reacting in time. The phenomenon of a computer's being able to fully emulate the functions of the human brain has been named by Kurzweil, borrowing from quantum physics, a "singularity." According to Kurzweil, singularity will be achieved before 2030, ushering in a whole new reality for making decisions.

The second aspect of improving decision-making processes in the future, and so eliminating the weaknesses of the human brain, looks a little terrifying. According to Kurzweil, the solution to poor memory will no longer be dubiously effective infusions of Chinese herbs. Their role will be taken over by microscopic hard drives implanted into our brains. If you're thinking right now that such a combination of nanotechnology and bioengineering—an artificial piece of equipment with living tissue—seems like an ethically unacceptable development, think back a little. Just such a fusion took place many years ago and is already commonplace. How else would you describe a pacemaker?

Furthermore, the cost of human genome sequencing dropped from $2.7 billion in 2003 to $1,000 in 2017, and one start-up has announced that it will bring it down to $100 very soon. With genetic engineering tools such as CRISPR-Cas9, we can not only read but also write DNA, which means we will at some point be able to modify the physical and intellectual capacities of a human being (which obviously raises hundreds of ethical issues).

Let's return, though, to the present, where, with all due regard to the intellectual scope of Ray Kurzweil's imagination, it's still arguable in which form such long-term prospects are likely to manifest. I believe that the really smart thing is to closely monitor the development of the key meta-trends (as they are less vulnerable to being overturned or destroyed by black swans), and avoid turkey syndrome and being too taken in by suspiciously precise predictions uttered by various silver-tongued orators. And let's hope that all this effort to support us does not lead to the total automation of the decision-making process. To err is human, and many wonderful innovations have emerged as a result of this "weakness." Thanks to gross negligence by scientists, we have acquired, among other things, penicillin (how lucky we are that Alexander Fleming was untidy) and Viagra (a side effect of developing a medicine designated UK92480, for people suffering from angina). Thanks to simple human error, William Roentgen discovered X-rays, the artificial sweetener saccharin was discovered by accident, the first fireworks were accidentally set off, the ability of microwaves to cook food was discovered unwittingly, the glue on Post-it notes was a failed super glue... and so on.

And then there are the decisions that we can't evaluate using a cold, binary logic, because while they might be the right choices, they may have little to do with rationalism.

THERE IS a most beguiling scene about making choices in Mikhail Bulgakov's fabulous novel *The Master and Margarita*. The eponymous heroine is having a difficult time. Her love, the Master, has been placed in a psychiatric hospital and subsequently become depressed and lost his inspiration for his work on a biography of Pontius Pilate. Meanwhile, on Earth (more precisely in Moscow), Woland, a.k.a. Satan, has appeared with his retinue, intending to celebrate his annual ball of the dead. The tradition is that Woland must be served by a local woman named Margarita who will be granted a wish after the ball. As you might guess, she agrees, and, after an extraordinary night stands once more before Woland, who awaits her wish.

> "And so, Margot," Woland went on, softening his voice, "what do you want for having been my hostess tonight? [...] Rouse your fantasy, spur it on!" [...]
>
> Silence ensued, interrupted by Koroviev, who started whispering in Margarita's ear: "Diamond donna [...] I advise you to be reasonable! Or else fortune may slip away."
>
> "I want my beloved master to be returned to me right now, this second," said Margarita.[10]

Margarita's choice of wish is rational only from her perspective, and also perhaps the Master's; for anyone else, including Woland's retinue, it is completely incomprehensible. I do hope, though, that despite the predictions of futurologists and science fiction authors, there will still be room in the future for making choices that might seem pointless to others but are the right ones for us, whatever any super-advanced fifteenth-generation quantum computer might think of them.

EPILOGUE

O
UR ODYSSEY THROUGH the twists and turns of decision-making began with reflections on a movie about a mad world, so it seems apt to end with a movie.

Producers Jerry Bruckheimer and Don Simpson have teamed up many times with director Tony Scott, and each time the results were better than average (certainly in terms of profit). Who doesn't remember *Top Gun* from the mid-eighties? Tom Cruise, Val Kilmer, Anthony Edwards, and the then little-known Tim Robbins sat behind the joystick of an F-14 as cadets at the elite United States Air Force Fighter Weapons School, with Tom Skerritt and Michael Ironside in the roles of their instructors.[1] A few years later, the production and direction trio went from sky to sea, resulting in the excellent *Crimson Tide*, which hit movie theaters in 1995. The action takes place onboard the nuclear-weapon–carrying submarine USS *Alabama*, commanded by Captain Frank Ramsey (played brilliantly by Gene Hackman), and the first officer, second in command, Lt. Cmdr. Ron Hunter (played equally brilliantly by Denzel Washington).

Ron Hunter is a highly educated officer, but somewhat green in combat conditions. His intelligence and expertise enable him to assess the state of play and analyze matters very broadly, something he is keen to do. Frank Ramsey, on the other hand, believes in total obedience and deference to the hierarchy. For him, following procedures and giving clear commands to the crew are sacrosanct. His conviction is reinforced by many years of combat experience and successful missions. The men's disparate perspectives rapidly descend into conflict. During a rocket-launching procedure, Captain Ramsey gives an order that Hunter is supposed to immediately repeat out loud without thinking, a double command being a formal requirement for a launch. Hunter, though, asks if the decision is correct, thus irritating Ramsey. Later, in private conversation, he explains the reasons for his anger to his first officer, at the same time clearly setting out his principles and values, which are essentially that those in command should present a united front at all times and not be seen questioning each other. Ramsey makes his views on the subject crystal clear: "We're here to preserve democracy, not to practice it."[2]

Later still, the situation becomes much more threatening. The plot isn't complicated—it resembles a somewhat improved and more realistic version of *Top Gun*. Russia is engulfed by civil war and the ultra-nationalist Vladimir Radchenko, backed by military units loyal to him, seizes a nuclear missile installation. The rebels make demands and the situation escalates, threatening nuclear war with the United States. As you might have guessed, the USS

Alabama is sent to an area near the Russian border with the aim of eliminating Radchenko and the threat to the USA. The Americans don't want to attack prematurely, so they wait for a signal that the rebels are genuinely preparing to launch missiles. When military satellites register the rockets being fueled, it can only mean one thing: Radchenko has ordered an attack. The captain of the USS *Alabama* receives an order to carry out a preemptive strike and launch ten Trident missiles at the nuclear base held by the rebels. But during launch preparations, the *Alabama* comes under attack by a Russian Akula-class submarine and is forced to hide in the depths, interrupting the launch procedure. While the *Alabama* is diving, it receives another order, but because of a sudden communications problem caused by the attack, the message is incomplete—it contains only the words "nuclear missile strike" and no solid, useable information. This leads to a heated exchange between the commander and his first officer, with each interpreting the situation differently. In Ramsey's view, in accordance with procedure, the last *complete* message is the binding one, and so they should again try to launch the missiles. The first officer, aware that the command center wanted to pass on new information, possibly amending the earlier order, demands that they surface and make contact with HQ in order to verify the order. The other officers on the bridge witness the ensuing argument between Ramsey and Hunter, with Hunter insisting that his superior take time to assess the situation rather than blindly following protocol. Frustrated, Hunter draws Ramsey's attention to a key aspect of that protocol:

> Captain Ramsey, under operating procedures governing the release of nuclear weapons we cannot launch our missiles unless both you and I agree! Now this is more than formality, sir. This is why your command must be repeated! It requires my assent! I do

not give it, and, furthermore, if you continue upon this course and insist upon this launch without confirming this message first . . .[3]

A furious Ramsey threatens to arrest Hunter for mutiny—only to find Hunter quoting from the regulations and effectively ordering Ramsey's own arrest.

Captain Ramsey never expected the procedure to be used in such a manner. Arrested by the COB (Chief of the Boat), he's led to his cabin and locked in. Hunter and the COB are extremely uneasy about how matters have unfolded, not least because they aren't convinced that Ramsey's orders were actually wrong.

As you've probably guessed, Ramsey, as an old salt, has no intention of giving in, but for those who haven't seen it (you should!), I won't issue a spoiler. We can, however, ask which of the protagonists in this case was right. The insubordinate Hunter, or the experienced captain, who acted precisely in accordance with the rules? Even if, in the final analysis, the first officer made the right decision in halting the attack, shouldn't breaking protocol and refusing to obey a superior officer have some consequences? What if the rebels had launched an attack while Hunter and Ramsey argued about procedures?[4]

Crimson Tide is just a movie about a fictional event, but when we consider the potential consequences of the wrong decision, it's enough to make your blood run cold. The terrifying fact is that a highly similar incident did actually take place.

At the beginning of the 1980s, there was a sharp downturn in relations between the superpowers. The reason for this was the hard line adopted by President Reagan, symbolized by the launching of the Strategic Defense Initiative (SDI), later referred to as Star Wars, coupled with the ongoing struggle for power within the Central Committee of the Communist party following the death of Leonid Brezhnev on November 10, 1982. These power plays were bookended by a number of other dangerous events: the outbreak of the war in Afghanistan, the deployment of SS-20 missiles by the Soviets, operation RJAN (a Soviet simulation of full readiness to launch nuclear missiles), and the USA's boycott of the 1980 Olympics in Moscow. On top of all this, on September 1, 1983, a Soviet Su-15 fighter shot down a Korean Air Lines Boeing 747 that had entered Soviet airspace near Kamchatka during a flight from Anchorage to Seoul. All 269 people on board were killed. Tensions reached a peak, and the prospect of nuclear war was increasingly likely, with every move of the enemy being closely observed.

The early warning system in the Soviet Union at that time was based on a network of military satellites known as Oko, which passed on data to the Serpukhov-15 monitoring station to the south of Moscow. One of the officers serving at Serpukhov was Stanislav Yevgrafovich Petrov, a forty-four-year-old Lt. Col. in the USSR Air Force. On September 26, 1983, at precisely four minutes past midnight, he saw a message on his screen that he had hoped never to see: the system told him a ballistic rocket was being launched from the Malmstrom Air Force Base in Montana. A minute later, another alarm went off in the command room, alerting Petrov to the launch of four more missiles from the same base.

Procedure clearly set out what actions Petrov should take. The first step was to inform the First Secretary at the time, Yuri Andropov, of a nuclear assault. Andropov was co-creator of Operation RJAN, and utterly convinced of the aggressive intentions of his country's adversary. Petrov was perfectly aware of what the consequences of passing on a sparse, terse message to the ailing former KGB boss would be: global nuclear war. So the colonel took an unusually bold decision: assessing the situation, he decided to disregard the procedure and not inform the authorities. He assumed that no one would initiate World War III by launching just five missiles, so the early warning system must be the result of a fault or error of some kind. Of course, he couldn't be certain, and like Ron Hunter in *Crimson Tide*, he went through twenty-five minutes of hell, not knowing if the American warheads would hit. If his decision to flout the rules had been wrong, the Soviet Union would have ceased to exist.

Ultimately, it turned out that the signal about the missile launch was a false alarm; the poorly designed satellite early warning system had interpreted the sun reflecting off a high layer of cloud as a sign of a missile launch and triggered the alert. If at that time in Serpukhov the equivalent of Captain Frank Ramsey had been perched in front of the monitors, you wouldn't be reading this book now. Fortunately, it was Stanislav Petrov sitting there, a man who had the courage to think for himself and most likely saved the world from nuclear destruction.[5]

Both these cases, fictional and true, have a common denominator—the justified breaking of established procedure. It is a classic dilemma that we often encounter in the business world. So why do we bother setting up decision-making procedures? To what end do we create management algorithms? What should we do in a black swan situation (e.g., receiving an incomplete order because of a communications breakdown)? Aren't procedures created for just such situations, guaranteeing a predictable response from a manager, team, or organization? Or is it precisely in those circumstances that we should abandon those procedures because they were created in ignorance of the ongoing situation? Do we need fixed rules, or an individual assessment of the situation?

Well-defined, regularly updated procedures provide several measurable benefits. First, they increase the likelihood of the right decision being made by an employee, because they're based on the accumulated experience of many individuals and have been repeatedly tested. In this way, we reduce the risk of poor decisions being made by a relatively inexperienced person. Second, procedures increase the predictability of an organization, which is important, not only from the management perspective, but also from the perspective of other employees (we know what to expect in any situation). Third, operating procedures can speed up responses in certain situations, as things happen along tried and tested lines. Fourth, in many cases, procedures provide an extra level of safety in key company processes, like the routine preflight checks before a plane takes off. In this sense, procedures guarantee that no fundamental issues will be ignored in any given instance.

So, it might seem that there is no simpler recipe for making the right decisions outside of a well-defined, comprehensively tested, and consistently improved set of procedures, with clearly identified roles, rights, and responsibilities assigned to individual employees. Unfortunately, the two situations described above show that there are situations in which even the best possible procedures turn out to be a poor advisor—just following the rules could lead to a nuclear catastrophe. So, the situation in which procedures might let you down are precisely those of a black swan. This shouldn't come as a surprise, seeing as they can also be called "events outside procedure" and are something for which we are entirely unprepared (so any established rules can't take into account the new realities). At that point, the human aspect becomes crucial. Bombarded by information, we are subject to emotions and exposed to all kinds of traps set up by our minds.

Such situations are a particular challenge to leaders.

The model of the single charismatic leader is now falling into disuse and though many of us still admire such visionaries as Steve Jobs, Richard Branson, Jack Welch, and Elon Musk, investors' attention is drawn more and more to highly effective and profitable firms led by—are you ready for this?—decidedly uncharismatic people. It turns out that the key to success lies in building great teams and shaping the organizational culture in such a way that many people display leadership, not just the chairperson or managing director. During one of the *Harvard Business Review* conferences I spoke at in Poland, I named this the "model of dispersed leadership."

Dispersed leadership means helping employees to develop certain habits and attitudes, encouraging them to be aware of changes taking place in the business world, to observe the world around them through a critical lens, and to feel able to speak about trends they're observing that could have an impact on the business. This entails empowering employees to assume a level of responsibility and make decisions that correlate with their level of authority. It also means understanding the influence that different people have on the quality of decision-making. Developing such attitudes in employees means that in any company, there will be dozens, hundreds, even thousands of "daily leaders," who operate just like the major decision-makers described elsewhere in this book. This will give any company the biggest gain it could wish for—minimized business risk. You might think that encouraging people to make independent decisions increases risk rather than reducing it, and it's true that in a dispersed leadership model the number of minor errors made by employees in good faith increases. However, it radically reduces the strategic risk of failing to spot a black swan on the horizon, and of making a decision that would be wrong for the organization as a whole. Think back to the story of *Encyclopædia Britannica*: an employee there spotted the approaching black swan (Wikipedia), recognized the threat, and told his superiors. However, they ignored the signal and just carried on operating in their tried and tested way. It wasn't long before they realized they'd made a terrible mistake. It's worth remembering, then, that while the predictability of employees' behaviors falls in a dispersed model, and the number of minor errors increases, the quality of the most important decisions improves. The enormous benefit of reducing strategic risk always outweighs the harm caused by smaller errors. Dispersed leadership counterbalances charismatic leadership, enabling us to avoid its central weakness—bad decisions made by a leader whom no one questions.

This isn't just a theory, as the world of aviation discovered.

IN THE 1970s, there were a number of catastrophes that shared a common denominator: flight crew rarely doubted the wisdom of a pilot's decision, and even if they did have doubts, they were too afraid to confront the pilot with their concerns. The rigorous recruitment procedures and training, as well as the requirement to accumulate experience amounting to thousands of flying hours logged, meant that passenger flight pilots had achieved almost god-like status among other employees. During a flight, the captain was the absolute authority and his (they were mostly men at that time) decisions were never to be questioned. The copilot, flight engineer, head of the cabin crew, and flight attendants simply did their jobs and obeyed the captain's orders. The system worked as long as the captain made the right choices. When he was wrong, the remaining crew members were in no position to oppose him—or even to express their opinions or concerns.

The air accident commission investigation into the biggest aviation disaster in history, which killed 583 people on Tenerife in 1977, revealed that the catastrophe was in large part caused by this flawed system. On March 27, a few minutes after midnight, a bomb went off in the terminal buildings of Gran Canaria Airport, the islands' main airport, injuring several people. Following this incident, most flights were redirected to Los Rodeos airport on the neighboring island of Tenerife. During the day, air traffic control at Los Rodeos buckled under the pressure of the extraordinarily crowded airspace and runway aprons, where plane after plane was landing. The situation was made worse by difficult weather conditions, including thick fog, as well as the fact that, as it was Sunday, there were only two controllers on duty to cope with the massively increased air traffic. Shortly after 5:00 pm, a catastrophic collision of two Boeing 747s occurred. A KLM plane that was taking off smashed into a Pan Am airliner at almost 125 miles per hour, killing everyone on board the Dutch jumbo jet (248 people) as well as 335 passengers and crew on the Pan Am aircraft; 61 people survived.

Among various issues highlighted as causes of the tragedy, one needs to be looked at here: the excessive authority enjoyed by the KLM captain and the context in which he made the decision to take off. Behind the joystick of the Dutch plane was KLM's most experienced pilot, fifty-year-old Jacob Veldhuyzen van Zanten, who was also an instructor for the airline. Irritated by the long wait on the apron,[6] he decided to begin taxiing, despite the thick fog and the fact that poor communications with air traffic control meant he couldn't be 100 percent certain that he had permission to take off. The captain's decision worried the flight engineer who, despite his lower position and significantly less experience, was bold enough to ask the commanding officer whether the Pan Am plane had really cleared the runway. The captain replied curtly, in a firm, assured voice, "*Jawel*" ("Yes, of course"), so the engineer acquiesced. Fifteen seconds later, the two aircraft collided.

The dangers resulting from the authority trap—the lack of psychological safety, lack of open communication, and the ensuing limited ability to analyze the situation—can be seen even more clearly in the disaster that took place barely eighteen months later in the USA. On December 28, 1978, a United Airlines DC-8 flying from Denver to Portland, piloted by the experienced fifty-two-year-old Malburn McBroom, ran out of fuel not far from its destination airport and crash-landed. The crash killed 10 people, including 2 crew members; 179 people survived. The investigation conducted by the National Transportation Safety Board (NTSB) showed that during the landing approach there was a fault with the landing gear: the indicator light showing that the gear had been deployed didn't come on. Captain McBroom decided to abort the landing to check the condition of the landing gear. He then focused on that issue so much that he didn't notice that he was almost out of fuel. It emerged later that he had also ignored the warnings of other crew members who raised the problem, a point stressed in the NTSB report:

> The probable cause of the accident was the failure of the captain to monitor properly the aircraft's fuel state and to properly respond to the low fuel state and the crew-member's advisories regarding fuel state. This resulted in fuel exhaustion to all engines. His inattention resulted from preoccupation with a landing gear malfunction and preparations for a possible landing emergency.
>
> Contributing to the accident was the failure of the other two flight members either to fully comprehend the criticality of the fuel state or to successfully communicate their concern to the captain.[7]

The report also included a recommendation that instigated a revolution in flight crew communications and in-flight decision-making:

> [It is recommended to] issue an operations bulletin to all air carrier operations inspectors directing them to urge their assigned operators to ensure that their flight crews are indoctrinated in

principles of flight deck resource management, with particular emphasis on the merits of participative management for captains and assertiveness training for other cockpit crewmembers.[8]

This recommendation provided the impetus to start work on CRM—Cockpit Resource Management, later renamed Crew Resource Management—a breakthrough approach that would increase aviation safety. Working on and implementing CRM radically improved the quality of decisions made by pilots and meant numerous tragedies were averted. The foundation of the system is very similar to the dispersed leadership model—in CRM, the key to better decision-making by pilots is the greater involvement of other crew members in the process, improving the flow of information, and ensuring the relevant level of psychological safety is in place. CRM requires all crew members to be proactive and assertive, immediately and openly inform their colleagues about any concerns or doubts, and cross-check all decisions. Today, this standard applies to all personnel flying on every commercial airline; its effectiveness was demonstrated on July 19, 1989, a few years after its introduction, when the crew of United flight 232 from Denver to Chicago was faced with a serious technical problem.

The McDonnell Douglas DC-10, used by airlines since 1971, had a very rare engine arrangement—as well as the standard two jet engines under the wings, it had a third engine, built into the vertical stabilizer. This engine was the cause of the United 232 catastrophe. At 3:16 pm, when the plane was at an altitude of 37,000 feet, the engine exploded, damaging all three independent hydraulic flight control systems. Alfred C. Haynes, piloting the aircraft, subsequently lost not only one of his engines, but worse still, all ability to steer the plane. The incident was a classic black swan, as the simultaneous failure of all three hydraulic systems had seemed highly implausible and so no standard response procedure was in place for it. Captain Haynes, a highly experienced fifty-seven-year-old pilot, knew that the chances of his finding a solution alone were virtually zero. From the very start, he involved his colleagues, first officer William Records and flight engineer Dudley Dvorak. In addition, when the captain informed the passengers of the necessity to carry out a crash-landing, first-class passenger Dennis Fitch stepped forward—he just happened to be a DC-10 flying instructor working for United, and he played a vital role in the preparations for landing. In the minutes that followed, the crew steered the plane using only engine numbers 1 and 3, trying to orient the plane toward the nearby Gateway Airport in Sioux City, and gradually losing altitude. Haynes, piloting in turns with Fitch, managed the impossible, flying the plane to its impromptu destination. Due to the damaged controls, the aircraft landed at a speed of 273 miles per hour (it's usually around 160 miles per hour) and with a rate of descent seven times the norm. The plane's right wing touched the runway and the aircraft broke up. Of the 296 people onboard, 111 were killed; the others were saved by the astounding cooperation between the crew and instructor, who adhered to CRM standards. Captain Haynes himself confirmed:

> But the preparation that paid off for the crew was something that United started in 1980 called Cockpit Resource Management, or Command Leadership Resource Training, or any number of things that you want to call it. I think we called it CLR to start with ... Up until 1980, we kind of worked on the concept that the captain was THE authority on the aircraft. What he says, goes. And we lost a few airplanes because of that. Sometimes the captain isn't as smart as we thought he was. And we would listen to him, and do what he said, and we wouldn't know what he's

talking about. And we had 103 years of flying experience there in the cockpit, trying to get that airplane on the ground, not one minute of which we had actually practiced, any one of us. So why would I know more about getting that airplane on the ground under those conditions than the other three? So if I hadn't used CLR, if we had not let everybody put their input in, it's a cinch we wouldn't have made it.[9]

RULE #16

Encourage and create leaders around you. Dispersed leadership involves many people, which means there is less risk of a single person making a poor strategic choice.

DISPERSED LEADERSHIP brings one more enormous, twofold benefit: agility and a rapid reaction to changing circumstances. Encouraging employees to be active observers of their work environment and involving them in communications and decision-making gives us a unique insight into what's going on in and around not only our own organization, but also in other sectors. Dozens, hundreds, even thousands of employee eyes are scanning the horizon for black swans, operating like a human super-radar, helping protect an organization from unpleasant surprises. This enables us to react instantly when a crisis does threaten, placing us ahead of our rivals, who probably still haven't spotted the threat. This is called business agility, and it is fast becoming one of the prerequisites for competing and succeeding in the modern world.

You've probably heard the story about the two hikers who went trekking in the Rockies. After a full day's hiking, they set up camp, had a light supper, and then went to bed in their tent. As they were dozing off, they were startled by the roar of a grizzly, who was angered by the intruders on his territory. The reactions of the two tourists were almost mirror images of each other. The first was hysterical, screaming and sobbing that he didn't want to die; the other, meanwhile, calmly emerged from his sleeping bag and started putting on his sneakers. His panicked friend looked at him as if he were insane, and said, "You have no chance of running faster than a grizzly!" The other finished tying his shoes and replied, "I don't want to outrun a grizzly. I want to run faster than you."

That's what the business world is like. There's no point in wondering how to become the fastest sprinter in the world, as there's only one person who can hold that title, so our chances are relatively small. In practice, it's about knowing that, like the hiker in the Rockies, we don't have to outrun the grizzly, but our direct competitors. Business agility means understanding this tale.

The combination of perspectives outlined on these pages leads us to a number of purely business conclusions. If we want to come out on top in an ever-more unpredictable world, we have to constantly work on increasing our competitive advantage. Yet this is a fragile and highly ephemeral advantage—technological and social revolution and changes in consumer behavior or breakthrough innovations can undermine it at any moment and floor even market leaders. So it's agility that counts, the ability to respond rapidly to new events and adapt an organization to fit the new circumstances. Today's "business Darwinism" can be summed up in one sentence: it's not the fittest that survive, but the fastest to adapt. Agility, then, demands the combining of up-to-date, tested decision-making procedures and improved and accelerated actions in repetitive processes and tasks with the ability to properly assess a state of affairs and adopt an inquiry approach in nonstandard situations.

In the most successful companies I've dealt with as an advisor and trainer, there has always been a combination of four elements directly affecting the quality of decision-making and business agility:

1. **Clear decision-making structures:** precisely defined rules for decision-making, complete with clearly defined parameters for specific individuals to make decisions, that have been communicated to all the relevant employees and are constantly monitored in terms of coherence and completeness (eliminating overlapping responsibilities, identifying "orphan" areas and elements—those not assigned to anyone—in the process).

2. **Continuous improvement:** consistently learning the lessons from errors (our own and others'), ongoing analysis of what the competition's doing, seeking out best practices in a variety of functions and sectors, creating a culture of "micro-innovations," with every employee looking for incremental improvements, and periodic stress-testing of procedures for resilience to extreme events.

3. **An organizational culture promoting psychological safety:** encouraging open communication, including the ability to express divergent opinions, promoting constructive conflict, encouraging new employees to voice their opinions and acting on what they say, maintaining a culture of consultation and participation regardless of employee status, providing a chance to avoid many of the traps set for us by our cognitive mechanisms (equivalent to the CRM approach in airlines).

4. **Dispersed leadership:** leadership attributes and attitudes are seen at various levels of the organization and in numerous employees,

leading to better monitoring of the business environment and shaping the attitudes of others; this can also happen through the creation of formal and informal "decision-making teams," along the lines of JFK's EXCOMM.

This combination of factors not only enables faster and better decisions to be made, but also helps us better understand the consequences of our decisions for other areas of an organization's operations. As a result, it's possible to identify potential side-effects, which, given the increasing interdependence and complexity of business systems, is priceless. Involving people from various positions and levels in the hierarchy in the decision-making process significantly increases the chances of spotting such problems.[10]

During a press conference in 2002, Donald Rumsfeld said, "[T]here are known knowns; there are things we know we know. We also know there are known unknowns; that is to say we know there are some things we do not know. But there are also unknown unknowns—the ones we don't know we don't know."[11] Many were less than complimentary about this word salad; the Plain English Campaign, an independent organization fighting for clarity in the use of the English language, gave the Defense Secretary its Foot in Mouth Award (awarded for "baffling quotes by public figures"). The fact is, though, that Rumsfeld was right, and differentiating between matters we know we know nothing about and things whose existence we don't even suspect is fundamental in terms of today's reality, the new normal, and effective decision-making processes. The unknown unknowns are the ugly ducklings that grow up into black swans and cause us real problems. And therein lies the beauty of dispersed leadership—it provides a broader spectrum from which we can observe the reality surrounding us, and it requires the involvement of a variety of types of experience, knowledge, and personalities, all of which enables us to locate problems in the three categories identified by Rumsfeld. Thanks to the input of others, we can identify our own areas of incompetence, whereby an unknown unknown turns into a known unknown, enabling us to take specific corrective or preventative actions. The experience of others can, in turn, change a known unknown into a known known, delivering knowledge and ideas that resolve a problem.[12]

In this way, dispersed leadership can be a highly effective weapon when used against black swans.

ALBERT CAMUS once said that life is the sum of all your choices. Who we are, where we are, how we are perceived, and where we are headed are the result of the choices we make every day—large and small, often unconscious, they can affect many others and can have consequences for the rest of our lives.

Just as I don't believe in the absolute decision-making powers of AI, neither do I believe in absolute determinism. I don't believe that humans are just flotsam and jetsam being tossed around by the waves. I don't believe that the world around us makes our decisions for us and pushes us in a given direction. I've come across too many tales of fascinating individuals who, seemingly doomed to failure, were able to turn their situation around and shape their own destiny, rather than being shaped by it.

I believe that our quality of life is directly related to how close to perfection our decisions are. The quality of a decision, in turn, depends on how far we are able to avoid the thousands of traps set for us by our own personalities and the pressures of the world around us. I am convinced that while no one has created, or ever will create, a formula for making only optimal decisions, there is a world where we can make better choices that we should actively seek out. A world in which we strive for perfection, expand our knowledge, gather experience, and, consequently, make better decisions. A world in which even if we make a mistake, it is the result of a bold experiment, an attempt to uncover far more effective ways of operating, and not the senseless repetition of yesterday's errors.

I hope the book you've just read will bring you closer to that world.

Rules Summary

Rule #1. Prepare for a black swan, because one thing is certain: sooner or later you will meet one.

Rule #2. The better it's going, and the more successful you are, the more you are at risk of turkey syndrome.

    The deeper you fall into turkey syndrome, the nastier your black swan will be.

Rule #3. The more you admire someone, the more critically you should examine their opinions.

    The more exciting somebody's vision seems, the more closely you should test its foundations in reality.

Rule #4. The more everyone around insists something is impossible, the more you should check it yourself. Several times.

Rule #5. The greater the investment of time, effort, money, and our own reputation, the harder it is to objectively assess a situation and make the right decision.

Rule #6. If you find yourself in a black swan situation, go into inquiry mode. Whatever your intuition or experience is telling you may be wrong.

Rule #7. Set up your own EXCOMM. Surround yourself with people who don't think like you. Value those who disagree with you, and who aren't afraid to say it.

Rule #8. When improving an organization, also pay attention to the best and most efficient processes.

    In a black swan situation, they can fail. Do you have a backup plan?

Rule #9. Shoot down Concordes and hunt for monkey habits.

Eliminating loss-making projects and ineffective practices frees up time for other things, increasing a company's agility and flexibility.

Rule #10. Recognize the value of your failures (and those of others).

Thoroughly analyze your past failures and draw in-depth, objective, and actionable conclusions for the future.

Rule #11. Never stop shaping the organizational culture. It can be your greatest ally, or your worst enemy, in making the right decisions.

Rule #12. Great leaders are distinguished by their awareness that greatness is no guarantee of infallibility.

Rule #13. Don't be a "decision drunk"—use data for illumination, not only for support. Data can be a great ally, when properly analyzed.

Rule #14. Never ignore the values and convictions of other generations, especially those only just entering the market. Even if their influence on decision-making today is minimal, the new normal means this may change sooner than you expect.

Rule #15. The world of data overload is also a world of new possibilities.

Actively seek out opportunities to engage a cost-free force that can radically improve the quality of your decision-making.

Rule #16. Encourage and create leaders around you. Dispersed leadership involves many people, which means there is less risk of a single person making a poor strategic choice.

ENDNOTES

Introduction

1. On April 25, 2015, an avalanche triggered by a powerful earthquake that hit Nepal killed twenty-two and injured more than sixty climbers.

Chapter 2: Turkey Trouble

1. I borrowed this tale of the poor turkey from Nassim Nicholas Taleb. It originated, though, with David Hume, the eighteenth-century Scottish philosopher, who used the example of fattened geese to illustrate inductive reasoning.
2. See gizmodo.com/5416781/top-5-assclown-iphone-quotes-in-2007
3. See jimcollins.com/books/how-the-mighty-fall.html

Chapter 3: In This Chapter, There Is No Good News

1. See nature.berkeley.edu/ucce50/ag-labor/7article/article35.htm
2. Professor Andrew McAfee, a lecturer at Harvard University and MIT, observed a similar phenomenon in his research. He named it the HiPPO effect, from the "highest-paid person's opinion."
3. Analyses carried out by Gregg Murray at Texas Tech University showed that, in US presidential elections, the taller of the two candidates is far more likely to win. See wsj.com/articles/voters-size-up-2016-presidential-candidates-whos-the-tallest-1445996933
4. S. Milgram, *Obedience to Authority: An Experimental View* (Harper and Row, 1974), 5.
5. AFP, "Jean-Marie Messier, l'homme qui se croyait 'maître du monde,'" *Le Point*, May 29, 2010. Available at lepoint.fr/bourse/jean-marie-messier-l-homme-qui-se-croyait-maitre-du-monde-dossier-portrait-29-05-2010-460652_81.php

6. Quoted in Nicholas Carlson, "Groupon CEO Andrew Mason's Honest, Charming Goodbye Memo: 'I Was Fired Today,'" www.businessinsider.com, February 28, 2013.

7. Rakesh Khurana, "The Curse of the Superstar CEO," *Harvard Business Review*, September 2002. Available at hbr.org/2002/09/the-curse-of-the-superstar-ceo

8. G.R. Stephenson, "Cultural Acquisition of a Specific Learned Response among Rhesus Monkeys," 1967. Available at scribd.com/doc/73492989/Stephenson-1966-Cultural-Acquisition-of-a-Specific-Learned-Response-Among-Rhesus-Monkeys

9. This roughly translates as "Even if it's not true, the underlying concept is sound."

10. Just how far Concorde was ahead of its time is testified to by the fact that it was nearly half a century after its unveiling before tentative talk began about reintroducing supersonic passenger planes. In the first half of 2017, Boom Technology, a startup founded in 2014, revealed its plans to develop such aircraft, attracting interest from none other than Sir Richard Branson. According to company representatives, the first planes should start appearing in the skies in 2023.

Chapter 4: Process

1. David A. Garvin and Michael Roberto, "What You Don't Know about Making Decisions," *Harvard Business Review*, September 2001. Available at hbr.org/2001/09/what-you-dont-know-about-making-decisions#

2. The mood of overwhelming uncertainty is captured well by the words of Secretary of Defense Robert McNamara, recorded at an EXCOMM meeting and quoted in the 2003 documentary film *The Fog of War*: "I have no idea what the world will look like after we attack Cuba. How do we stop there?" E. Morris [director], *The Fog of War* (USA, 2003).

3. Quoted in Morris, *The Fog of War*.

4. More behind-the-scenes negotiations led to the withdrawal of the US Jupiter missiles from Italy and Turkey.

5. It's no accident that DARPA was established in the same period. Its activities initially focused on protecting the United States from a Soviet missile attack, but in time it played a key role in the development of inventions such as GPS and the Internet (whose precursor was the ARPANET network, built by DARPA), to name but two.

6. Jack Swigert joined the crew of *Apollo 13* just two days before liftoff, replacing Thomas Kenneth Mattingly II (better known as Ken Mattingly), who had come

into contact with someone suffering from German measles and so was at risk of falling ill and infecting the others during the mission.

7. In N. Buckner and R. Whittlesey [directors], *Apollo 13: To the Edge and Back* (USA, 1994).

8. G. Kranz, *Failure Is Not an Option: Mission Control from Mercury to Apollo 13 and Beyond* (Simon & Schuster, 2000), 320–21.

9. Kranz, *Failure Is Not an Option*, 321.

10. Kranz, *Failure Is Not an Option*, 335.

11. In the context of managing innovations, you might know this approach as a Stage-Gate (there are others, as well). Its creators, Robert Cooper and Scott Edgett, defined five stages in the process of introducing a new product or service, separated by four gates. Each gate is a set of indicators that must be achieved before a project moves into the next phase.

Chapter 5: 改 善

1. This incident attracted a great deal of media attention. A myriad of books were written, in the form of both first-hand accounts and expert opinions, and two films were produced, 1997's *Into Thin Air*, directed by Robert Markowitz and based in large part on the experience of Jon Krakauer, and 2015's *Everest*, directed by Baltasar Kormákur.

2. This is, in fact, true, as climbing demands enormous courage bordering on insanity. It's interesting, though, that these negative opinions are, in my experience, mostly offered by people with nearly triple-figure BMIs with awful cholesterol levels who spend hours sitting in front of the TV munching fries and downing beers. Strangely, such a lifestyle is not regarded as risky, despite the numerous studies showing the serious health risks resulting from poor diet, alcohol abuse, or lack of physical activity.

3. This is, of course, the 8,000-meter barrier, which gives Everest and its equally tall fellow mountains their informal name: the eight-thousanders.

4. Sir John Hunt, though recognized for his undisputed contribution to the organization and logistics of the expedition, remained in the shadow of Edmund Hillary. Hillary himself, in his book *View from the Summit*, recalls an extremely awkward situation he witnessed. US President Eisenhower, when handing John Hunt the Hubbard Medal awarded him in 1954, addressed him as "Sir Edmund," evidently confusing him with Hillary, standing alongside, who proceeded to whisper the actual name of the laureate to the president. For the record, the Hubbard Medal was also awarded to Tenzing Norgay (in this case without mistaken identity).

5. According to Jon Krakauer, four experienced climbers from the South African expedition abandoned the push for the summit as they didn't agree with Woodall's domineering style. In the following days, one of the participants who went up to the summit too late and died on the way back to base camp became yet another victim of the mountain.

6. The tragic earthquake that struck Nepal in April 2015 altered the shape of the Hillary Step. As climbers found in 2016 and 2017, it is now easier to cross and is covered in a large amount of snow and ice.

7. This issue divided many in the climbing community. There were those who regarded Boukreev as a hero, pointing out his heroic behavior during the night, when he left the camp three times in appalling conditions to lead down clients lost in the blizzard. Discussions about his behavior only ceased with his death—eighteen months after the events on Everest, on Christmas Day in 1997, Anatoli Boukreev died in an avalanche on Annapurna.

8. Adventure Consultants brochure. See A. Boukreev and G. Weston DeWalt, *The Climb: Tragic Ambitions on Everest* (St. Martin's Griffin Edition, 1999), 6.

9. Scott Fischer, quoted in J. Krakauer, *Into Thin Air* (Anchor Books, 1998), 85–86.

10. Krakauer, *Into Thin Air*, 85–86.

11. Krakauer, *Into Thin Air*, 91.

12. Cited in B. Weathers and S.G. Michaud, *Left for Dead: My Journey Home from Everest* (Dell Publishing, 2001), 64, 65.

13. Cited in A. Boukreev and G. Weston DeWalt, *The Climb: Tragic Ambitions on Everest* (St. Martin's Press, 1997).

14. Unfortunately, we don't learn from our mistakes. While the Polish expedition up Broad Peak in 2013 achieved its aim of being the first winter ascent, the following days brought tragedy. Only two of the four climbers made it back to base, and Maciej Berbeka and Tomasz Kowalski lost their lives on the slopes of the mountain they'd just conquered. As an investigation by the Polish Mountaineering Association showed, many of the errors that led to Hall's and Fischer's disaster were repeated.

Chapter 6: Something in the Air

1. "Power distance can therefore be defined as the extent to which the less powerful members of institutions and organizations within a country expect and accept that power is distributed unequally." G. Hofstede, G. J. Hofstede, and M. Minkov, *Cultures and Organizations* (McGraw-Hill, 2010), 61.

2. "Individualism pertains to societies in which the ties between individuals are loose: everyone is expected to look after him- or herself and his or her

immediate family. Collectivism as its opposite pertains to societies in which people from birth onward are integrated into strong, cohesive in-groups, which throughout people's lifetime continue to protect them in exchange for unquestioning loyalty." Hofstede, Hofstede, and Minkov, *Cultures and Organizations*, 92.

3. "A society is called masculine when emotional gender roles are clearly distinct: men are supposed to be assertive, tough, and focused on material success, whereas women are supposed to be more modest, tender, and concerned with the quality of life. A society is called feminine when emotional gender roles overlap: both men and women are supposed to be modest, tender, and concerned with the quality of life." Hofstede, Hofstede, and Minkov, *Cultures and Organizations*, 140.

4. "Uncertainty avoidance can therefore be defined as the extent to which the members of a culture feel threatened by ambiguous or unknown situations." Hofstede, Hofstede, and Minkov, *Cultures and Organizations*, 191.

5. See presidency.ucsb.edu/ws/?pid=42705

6. The fifth shuttle built, *Endeavour*, was finished in 1991 to replenish the fleet after the *Challenger* disaster. *Endeavour* was constructed of spare parts intended for the remaining shuttles.

7. John Quinones, "World's News Today," ABC TV.

8. See D. Vaughan, *The Challenger Launch Decision* (The University of Chicago Press, 1996), 2–6.

9. P.M. Boffey, "NASA Had Warning of a Disaster Risk Posed by Booster," *New York Times*, February 9, 1986.

10. The mission was finally completed in 2007, when Barbara Morgan went up on the shuttle *Endeavour*. In 1986, Morgan had been Christa McAuliffe's backup.

11. As you read this sad story, please remember the words of President George W. Bush, from his memorial speech on February 4, 2003: "This cause of exploration and discovery is not an option we choose; it is a desire written in the human heart. We find the best among us, send them forth into unmapped darkness, and pray they will return. They go in peace for all mankind, and all mankind is in their debt." Available at https://history.nasa.gov/columbia /Troxell/Columbia%20Web%20Site/Documents/Executive%20Branch /President%20Bush/pres_memorial.html

12. See, for example, imd.org/publications/articles/why-so-many-corporate-failures

13. See nasa.gov/columbia/home/CAIB_Vol1.html

14. M. Cabbage, "Still Haunted by Columbia's End: Space-Shuttle Manager Left NASA after Disaster," *Orlando Sentinel*, February 1, 2004.

15. NASA, *Report of Columbia Accident Investigation Board*, Volume I (NASA, 2003), 177. Available at nasa.gov/columbia/home/CAIB_Vol1.html

16. Cited in M.S. Smith, *NASA's Space Shuttle Columbia: Synopsis of the Report of the Columbia Accident Investigation Board*, September 2, 2003. Available at https://history.nasa.gov/columbia/Troxell/Columbia%20Web%20Site/Documents/Congress/CRS%20Summary%20of%20CAIB%20Report.pdf

17. NASA, *Assessment and Plan for Organizational Culture Change at NASA* (NASA, March 15, 2004), Appendix A. Available at http://www.spaceref.com/news/viewsr.html?pid=12540

18. NASA, *Assessment*, 33.

19. See nytimes.com/2005/04/04/politics/some-at-nasa-say-its-culture-is-changing-but-others-say-problems.html

20. See nytimes.com/1964/03/27/archives/37-who-saw-murder-didnt-call-the-police-apathy-at-stabbing-of.html

Chapter 7: In Search of Authentic Leaders

1. Some historians claim that, in the final stages of the war, desperate French politicians and military seriously considered using nuclear weapons.

2. H.R. McMaster, *Dereliction of Duty: Lyndon Johnson, Robert McNamara, the Joint Chiefs of Staff, and the Lies That Led to Vietnam* (Harper Perennial, 1998), 125.

3. McMaster, *Dereliction of Duty*, 26.

4. Cited in www.nsa.gov/news-features/declassified-documents/gulf-of-tonkin/articles/assets/files/release-2/rel2_gulf_tonkin_incident_desoto.pdf (page 49).

5. Sharp, speaking in Morris, *The Fog of War*.

6. President Johnson, calling McNamara at 11 pm, shouted into the phone: "Bob, I am exposed here! I have got to make my speech right now!" (McMaster, *Dereliction of Duty*, 132).

7. See presidency.ucsb.edu/ws/index.php?pid=27126

8. In Morris, *The Fog of War*.

9. R.S. McNamara, *In Retrospect: The Tragedy and Lessons of Vietnam* (Vintage Books, 1996), 96.

10. Cited in D. Stahel, *Operation Barbarossa and Germany's Defeat in the East*, 38.

11. When word of the Allies' victory reached Winston Churchill, he uttered the memorable words, "Now this is not the end. It is not even the beginning of the end, but it is, perhaps, the end of the beginning."

12. C.G. von Clausewitz, *On War* (Princeton University Press, 1976), 627–628.

13. It is worth recalling, though, that the geopolitical situation was far more complex at the time. According to some historians (e.g., Viktor Suvorov and

Igor Bunich), Stalin had been preparing an attack on Germany for months; it was supposed to begin in mid-1941. The Nazis themselves stated in their propaganda that Operation Barbarossa was intended to stop the Soviets from invading Western Europe, which in turn was regarded as an invention of the Nazi propaganda machine. In this light—although the thesis is both controversial and questionable—the decision to attack the USSR could be viewed as an act by which Hitler saved Germany from the threat of invasion.

14. See 6sigma.us/six-sigma-articles/six-sigma-certification-levels-explained
15. The transformation is described brilliantly by Bryce G. Hoffman in *American Icon: Alan Mulally and the Fight to Save Ford Motor Company* (Crown Publishing Group, 2012).
16. *Pentiti* also translates into English as "turncoats"—interesting, don't you think?
17. The rules were brilliantly extracted from the letters by Clare Longrigg. See theguardian.com/world/2008/apr/09/internationalcrime.italy
18. See H. Bruch and S. Ghoshal, "Beware the Busy Manager," *Harvard Business Review*, February 2002. Available at https://hbr.org/2002/02/beware-the-busy-manager
19. Research shows that younger employees—Millennials, Generation Z—react even more strongly to micromanagement, quickly losing their sense of purpose and, consequently, their sense of engagement. See, for example, theglobeandmail.com/report-on-business/careers/management/guilty-of-micromanaging-stop-before-its-too-late/article38092554

Chapter 8: My Favorite Enemy

1. Questions and data from D. Ariely, *Predictably Irrational: The Hidden Forces That Shape Our Decisions* (HarperCollins, 2009).
2. This is in no way an attempt to justify infidelity!
3. Serge Stoléru, Jérôme Redouté, Marie-Claude Gregoire, and Jean-François Pujol, "Brain Processing of Visual Sexual Stimuli in Human Males," *Human Brain Mapping*, 11(3), November 2000.
4. Please forgive me—the sentence in bold was a shameless piece of manipulation on my part. In no way do I consider you unable to make good decisions. After all, you chose to buy my book... and that was a good decision!
5. See tmz.com/2014/04/26/donald-sterling-clippers-owner-black-people-racist-audio-magic-johnson
6. Sterling was severely punished. The commissioner of the NBA, Adam Silver, gave the Los Angeles team's owner the severest possible punishment—a lifetime ban, to which he added a $2.5 million fine and appealed to the NBA Board of Governors to force Sterling to sell his shares in the Clippers. Sterling

apologized for his words in an interview on May 12, 2014, on CNN, and three weeks later announced he was selling the team. On August 12, 2014, it was bought by Steve Ballmer, a former CEO of Microsoft.

7. The court had no doubts: in November 2017, Oscar Pistorius was sentenced to thirteen years and five months imprisonment.

8. Mel Gibson, cited in D. Eagleman, *Incognito: The Secret Lives of the Brain* (Vintage, 2012), 101.

9. Eagleman, *Incognito*, 102.

10. To get the fullest picture, to Kahneman's proposal, I would add our instincts and the operation of the parasympathetic nervous system, which in a sense constitutes System 0. System 0 lies beyond our control, as it governs our body's fundamental functions, such as heartbeat; obviously, we can't use System 1 or 2 to "decide" to switch these functions off.

11. Burma, with a population of 55,123,814, is generally referred to these days as Myanmar. See, for example, news.bbc.co.uk/2/hi/7013943.stm for more on its name.

12. The creator of this simple, surprising experiment is David Eagleman.

13. And anyway, everyone knows there's nothing better than a Tuscan bottle of Brunello di Montalcino from a good producer! Just a small attempt on my part at instilling in you a non-threatening, but extremely pleasurable heuristic...

Chapter 9: Peering through the Looking Glass

1. There was one further prediction by the RAND Corporation: according to the experts, by 2070 we are expected to make contact with extraterrestrial beings.

2. Some experts forecast there would be 300 billion networked devices by 2022.

3. McKinsey Global Institute, "The Internet of Things: Mapping the Value Beyond the Hype" (McKinsey & Company, 2015). See mckinsey.com/~/media/McKinsey/Business%20Functions/McKinsey%20Digital/Our%20insights/The%20internet%20of%20things%20the%20value%20of%20digitizing%20the%20physical%20world/The-Internet-of-things-Mapping-the-value-beyond-the-hype.ashx

4. Various sources give various dates, but typically Baby Boomers are regarded as those born during the postwar demographic peak, which ended in the middle of the 1960s.

5. In the case of Generation X, there is similar confusion over the dates; some researchers give the end date as 1982, others as 1984.

6. It will be even more interesting when Generation Z, born around 1995–2012, starts turning up in the workplace. The successors to the Millennials, these are young people for whom a world without social media has never existed.

7. D. Tapscott, *Grown Up Digital* (McGraw-Hill, 2009), 19–20.
8. Tapscott, *Grown Up Digital*, 19–20.
9. Tapscott, *Grown Up Digital*, 19–20.
10. M. Bulgakov, *The Master and Margarita* (Penguin Books, 1997), 293–295.

Epilogue

1. The United States Air Force Fighter Weapons School actually exists, although since 2005 it has been named the United States Air Force Warfare Center. Interestingly, to this day, there's a $5 fine for any employee who mentions the film *Top Gun* while on base.
2. Tony Scott [director], *Crimson Tide* (USA, 1995).
3. Scott, *Crimson Tide*.
4. The film doesn't answer the question of which officer was right one way or the other—Captain Ramsey, blindly putting his faith in procedure (the last complete order), or his subordinate, who, in the light of the interrupted, incomplete replacement directive tries to initiate an inquiry approach and verify the information. When the two sailors ultimately stand before an investigative commission, its head, Admiral Anderson, concludes, "You were both right, and you were also both wrong."
5. Several months after these events, Stanislav Petrov left the military; he spent the rest of his life in the town of Fryazino, near Moscow, where he died on May 19, 2017. Sadly, he never received the fame and recognition his decision deserved. In 2004, he received the World Citizens Foundation award of a meager $1,000 (you read it right—it's not something the editor missed). For anyone interested in learning more, I recommend the excellent Polish documentary film *The Red Button*, directed by Mirosław Grubek and the late Ewa Pięta.
6. There was a serious risk of exceeding the uninterrupted working time permitted by the regulations, which, in the event of further delay, would mean compulsory rest for the crew, who would have had to remain on the island for one more day.
7. See ntsb.gov/investigations/AccidentReports/Pages/AAR7907.aspx
8. See ntsb.gov/investigations/AccidentReports/Pages/AAR7907.aspx
9. See https://yarchive.net/air/airliners/dc10_sioux_city.html
10. An example of this is the less than obvious consequences of the increased checks on passengers at airports following the attacks of September 11, 2001. The longer checks and baggage restrictions have meant that many passengers have given up flying and turned to the far more dangerous form of transport that is the automobile (especially on shorter trips). This has led to an increase

in accidents: three economists from Cornell University have estimated that in the United States alone the increase in road accident victims that can be ascribed to this trend is over five hundred people annually.

11. See https://www.nato.int/docu/speech/2002/s020606g.htm

12. Slovenian philosopher Slavoj Žižek added a category to the three listed by Donald Rumsfeld, one that quite naturally suggests itself. He estimated that serious danger lurks in "unknown knowns," or unarguable facts that we deny, especially when they run counter to our publicly stated values.

BIBLIOGRAPHY AND FURTHER READING

Books

Ariely, Dan. *Predictably Irrational: The Hidden Forces That Shape Our Decisions.* HarperCollins, 2009.

———. *The Upside of Irrationality: The Unexpected Benefits of Defying Logic at Work and at Home.* HarperCollins, 2010.

Boukreev, Anatoli, and G. Weston DeWalt. *The Climb: Tragic Ambitions on Everest.* St. Martin's Press, 1997.

Breashears, David. *High Exposure: An Enduring Passion for Everest and Unforgiving Places.* Simon & Schuster, 1999.

Brynjolfsson, Erik, and Andrew McAfee. *The Second Machine Age: Work, Progress, and Prosperity in a Time of Brilliant Technologies.* W.W. Norton & Company, 2014.

Bulgakov, Mikhail. *The Master and Margarita.* Penguin Books, 1997.

Bullock, Alan. *Hitler: A Study in Tyranny.* Harper Perennial, 1991.

Carr, Nicholas. *The Shallows: What the Internet Is Doing to Our Brains.* W.W. Norton & Company, 2010.

Christian, Brian, and Tom Griffiths. *Algorithms to Live By: The Computer Science of Human Decisions.* Henry Holt & Company, 2016.

Clark, Alan. *Barbarossa.* William Morrow Paperbacks, 1985.

Collins, Jim. *How The Mighty Fall: And Why Some Companies Never Give In.* HarperCollins, 2009.

Damásio, António R. *Descartes' Error: Emotion, Reason and the Human Brain.* Penguin Books, 2005.

Dickie, John. *Cosa Nostra: A History of the Sicilian Mafia.* Hodder & Stoughton, 2004.

Diehl, Alan. *Air Safety Investigators: Using Science to Save Lives—One Crash at a Time*. Xlibris Corporation, 2013.

Eagleman, David. *Incognito: The Secret Lives of the Brain*. Vintage Books, 2012.

Evans, Dylan. *Risk Intelligence: How to Live with Uncertainty*. Atlantic Books, 2013.

Evans, Philip, and Thomas S. Wurster. *Blown to Bits: How the New Economics of Information Transforms Strategy*. Harvard Business Review Press, 1999.

Fall, Bernard B. *Hell in a Very Small Place: The Siege of Dien Bien Phu*. Da Capo Press, 2002.

Ford, Martin. *Rise of the Robots: Technology and the Threat of a Jobless Future*. Basic Books, 2015.

Frankel, Max. *High Noon in the Cold War: Kennedy, Khrushchev, and the Cuban Missile Crisis*. Presidio Press, 2004.

Fukuyama, Francis. *Our Posthuman Future: Consequences of the Biotechnology Revolution*. Farrar, Straus and Giroux, 2002.

Gazzaniga, Michael S. *Who's in Charge? Free Will and the Science of the Brain*. Ecco, 2011.

Gerrig, Richard J., and Philip G. Zimbardo. *Psychology and Life*. Pearson, 2010.

Gladwell, Malcolm. *Blink: The Power of Thinking without Thinking*. Back Bay Books, 2005.

Goldsmith, Marshall. *Triggers: Creating Behavior That Lasts—Becoming the Person You Want to Be*. Crown Business, 2015.

———. *What Got You Here Won't Get You There: How Successful People Become Even More Successful*. Hyperion Books, 2007.

Goleman, Daniel. *Emotional Intelligence: Why It Can Matter More Than IQ*. Bantam Books, 1996.

Hackman, J. Richard. *Leading Teams: Setting the Stage for Great Performances*. Harvard Business School Publishing Corporation, 2002.

Harari, Yuval Noah. *Homo Deus: A Brief History of Tomorrow*. Harvill Secker, 2015.

Heifetz, Aviad. *Game Theory: Interactive Strategies in Economics and Management*. Cambridge University Press, 2012.

Herring, George C. *America's Longest War: The United States and Vietnam, 1950-1975*. McGraw-Hill, 2001.

Hoffman, Bryce G. *American Icon: Alan Mulally and the Fight to Save Ford Motor Company*. Crown Publishing Group, 2012.

Hofstede, Geert, Geert Jan Hofstede, and Michael Minkov. *Cultures and Organizations: Software of the Mind*. McGraw-Hill Professional, 2010.

Howe, Jeff. *Crowdsourcing: Why the Power of the Crowd Is Driving the Future of Business*. Three Rivers Press, 2009.

Hubbard, Douglas W. *The Failure of Risk Management: Why It's Broken and How to Fix It*. John Wiley & Sons, 2009.

Kahneman, Daniel. *Thinking, Fast and Slow*. Farrar, Straus and Giroux, 2011.

Karnow, Stanley. *Vietnam: A History*. Penguin Books, 1997.

Kochanski, Halik. *The Eagle Unbowed: Poland and the Poles in the Second World War*. Harvard University Press, 2012.

Krakauer, Jon. *Into Thin Air: A Personal Account of the Everest Disaster*. Mayfly, 1998.

Kranz, Gene. *Failure Is Not an Option: Mission Control from Mercury to Apollo 13 and Beyond*. Simon & Schuster, 2000.

Kurzweil, Ray. *The Singularity Is Near: When Humans Transcend Biology*. Penguin Books, 2005.

Lee, Edward Ashford. *Plato and the Nerd: The Creative Partnership of Humans and Technology*. MIT Press, 2017.

LeGault, Michael R. *Think! Why Crucial Decisions Can't Be Made in the Blink of an Eye*. Threshold Editions, 2006.

Lehrer, Jonah. *How We Decide*. Mariner Books, 2010.

Levitt, Steven D., and Stephen J. Dubner. *Freakonomics: A Rogue Economist Explores the Hidden Side of Everything*. William Morrow, 2005.

——. *Think Like a Freak*. Allen Lane, 2014.

Lindstrom, Martin. *Brand Sense. Sensory Secrets behind The Stuff We Buy*. Free Press, 2005.

Longrigg, Clare. *Boss of Bosses: How Bernardo Provenzano Saved the Mafia*. John Murray, 2008.

Lowenstein, Roger. *When Genius Failed: The Rise and Fall of Long-Term Capital Management*. Random House, 2001.

McClelland, David. *Human Motivation*. Cambridge University Press, 1973.

McMaster, H.R. *Dereliction of Duty: Lyndon Johnson, Robert McNamara, the Joint Chiefs of Staff, and the Lies That Led to Vietnam*. Harper Perennial, 1998.

McNamara, Robert S. *In Retrospect: The Tragedy and Lessons of Vietnam*. Vintage Books, 1996.

Nadella, Satya, Greg Shaw, and Jill Tracie Nichols. *Hit Refresh: The Quest to Rediscover Microsoft's Soul and Imagine a Better Future for Everyone*. Harper Business, 2017.

Plous, Scott. *The Psychology of Judgement and Decision Making*. McGraw-Hill, 1993.

Ratcliffe, Graham. *A Day to Die For*. Mainstream Publishing, 2011.

Rollins, Thomas, and Darryl Robert. *Work Culture, Organizational Performance and Business Success: Measurement and Management*. Quorum Books, 1998.

Schein, Edgar H. *Organizational Culture and Leadership*. Jossey-Bass, 2004.

Stahel, David. *Operation Barbarossa and Germany's Defeat in the East*. Cambridge University Press, 2009.

———. *Operation Typhoon. Hitler's March on Moscow*. Cambridge University Press, 2013.

Suworow, Wiktor. *Icebreaker: Who Started the Second World War?* Hamish Hamilton, 1990.

Taleb, Nassim Nicholas. *Antifragile: Things That Gain from Disorder*. Random House, 2014.

———. *Black Swan: The Impact of the Highly Improbable*. Random House, 2010.

Tapscott, Don. *Growing Up Digital: The Rise of the Net Generation*. McGraw-Hill, 1998.

———. *Grown Up Digital: How the Net Generation Is Changing Your World*. McGraw-Hill, 2009.

Toffler, Alvin. *The Third Wave*. Bantam Books, 1980.

Trompenaars, Fons, and Charles Hampden-Turner. *Riding the Waves of Culture: Understanding Cultural Diversity in Business*. Nicholas Brealey Publishing, 1997.

Vaughan, Diane. *The Challenger Launch Decision*. University of Chicago Press, 1996.

Weathers, Beck, with Stephen G. Michaud. *Left for Dead: My Journey Home from Everest*. Dell Publishing, 2001.

Articles and Blog Posts

AFP. "Jean-Marie Messier, l'homme qui se croyait 'maître du monde.'" *Le Point*, May 29, 2010. Available at lepoint.fr/bourse/jean-marie-messier-l-homme-qui-se-croyait-maitre-du-monde-dossier-portrait-29-05-2010-460652_81.php

Aksenov, Pavel. "Stanislav Petrov: The Man Who May Have Saved the World." BBC News, September 26, 2013. Available at bbc.com/news/world-europe-24280831

Barrionuevo, Alexei. "Enron Chiefs Guilty of Fraud and Conspiracy." *New York Times*, May 25, 2006. Available at nytimes.com/2006/05/25/business/25cnd-enron.html

Barton, Christine, Jeff Fromm, and Chris Egan. "The Millennial Consumer: Debunking Stereotypes." Boston Consulting Group, 2012. Available at https://www.bcg.com/documents/file103894.pdf

BBC News. "Harvey Weinstein Timeline: How the Scandal Unfolded." May 25, 2018. Available at bbc.com/news/entertainment-arts-41594672

———. "Nokia's Mobile Chief Anssi Vanjoki Steps Down." September 13, 2010. Available at bbc.co.uk/news/technology-11281971

Berman, Alison E. "The Technologies We'll Have Our Eyes on in 2018." SingularityHub. December 30, 2017. Available at singularityhub.com/2017
/12/30/the-technologies-well-have-our-eyes-on-in-2018

Biotechnologia. "Helicobacter pylori—odkrycie dzięki poświęceniu."
September 10, 2013. Available at biotechnologia.pl/biotechnologia/
helicobacter-pylori-odkrycie-dzieki-poswieceniu,12852 [Polish only].

Blalock, Garrick, Vrinda Kadiyali, and Daniel H. Simon. "The Impact of
Post–9/11 Airport Security Measures on the Demand for Air Travel."
Cornell University, April 30, 2007. Available at blalock.dyson.cornell.
edu/wp/JLE_6301.pdf

Blank, Steve. "Why Visionary CEOs Never Have Visionary Successors."
Harvard Business Review, October 20, 2016. Available at hbr.org/2016
/10/why-visionary-ceos-never-have-visionary-successors

Bloomberg. "Steve Ballmer's Six Big Misses at Microsoft." August 26,
2013. Available at economictimes.indiatimes.com/tech/software/steve-
ballmers-six-big-misses-at-microsoft/articleshow/22056511.cms

Boudette, Neal E., and Jeff Bennett. "Pigment Shortage Hits Auto Makers."
Wall Street Journal, March 26, 2011. Available at wsj.com/articles/SB10001
424052748703696704576222990521120106

Byrne, John A. "How Jack Welch Runs GE." *Businessweek*, June 8, 1998.

Cabbage, Michael. "Still Haunted by Columbia's End: Space-Shuttle Manager
left NASA after Disaster." *Orlando Sentinel*, February 1, 2004.

Campbell, Andrew, Jo Whitehead, and Sydney Finkelstein. "Why Good
Leaders Make Bad Decisions." *Harvard Business Review*. February 2009.
Available at hbr.org/2009/02/why-good-leaders-make-bad-decisions

Cave, Andrew. "Former Microsoft CEO Steve Ballmer's Biggest Regret." *Forbes*,
March 4, 2014. Available at forbes.com/sites/andrewcave/2014/03/04
/former-microsoft-ceo-steve-ballmer-my-biggest-regret/#6ee109f91603

Chandler, David L. "'Kitchen Physics' Haunts NASA Inquiry." *New Scientist,*
June 21, 2003. Available at newscientist.com/article/mg17824001-100-
kitchen-physics-haunts-nasa-inquiry

Collins, Jim. "How the Mighty Fall: A Primer on the Warning Signs."
Businessweek, May 2009. Available at jimcollins.com/books/how-the-
mighty-fall.html

Cox, Josie. "Weinstein Company Files for Bankruptcy after Sexual Harassment
Scandal." *Independent*, February 26, 2018. Available at independent.co.uk
/news/business/news/weinstein-company-bankrupt-file-film-sexual-
harassment-harvey-women-producer-a8228591.html

Craig, William. "5 Qualities an Exponential Leader Must Embody." *Forbes*,
May 22, 2018. Available at forbes.com/sites/williamcraig/2018/05/22/5-
qualities-an-exponential-leader-must-embody/#5fc7a53e1dce

Curtis, Sophie. "How British Satellite Company Inmarsat Tracked Down MH370." *Telegraph*, May 25, 2014. Available at telegraph.co.uk /technology/news/10719304/How-British-satellite-company-Inmarsat-tracked-down-MH370.html

Czerwińska, Anna, Bogdan Jankowski, Michał Kochańczyk, Roman Mazik, and Piotr Pustelnik. Raport Zespołu Wypadkowego Broad Peak, August 2013. Available at pza.org.pl/download/2117948.pdf [Polish only].

Davenport, Thomas H. *Analytics 3.0. Harvard Business Review*, May 2013. Available at hbr.org/2013/12/analytics-30

Der Spiegel. "October Launch Scrapped: Berlin Airport Opening Delayed Yet Again." January 7, 2013. Available at spiegel.de/international/germany /opening-of-berlin-airport-delayed-again-due-to-technical-problems-a-876103.html

Diamandis, Peter H. "Exponential Growth Will Transform Humanity in the Next 30 Years." SingularityHub, December 21, 2016. Available at singularityhub.com/2016/12/21/exponential-growth-will-transform-humanity-in-the-next-30-years

———. "4 Billion New Minds Online: The Coming Era of Connectivity." SingularityHub, July 27, 2018. Available at singularityhub.com/2018/07 /27/4-billion-new-minds-online-the-coming-era-of-connectivity

———. "Ray Kurzweil's Mind-Boggling Predictions for the Next 25 Years." SingularityHub, January 26, 2015. Available at singularityhub.com/2015/01/26 /ray-kurzweils-mind-boggling-predictions-for-the-next-25-years

Dickey, Beth. "Culture Crash." Government Executive, April 1, 2004. Available at govexec.com/magazine/magazine-news-and-analysis/2004/04 /culture-crash/16417

Dinerman, Taylor. "Return to Flight: Has NASA Changed Enough?" *Space Review*, June 11, 2005. Available at thespacereview.com/article/406/1

Ericson, Paul. "Is Kodak's Epic Decline the Fault of Its Leaders?" *Rochester Business Journal*, February 3, 2012. Available at rbj.net/2012/02/10 /is-kodaks-epic-decline-the-fault-of-its-leaders

Eurocontrol. "Ash-Cloud of April and May 2010: Impact on Air Traffic" [report]. Eurocontrol, June 28, 2010. Available at eurocontrol.int/sites /default/files/content/documents/official-documents/facts-and-figures /statfor/ash-impact-air-traffic-2010.pdf

Fan, Shelly. "Is the Brain More Powerful Than We Thought? Here Comes the Science." SingularityHub, March 22, 2017. Available at singularityhub.com /2017/03/22/is-the-brain-more-powerful-than-we-thought-here-comes-the-science

Finkelstein, Sydney. "Lessons in Failure." *Inc.*, October 1, 2004. Available at inc.com/articles/2004/10/failure.html

Gaines, Cork. "Injuries, Infidelities, and Poor Choices: How Tiger Woods Unraveled from the Greatest Golfer in the World." *Business Insider*, May 31, 2017. Available at businessinsider.de/tiger-woods-controversies-2017-5? r=US&IR=T

Gansberg, Martin. "Thirty-Eight Who Saw Murder Didn't Call the Police." *New York Times*, March 27, 1964. Available at nytimes.com/1964/03/27 /archives/37-who-saw-murder-didnt-call-the-police-apathy-at-stabbing-of.html

Gelles, David. "*Encyclopaedia Britannica* to Cease Print Edition." *Financial Times*, March 13, 2012. Available at ft.com/content/7382302e-6d1f-11e1-ab1a-00144feab49a

Gillmor, Dan. "Encyclopedia Britannica in the Age of Wikipedia." *Guardian*, March 14, 2012. Available at theguardian.com/commentisfree /cifamerica/2012/mar/14/encyclopedia-britannica-wikipedia

Greenberg, Herb. "Worst CEO of 2012." CNBC, December 17, 2012. Available at cnbc.com/id/100320782

Griffith, Erin. "Counterpoint: Groupon Is Not a Success." *Fortune*, March 20, 2015. Available at fortune.com/2015/03/20/groupon-success

Guerrasio, Jason. "Mel Gibson Opens Up about His Anti-Semitic Comments: 'I Was Loaded and Angry and Arrested.'" *Business Insider Deutschland*, October 27, 2016. Available at businessinsider.de/mel-gibson-anti-semitic-comments-2016-10?r=US&IR=T

Häcker, Joachim. "Volkswagen and Porsche—Corporate Finance Case Study." Deutsches Institut fur Corporate Finance. Available at dicf.de/fileadmin /user_upload/sgbs/VW_Porsche_Case_study_final.pdf

Hamann, Greta. "Dominique Strauss-Kahn: The Rise and Fall of a Political Star." *Deutsche Welle*, February 2, 2015. Available at dw.com/en /dominique-strauss-kahn-the-rise-and-fall-of-a-political-star/a-18229157

Hartung, Adam. "Oops! Five CEOs Who Should Have Already Been Fired (Cisco, GE, WalMart, Sears, Microsoft)." *Forbes*, May 12, 2012. Available at forbes.com/sites/adamhartung/2012/05/12/oops-5-ceos-that-should-have-already-been-fired-cisco-ge-walmart-sears-microsoft /#35f4b5b427c0

Hirschhorn, Larry, and Thomas Gilmore. "The New Boundaries of the 'Boundaryless' Company." *Harvard Business Review*, May 1992. Available at hbr .org/1992/05/the-new-boundaries-of-the-boundaryless-company

Hoffman, David. "I Had a Funny Feeling in My Gut." *Washington Post*, February 10, 1999. Available at washingtonpost.com/wp-srv/inatl/longterm /coldwar/soviet10.htm

Howe, Jeff. "The Rise of Crowdsourcing." *Wired*, June 14, 2006. Available at wired.com/2006/06/crowds

Howell, Elizabeth. "Columbia Disaster: What Happened, What NASA Learned." Space.com, November 14, 2017. Available at space.com/19436-columbia-disaster.html

Jackson, Harold. "Robert McNamara." *Guardian*, July 6, 2009. Available at theguardian.com/world/2009/jul/06/robert-mcnamara-obituary

Johnson, John Jr. "NASA Chief Michael Griffin Praises Post–*Columbia* Effort in Farewell." *Los Angeles Times*, January 17, 2009. Available at articles.latimes.com/2009/jan/17/nation/na-nasa17

Kahneman, Daniel, and Amos Tversky. "Prospect Theory: An Analysis of Decision under Risk." *Econometrica* 47(2), March 1979. Available at jstor.org/stable/1914185?seq=1#page_scan_tab_contents

Karabell, Shellie. "After The Fall: How to Make a Comeback." *Forbes*, August 4, 2016. Available at forbes.com/sites/shelliekarabell/2016/08/04/after-the-fall-how-to-make-a-comeback/#2048c25539f6

Kim, W. Chan, and Renée Mauborgne. "Fair Process: Managing in the Knowledge Economy." *Harvard Business Review*, January 2003. Available at hbr.org/2003/01/fair-process-managing-in-the-knowledge-economy

Komorowski, Matthew. "A History of Storage Cost." mkomo.com, September 8, 2009. Available at mkomo.com/cost-per-gigabyte-update

Leske, Nicola, and Edward Taylor. "Porsche's Wiedeking Falls on VW Gamble." *Reuters*, July 23, 2009. Available at reuters.com/article/us-wiedeking-newsmaker-sb-idUSTRE56M10I20090723?mod=related&channelName=innovationNews

Lindstroem, Martin. "How Whole Foods 'Primes' You To Shop." *FastCompany*, September 15, 2011. Available at fastcompany.com/1779611/how-whole-foods-primes-you-shop

Longrigg, Clare. "How to Do Business Like the Mafia." *Guardian*, April 8, 2008. Available at theguardian.com/world/2008/apr/09/international-crime.italy

McClelland, David C., and David H. Burnham. "Power Is the Great Motivator." *Harvard Business Review*, January 2003. Available at hbr.org/2003/01/power-is-the-great-motivator

McShane, Sveta, and Jason Dorrier. "Ray Kurzweil Predicts Three Technologies Will Define Our Future." SingularityHub, April 19, 2016. Available at singularityhub.com/2016/04/19/ray-kurzweil-predicts-three-technologies-will-define-our-future

Merkle, Ralph C. "How Many Bytes in Human Memory?" *Foresight Update* 4, September 1988. Available at merkle.com/humanmemory.html

Metscher, Donald S., Marvin Smith, and Abdullah Alghamdi. "Multi-Cultural Factors in the Crew Resource Management Environment: Promoting Aviation Safety for Airline Operations." *Journal of Aviation/Aerospace*

Education and Research 18, Winter 2009. Available at researchgate.net
/publication/325273456_Crew_Resource_Management_CRM_and_Cultural
_Differences_Among_Cockpit_Crew_-_the_Case_of_Turkey

Milgram, Stanley. *Obedience to Authority: An Experimental View.* Harper and
Row, 1974.

———. "The Perils of Obedience." *Harper's,* December 1973. Available at
harpers.org/archive/1973/12/the-perils-of-obedience

Motor Trend. "Japan's Earthquake and Tsunami Hit Parts Supplies."
Motor Trend, April 4, 2011. Available at motortrend.com/news/japan-
earthquake-tsunami-hit-parts-supplies

Musser, George. "Time on the Brain: How You Are Always Living in the Past,
and Other Quirks of Perception" [blog entry]. Available at blogs.scientific
american.com, entry on September 15, 2011.

NASA. "Actions to Implement the Recommendations of the Presidential Commission on the Space Shuttle Challenger Accident." Available at history
.nasa.gov/rogersrep/actions.pdf

———. "*Columbia* Accident Investigation Board Report." NASA, August 26,
2003. Available at history.nasa.gov/columbia/CAIB_reportindex.html

National Transport Safety Board Report on Avianca AVA052 Accident.
Available at ntsb.gov/investigations/AccidentReports/Reports
/AAR9104.pdf

National Transport Safety Board Report on Crash of DC-8-61, N8082U,
Portland, Oregon, December 28, 1978. Available at libraryonline.erau.edu

Netherlands Aviation Safety Board Report on KLM4805 and PanAm 1736
Crash on March 27, 1977. Available at project-tenerife.com/engels/
Airmanshiponline.com.htm

Pasztor, Andy, Jon Ostrower, and James Hookway. "Critical Data Was Delayed
in Search for Missing Malaysia Airlines Flight." *Wall Street Journal,* March
20, 2014. Available at wsj.com/articles/critical-satellite-data-was-delayed-
in-search-for-missing-malaysia-airlines-flight-370-1395284863

Patterson, John. "Is All Forgiven? The Strange, Troubling Resurgence of Mel
Gibson." *Guardian,* November 23, 2017. Available at theguardian.com
/film/2017/nov/23/mel-gibson-hollywood-road-rehabilitation

Phillips, Kristine. "The Former Soviet Officer Who Trusted His Gut—And
Averted a Global Nuclear Catastrophe." *Washington Post,* September 18,
2017. Available at washingtonpost.com/news/retropolis/wp/2017/09/18
/the-former-soviet-officer-who-trusted-his-gut-and-averted-a-global-
nuclear-catastrophe

Reber, Paul. "What Is the Memory Capacity of the Human Brain?" *Scientific American,* June 2010. Available at scientificamerican.com/article
/what-is-the-memory-capacity

Rejcek, Peter. "Can Futurists Predict the Year of the Singularity?" Singularity-Hub, March 31, 2017. Available at singularityhub.com/2017/03/31/can-futurists-predict-the-year-of-the-singularity

Ross, Jeanne W., Cynthia M. Beath, Anne Quaadgrass, "You May Not Need Big Data After All." *Harvard Business Review*, December 2013. Available at hbr.org/2013/12/you-may-not-need-big-data-after-all

Schneider, Stacey. "20+ Examples of Getting Results with Big Data" [blog post]. blog.pivotal.io, May 15, 2013.

Schonbrun, Zach. "Tiger Woods Is Back: Will Sponsors Buy In?" *New York Times*, March 31, 2018. Available at nytimes.com/2018/03/31/business/tiger-woods-advertising.html

Schroeder, Stan. "More Turmoil at Nokia: Head of Mobile Solutions Anssi Vanjoki Resigns." Mashable, September 13, 2010. Available at mashable.com/2010/09/13/anssi-vanjoki-resigns/?europe=true#dicbC_w.N5qR

Schwartz, John. "Some at NASA Say Its Culture Is Changing, but Others Say Problems Still Run Deep." *New York Times*, April 4, 2005. Available at nytimes.com/2005/04/04/politics/some-at-nasa-say-its-culture-is-changing-but-others-say-problems.html

Scott, David. "GOP Debate: Does Height Matter in Presidential Politics?" *Christian Science Monitor*, October 18, 2011. Available at csmonitor.com/Science/2011/1018/GOP-debate-does-height-matter-in-presidential-politics

SETI Institute. "Early SETI: Project Ozma, Arecibo Message." Available at seti.org/seti-institute/project/details/early-seti-project-ozma-arecibo-message

Shubber, Kadhim, and Naomi Rovnick. "Harvey Weinstein Appears in New York Court on Rape Charges." *Financial Times*, May 25, 2018. Available at ft.com/content/e0e8d166-6009-11e8-9334-2218e7146b04

Smith, Marcia S. "NASA's Space Shuttle Columbia: Synopsis of the Report of the *Columbia* Accident Investigation Board." CRS Report for Congress, September 2, 2003. Available at history.nasa.gov/columbia/Troxell/Columbia%20Web%20Site/Documents/Congress/CRS%20Summary%20of%20CAIB%20Report.pdf

Smith, Oliver. "Whatever Happened to German Efficiency? Berlin's New Airport Is a Contender for the World's Most Useless." *Telegraph*, January 9, 2018. Available at telegraph.co.uk/travel/news/berlin-new-airport-delayed-again

Solomon, Lisa Kay. "How the Most Successful Leaders Will Thrive in an Exponential World." SingularityHub, January 11, 2017. Available at singularityhub.com/2017/01/11/how-the-most-successful-leaders-will-thrive-in-an-exponential-world

Sorge, Marjorie, and Mark Phelan. "The Deal of the Century." *Automotive Industries*, June 1, 1998.

Statista. "Global Market Share Held by Nokia Smartphones from 1st Quarter 2007 to 2nd Quarter 2013. Statista. Available at statista.com /statistics/263438/market-share-held-by-nokia-smartphones-since-2007

Statistic Brain Research Institute. "Average Cost of Hard Drive Storage." Statistic Brain, June 18, 2013. Available at statisticbrain.com/average-cost-of-hard-drive-storage

Sulopuisto, Olli. "Nokia: Where It All Went Wrong, by the Man Who Made It the World's Biggest Mobile Company." ZDNet, November 12, 2013. Available at zdnet.com/article/nokia-where-it-all-went-wrong-by-the-man-who-made-it-the-worlds-biggest-mobile-company

Suvorow, Viktor. "Who Was Planning to Attack Whom in June 1941, Hitler or Stalin?" June 1985. Available at tandfonline.com/doi/abs/10.1080 /03071848508522704

Taleb, Nassim N., Daniel G. Goldstein, and Mark W. Spitznagel. "The Six Mistakes Executives Make in Risk Management." *Harvard Business Review*, October 2009. Available at hbr.org/2009/10/the-six-mistakes-executives-make-in-risk-management

Tedor, Richard. "Stalin's Secret War Plans: Why Hitler Invaded the Soviet Union." *Barnes Review*, November–December 2000. Available at winterson nenwende.com/scriptorium/english/archives/articles/stalwarplans.html

Telegraph. "Human Brain Can Store 4.7 Billion Books—Ten Times More Than Originally Thought." *Telegraph*, January 21, 2016. Available at telegraph .co.uk/news/science/science-news/12114150/Human-brain-can-store-4.7-billion-books-ten-times-more-than-originally-thought.html

Thompson, Nicholas. "Why Steve Ballmer Failed." *New Yorker*, August 23, 2013. Available at newyorker.com/business/currency/why-steve-ballmer-failed

Tichy, Noel, and Warren Bennis. "Making Judgment Calls." *Harvard Business Review*, October 2007. Available at hbr.org/2007/10/making-judgment-calls

TMZ. "L.A. Clippers Owner to GF: Don't Bring Black People to My Games." April 26, 2014. Available at tmz.com/2014/04/26/donald-sterling-clippers-owner-black-people-racist-audio-magic-johnson

Troianovski, Anton, and Sven Grundberg. "Nokia's Bad Call on Smartphones." *Wall Street Journal,* July 18, 2012. Available at wsj.com/articles/SB1000142 4052702304388004577531002591315494

Wei, Will. "Tiger Woods Lost $22 Million in Endorsements in 2010." *Business Insider*, July 21, 2010. Available at businessinsider.com /tiger-woods-lost-22-million-in-2010-endorsements-2010-7?IR=T

Wielicki, Krzysztof. "Górska edukacja." *Góry* nr 1/2014 [Polish only].

Williams, Matt. "Dominique Strauss-Kahn Settles Sexual Assault Case with Hotel Maid." *Guardian*, December 10, 2012. Available at theguardian.com /world/2012/dec/10/dominique-strauss-kahn-case-settled

Yang, Stephanie. "The Epic Story of How a 'Genius' Hedge Fund Almost Caused a Global Financial Meltdown." *Business Insider*, July 10, 2014. Available at businessinsider.com/the-fall-of-long-term-capital-management-2014-7?IR=T

Zeitchik, Steven. "Gibson Scandal Could Doom His Movie Career." *Los Angeles Times*, July 13, 2010. Available at articles.latimes.com/2010/jul/13 /entertainment/la-et-mel-gibson-20100713

Žižek, Slavoj. "The Empty Wheelbarrow." *Guardian*, February 19, 2005. Available at theguardian.com/comment/story/0,3604,1417982,00.html

Documentaries

Buckner, Noel, and Rob Whittlesey [directors]. *Apollo 13: To the Edge and Back*, USA, 1994.

Morris, Eroll [director]. *The Fog of War*, USA, 2003.

Pięta, Ewa, and Mirosław Grubek Film [directors]. *The Red Button*, Poland, 2011.

INDEX

absolute determinism, 320

accidents. *See* mistakes/accidents

accountability, 180

acculturation, 50–3

Adventure Consultants, 4–5, 101–2, 105–17, 118–21, 122–4

advocacy decision-making, 65, 69, 202–3

agents of change, 216–8, 220, 248–9

agility, 317–8

airplane crashes, 9, 20, 311–6

Åland Islands, 148–9

Aldrich, Arnold, 83–4

amygdala hijack, 263, 266–7

anchoring trap, 273–4

Android operating system, 32

Andropov, Yuri, 307

anger, 263–5, 266–7

anti-Semitism, 267–8

Apollo space missions, 76

Apollo 13 space shuttle, 75–85, 326n6

Apollo 13: To the Edge and Back (film), 85

Apple, 134

Ariely, Dan, 257–60

authentic leaders

    importance of, 133

    NASA, 172, 174, 181–2

    as rare, 192

    roles of, 135

authority/experts. *See also* charismatic leadership

    in collectivist cultures, 146–7

    and mental security, 88

    and mistakes, 60

    Mount Everest climb, 115–6, 123–4

    NASA, 170–1

    shock experiment, 42–4

    Tenerife airport disaster, 312

    United Airlines 1978 crash, 313–4

    Vietnam War, 203

Baby Boomers, 289–90, 332n4

Bagian, James P., 7–8, 171

Ball, Gary, 105

Ballmer, Steve, 48

Bargh, John, 271–2

baseball bat and ball puzzle, 269–70

Bass, Richard, 4–5, 105

Bay of Pigs, 69–70
Behavioral Science Technology
    Solutions (BST), 176–81
Beidleman, Neal, 119
Berlin Brandenburg Airport, 57–8
Big Data, 287–8, 297
bioengineering, 297–8
black swan events. *See also*
    individual events
    and charismatic leaders of
        conformist team, 53
    definition, 19, 21–2
    global, 22
    individuals, 23
    and inquiry decision-making,
        85–7
    organizational, 23
    as positive, 21–2
    preparing for, 23
    and process, 90–1
    sectoral, 22
    and signs, 29–30, 33
    small group, 23
    and timing, 88–9
    and turkey syndrome, 33, 90
*The Black Swan: The Impact of the
    Highly Improbable* (Taleb), 19
blockchain technology, 289
Bontade, Stefano, 232, 233
book overview, 11–13
Boom Technology, 326n10
Boukreev, Anatoli, 109–10, 119–20,
    328n7
brains
    and accelerating technology, 286
    amygdala hijack, 263, 266–7
    capacity of, 296
    computer brains, 297
    hostages to, 281
    overview, 260–1

and sexual drive, 261–2
    and wine, 277–8
Branson, Richard, 326n10
Breashears, David, 105
Brin, Sergey, 21–2
British Aircraft Corporation, 54–7
British Petroleum (BP), 5, 23
Bruce, Charles Granville, 102
Bruch, Heike, 241–3
Bruno, Giordano, 51–2, 326n9
Bulgakov, Mikhail, 299
Burleson, Todd, 116–7
Buscetta, Tommaso, 234–5
Bush, George W., 329n11
bystander effect, 184–5

Camus, Albert, 320
Castro, Fidel, 69–70
Catch-22, 24–5
cell phones, 31–2
Challenger space shuttle, 7–8, 155–64
change, 36–7, 192. *See also* agents
    of change
charismatic leadership, 44–50, 240, 281,
    309–10. *See also* authority/experts
Chhetri, Madan Khatri, 117
Chrysler, 10–11, 66–7, 142–3
Churchill, Winston, 330n11
CIA, 69–70
Clausewitz, Carl von, 215
clear structures, 318
cloning, 52–3
Cockpit Resource Management, 314–6
collapse, process of, 34–5
collectivism, 145–7, 328n2
Collins, Jim, 34–5
Columbia Accident Investigation Board
    (CAIB), 168–82
Columbia space shuttle, 8, 154–60,
    166–8

communication, 179, 220-1
Compagnie Générale des Eaux (CGE),
    45-6
competitive advantage, 317-8
concessions, gaining small, 132-3
Concorde, 54-7, 326n10
Concorde fallacy, 56-8
conformity, 50-4, 87-8, 92
Cooper, Robert, 327n11
Corleo, Luigi, 231
Cosa Nostra
    organization, 225-39
    rules, 239-40
cost-cutting, 113-4, 164-6
Crimson Tide (film), 303-5, 333n4
crowdsourcing, 292-5
Cuban Missile Crisis, 68-9,
    70-4, 171
cultural differences, 67-8, 142-4
culture, 142-3. *See also* individualism;
    masculinity (MAS) index; power
    distance index (PDI); uncertainty
    avoidance
culture, organizational, 141-2, 151-3,
    170, 173-5, 182

daily leaders, 310
Daimler-Benz and Chrysler merger,
    10-11, 66-7, 142-3
Dalla Chiesa, Carlo Alberto, 233-4
DARPA, 326n5
data
    Big Data, 287-9, 297
    as growing exponentially, 18-9
    as ignored, 66
    overload, 296
    storage, 287
    unreliable, 24, 131
Deal, Duane, 175
decision narcissism, 86

decision salami, 132-3
decision-makers, 25, 30, 35,
    86, 145
decision-making
    automation, 132, 289, 298
    conflict due to difference in,
        304, 305-6, 333n4
    democratic, 145, 304
    elements affecting, 318-9
    as game, 187
    improving process, 132
    infrastructure, 241, 245
    and leader formation, 246
    as process, 64-5. *See also* advo-
        cacy decision-making; inquiry
        decision-making
Deepwater Horizon, 5, 23
delusions, 274-8
Diallo, Nafissatou, 254-5
difference, 87-8
dispersed leadership, 310-1,
    314-6, 318-9
Draper Labs, 81-2
Drucker, Peter, 171, 192

Eaton, Robert J., 10, 66
Edgett, Scott, 327n11
Eichmann, Adolf, 41-2
El-Erian, Mohamed A., 24
emotion, 124-5, 128, 150, 263-5,
    266-9
Encyclopædia Britannica, 35-6, 295
Enron, 49
errors, avoidable. *See* mistakes/
    accidents
Eurocontrol, 9-10, 66
EXCOMM (the Executive Committee
    of the National Security Council),
    71-4, 326n2
experts. *See* authority/experts

experts/authority, 42–4, 60, 80–1, 88
    See also charismatic leadership
Eyjafjallajökull volcano, 9–10, 66

failures, analyzing, 128–30
Falcone, Giovanni, 234–5
Falkland Islands, 148–9
Fastow, Andrew, 49
femininity, 147–50, 329n3
financial crisis 1997/98, 7
financial crisis 2008, 22, 24–5, 31, 223–4
Fischer, Scott, 4–5, 101–2, 106–13,
    106–17, 118–21, 122–4
Fitch, Dennis, 315
5 Whys, 100–1
flight ban, 9–10, 66
The Fog of War (film), 203, 204–5, 326n2
Ford Motor Company, 220–1

García Márquez, Gabriel, 5
General Electric (GE), 217–9
Generation X, 290, 332n5
Generation Y, 290, 331n19
Generation Z, 332n6
generations, 289–92, 331n19,
    332nn4–6
Genovese, Kitty, 184–5
Getty, John Paul, III, 230
Gibson, Mel, 267–8
globalization, 20–1
Godfather (film trilogy), 225
Goldin, Daniel, 164–5
Goldsmith, Marshall, 100 Coaches
    program, 220–1
Goleman, Daniel, 263
Google, 21–2, 47–8
Groupon, 46–8
Grove, Andy, 35
Grown Up Digital (Tapscott), 290
Gulf of Tonkin, 3–4, 198–203

habits, 24, 91–2
Hackman, J. Richard, 245
Haise, Fred, 74–5
Halder, Franz, 209, 210
Hall, Rob, 4–5, 101–2, 105–17,
    118–21, 122–4
Hallock, James, 164–5
Ham, Linda, 8, 166–7, 172–3
Hamann, Stephan, 262
Hansen, Doug, 109, 110, 124
Haynes, Alfred C., 314–6
height, 43, 325n3
Herrick, John J., 3–4, 201, 203
high-context communication, 146–7
Hillary, Edmund, 104, 327n4
HIPPO effect, 325n2
Hitachi, 21
Hitler, Adolf, 193, 206–16, 330n13
Hofstede, Geert, 142, 143–4, 146
How the Mighty Fall (Collins), 34–5
Hunt, John, 104, 327n4
Husband, Rick, 8
Hyundai, 223–4

IBM, 144
identifying issues, 133
implementation, 134–5
individualism, 145–6, 328n2
individualism index (IDV), 145–6
infallibility, 216
inquiry decision-making
    Big Data, 288
    Columbia space shuttle, 168
    in *Crimson Tide*, 305
    and crowdsourcing, 295
    Cuban Missile Crisis, 70–4
    and intuition, 85–6
    Mount Everest climb, 111–2,
        114, 115
    NASA, 80–2, 179

overview, 68-9
and time, 131
Vietnam War, 204
Internet, 19, 290-1, 293, 294
Internet of Things (IoT), 288-9
investors, 30-1
Irvine, Andrew "Sandy," 102-3

Jobs, Steve, 134
Johnson, Lyndon B., 4, 195, 198-201,
202-5, 330n6

Kaczyński, Lech, 9
Kaczyński, Maria, 9
Kahneman, Daniel, 269-71, 332n10
Kaizen, 97-8, 133, 318
Kennedy, John F., 68-9, 70-5, 171, 205
Kerwin, Joseph, 83-4
Khrushchev, Nikita, 72-4
Khurana, Rakesh, 49
KLM, 312
Koyaanisqatsi (film), 17-8
Krakauer, Jon, 106, 109-10, 112, 115,
32n5
Kranz, Gene, 74-81, 77-85, 84-5
Kruse, Dale, 124-5
Kurzweil, Ray, 297

leadership. *See also* authentic leaders
agents of change, 216-8, 220,
248-9
as architect, 222, 240-1, 249
and black swan events, 53
and burdens, 245-6
charismatic leadership, 44-50, 240,
281, 309-10
dispersed leadership, 310-1, 314-6,
318-9
formation of, 246-7
and inclusivity, 220-1

vs. managers, 133, 172, 193-4
overview, 191-4
and people, 220
roles of, 248-9
and solutions, 221-2
and trust, 221
and values, 221
vision and strategy, 195, 205-6,
215-6, 238-9, 248
LeDoux, Joseph, 263
Lefkofsky, Eric, 47-8
Leggio, Luciano, 229-31
Lem, Stanislaw, 285-6
libido, 255-62
Liebergot, Seymour, 77
logic, 268-71, 278, 298
Long-Term Capital Management
(LTCM), 7
Lopsang Jangbu, 107, 109, 114
Lovell, James, 74-5

Macondo, 5
Mafia, 225-39
Mafia rules, 239-40
Mallory, George Herbert Leigh, 102-3
managers
and achievement motive, 280
candidates for, 120-2
and decision-making, 218
groups of, 241-3
vs. leaders, 133, 172, 193-4
Mount Everest climbers, 122-3
at NASA, 156-7, 166, 169, 172-3,
177-8, 180
as scapegoats, 130-1
Marcks, Erich, 209-10
Marshall, Barry James, 99-100
Mason, Andrew, 46-7
masculinity (MAS) index, 147-50,
329n3

The Master and Margarita
  (Bulgakov), 299
Matteo, Giuseppe Di, 237
McAfee, Andrew, 325n2
McBroom, Malburn, 313
McClelland, David, 278-9
McNamara, Robert S., 73, 199-205,
  326n2, 330n6
mental security, 88
Mercury space project, 75
Merkle, Ralph, 296
Merton, Robert C., 6-7, 33-4
Messier, Jean-Marie, 45-6
Messner, Reinhold, 104-5
Microsoft, 48
Milgram, Stanley, 41-2
Millennials, 290, 331n19
mistakes/accidents
  and airport security, 333n10
  and authority/experts, 60
  and innovations, 298, 321
  overview, 11
  repeated, 328n14
  scapegoats, 100
  value of, 128, 206, 328n14
  World War II, 215
monkey hunting, 91-3
monkey ladder experiment,
  50-1, 141
Moore's Law, 18
Morton-Thiokol, 156-7, 159
Moseley, Winston, 184
motives. *See* social motives
Mount Everest
  climbing as risky, 101, 327n2
  deaths, 5, 101, 103, 105, 110, 123,
    328n5, 328n14
  Hall and Fischer climbing events,
    107-17, 118-21, 122-3, 328n7

history of climbing, 102-5
  Hubbard Medal awards, 327n4
  overview, 4-5, 101-2, 105-7
Mountain Madness, 4-5, 101-2, 106-17,
  118-21, 122-4
Mulally, Alan, 219-22
Mulloy, Lawrence, 156

Nadella, Satya, 48-9
Nagy, Piroska, 254-5
nanotechnology, 297
NASA
  Apollo space missions, 75-85, 85,
    326n6
  authentic leaders, 172, 174, 181-2
  and authority/experts, 170-1
  CAIB report results, 168-82
  Challenger space shuttle, 7-8,
    155-64
  Columbia space shuttle, 8, 154-60,
    166-8
  cost-cutting, 164-6
  inquiry decision-making, 80-2, 179
  managers, 156-7, 166, 169,
    172-3, 177-8, 180
  and risk, 161
  rules and procedures, 179-81
  and time, 177-8
Navarra, Michele, 228-30
Nazi Germany, 193, 207-16, 330n11,
  330n13
new normal, 24-5, 37, 192, 246, 292
Ngô Đình Diệm, 197-8
9/11, 20
Nokia, 31-3
Norgay, Tenzing, 104, 327n4
North American Aerospace Defense
  Command (NORAD), 20
Nuovo, Frank, 33

obedience, 188–9
O'Donnell, Kenneth, 200
O'Keefe, Sean, 164–5
On War (Clausewitz), 215
One Hundred Years of Solitude
　(García Márquez), 5
Operation Barbarossa, 210–2,
　330n13
organizational culture
　adopting, 173–4
　definition, 141
　as important, 222
　overview, 318
　power of, 170
　shaping, 151–3, 182
　values, 221, 222–5, 227, 237, 239–40

Page, Larry, 21–2
PageRank algorithm, 21–2
Palo Alto Research Center (PARC),
　134–5
Paul, Getty, John, 230
Paulus, Friedrich Wilhelm, 213–4
PDSA (Plan-Do-Study-Act), 98
Petrov, Stanislav Yevgrafovich, 307–8,
　333n5
Pistorius, Oscar, 265, 332n7
Pittman, Sandy Hill, 106–7, 110,
　112, 114
Porsche, 6–7
positive paranoia, 89–90
positivity, 29–30, 31, 34, 60
Powell, Colin, 59
power distance index (PDI), 144–5,
　146, 328n1
power of habit, 24
pressure, 161–3, 171, 187–8, 203
priming, 271–3
process audits, 90

project elimination, 91, 132
Provenzano, Bernardo, 230, 231, 237,
　237–9

racism, 264–5
RAND Corporation, 285–6, 332n1
rapid response teams, 89–92, 93–4, 132
rationality. *See* logic
RCA (root cause analysis)
　Challenger space shuttle, 160–2
　and collectivist cultures, 147
　and emotion, 128
　implementation of, 182
　Mount Everest climb, 111–7,
　　118–21, 122–4
　overview, 100–1
　vs. scapegoating, 131
　step-by-step, 136–7
　and time, 131
　ulcers, 98–100
　and winning organizations, 133
Reagan, Ronald, 154–5, 158, 162
Reber, Paul, 296
Reggio, Godfrey, 17–8
responsibility, 179–80, 183–6, 215–6,
　242, 244–5
Riina, Salvatore, 230–5, 237
risk
　Challenger space shuttle, 160
　denial of, 34
　and dispersed leadership, 310
　Hyundai, 224
　and libido, 258
　Mount Everest climb, 111–4
　NASA, 161
　and psychological safety, 88
　routinized decision-making, 65
　and success, 36–7
Rocha, Rodney, 170, 181

Rogers Commission, 158–60, 162, 163, 164
routinized decision-making, 64–5
rowing teams joke, 129
rules and procedures
  in Cosa Nostra, 239–40
  in *Crimson Tide* (film), 305–6
  Daimler/Chrysler conflict, 142–3
  following, 152
  going against, 152, 307–8, 333n5
  Mount Everest climb, 106, 123
  NASA operation, 179–81
  overview, 308–9
  of RCA, 100–1
  and turkey syndromes, 185–6
rules of decision making. *See under*
  decision-making
Rumsfeld, Donald, 319

Saint-Exupéry, Antoine de, 245
Sarkozy, Nicolas, 254–5
scapegoats, 100, 128, 130, 133
Schrempp, Jürgen E., 10, 66
Search for Extraterrestrial Intelligence
  (SETI), 292–3
sexual drive. *See* libido
sexual harassment/assault, 7, 256–7, 260, 262
Sharp, Ulysses S. Grant, 4, 201–2
shock experiment, 41–2
Sicily, 225–6. *See also* Cosa Nostra
signals from space, 292–3
signs, 30, 31–2, 35
singularity, 297
Six Sigma system, 218
Skilling, Jeffrey, 49
smart devices, 288
Smircich, Linda, 142
social motives, 278–81

Southeast Asia, 195–7. *See also*
  Vietnam; Vietnam War
Soviet Union, 209–15, 306–7, 330n13, 333n5
Spurrier, Steven, 274–7
Stage-Gate, 84–5, 327n11
Star Wars defense, 306–7
Steenkamp, Reeva, 264–5
Sterling, Donald, 264–5, 331n6
Stiviano, V., 263–4
Stoléru, Serge, 261
stomach ulcers, 98–100
Strategic Defense Initiative (SDI), 306–7
Strauss-Kahn, Dominique, 254–6
success, 34, 37
Sud Aviation, 54–7
sunk costs effect, 56–8, 205, 215
Swigert, Jack, 74–5, 83–4, 326n6
Symbian operating system, 31–2
System 0, 332n10
System 1 & System 2, 269–71, 332n10

Taleb, Nassim Nicholas, 19
Tapscott, Don, 290–1
technological evolution, 18, 285–9, 293–8, 332n2
terrorism, 20
Thompson, Llewellyn "Tommy," 72–4
time
  and advocacy mode, 65
  considering, 63
  and inquiry decision-making, 131
  at NASA, 80–1, 177–8
  and teams, 88–9
Titanics, 56–9
Toffler, Alvin, 18
Top Gun (film), 303, 333n1
Total Quality Management (TQM), 97

trends, 30-1
Trinsum Group, 7
trust, 221
trusted methods, 12, 24-5
tsunami, 20-1
TU-144 aircraft, 54
turkey syndrome
    and black swan events, 33, 90
    Columbia space shuttle, 169
    Mount Everest climb, 112
    Nokia, 32-3
    story of, 29-30
    Vietnam War, 204
Twain, Mark, 206, 287

uncertainties, 150-1, 319-30, 334n12
uncertainty avoidance, 150-1, 329n4
unknowns, 150-1, 319-20, 334n12
USS *Maddox*, 3-4, 198, 201
USS *Turner Joy*, 3-4

values, 221, 222-5, 227, 237, 292
Vanjoki, Anssi, 33
Veldhuyzen van Zanten,
    Jacob, 312
Vietnam, 195-6

Vietnam War, 3-4, 195, 200-6, 330n6
View from the Summit (Hillary), 327n4
Vivendi, 45-6
Vo Nguyen Giap, 205
Voronezh Aircraft Production
    Association, 54

warning signs. *See* signs
Warren, John Robin, 99-100
Wear, Larry, 156
Weathers, Beck, 114-7
Weinstein, Harvey, 7, 247
Welch, Jack, 217-9
Wiedeking, Wendelin, 6-7, 33-4
Wikipedia, 36, 294
wine, 274-8
Woods, Eldrick "Tiger," 254-5
workgroups, 118-9
World War II, 207-21, 330n11,
    330n13
Wowereit, Klaus, 57-8

Xerox, 134-5
Xirallic, 21

Žižek, Slavoj, 334n12

ABOUT
THE AUTHOR

ONE OF the leading European experts in leadership, decision-making, and talent management, Pawel Motyl passionately combines these topics by applying a lens of technology revolution and its impact on the effectiveness of organizations, teams, and individuals.

Pawel is the co-founder and managing partner of Leadership Lab; a valued inspirational speaker, strategic consultant, and trainer; and a certified Stakeholder-Centered Coaching executive coach. From 2007 to 2014 he was the CEO of the ICAN Institute, publisher of the *Harvard Business Review Polska*. Prior to that, he worked for over eight years with the Hay Group as a consultant and as a leader of the diagnostics team for Central and Eastern Europe.

In 2016, he was selected from over sixteen thousand candidates for the first cohort of the elite global group of Marshall Goldsmith's "100 Coaches" initiative.

Pawel spends his free time in the mountains, and he has climbed numerous peaks in the Himalayas and Pamir.

Pawel lives in Warsaw, Poland, and works throughout the world.

For more information, see www.pawelmotyl.com